Towards
Sherlock Holmes

Towards Sherlock Holmes

A Thematic History of Crime Fiction in the 19th Century World

STEPHEN KNIGHT

McFarland & Company, Inc., Publishers

Jefferson, North Carolina

Chapter 7, in shorter form, originally appeared as "Watson's Wound and the Speckled Band: Imperial Threats and English Crimes in Conan Doyle," *Linguæ* & 1 (2006): 11–24.

ISBN (print) 978-1-4766-6616-7
ISBN (ebook) 978-1-4766-2751-9

LIBRARY OF CONGRESS CATALOGUING DATA ARE AVAILABLE

British Library cataloguing data are available

Front cover: Frederick Childe Hassam, *Cab Stand at Night, Madison Square, New York*, oil on paper, 13.75" × 8.25", 1891 (Pictures Now)

Printed in the United States of America

McFarland & Company, Inc., Publishers
Box 611, Jefferson, North Carolina 28640
www.mcfarlandpub.com

Table of Contents

Preface

This book has developed through several variations of time and space, and in response to the developing patterns of crime fiction criticism. After feeling nearly 20 years ago that the single-volume histories of crime fiction which were regularly appearing tended to simplify the development of the form and its variation over two centuries, I decided to write a history of it which paid more attention than usual to the genre's social and political contexts, and took note of its revealing but generally unmentioned features, from the 1838 "Philadelphia Lawyer" to indigenous Australian crime fiction of the present. That attempt to make the standard survey more veridical was published by Palgrave Macmillan in 2004 and then revised in 2010, but I continued to feel the historicist model itself made it hard to chronicle how crime fiction both developed from and in turn realized the new urban and volatile social structures of the past two centuries—especially the seriously under-examined nineteenth.

So I started to research, develop, and at times deliver papers on topics that were excavations of areas which seemed in special need of the criminographical archaeologist's shovel and lamp. I was then working at Cardiff University, a train ride away from the riches of the British Library; I was also able to access French material both through academic interchanges and familial investment in a small flat equally convenient for dejeuner at the beach and the Montpellier libraries. The ease of Heathrow-avoiding travel from Cardiff via Amsterdam to American conferences and campus visits meant the New York Public Library was a readily available fine source of material, by no means all of it merely American. Wales's long-delayed devolution from England brought formal Euro-connections to that rediscovered country, and I was able to meet colleagues like Gustav Klaus at Rostock, Peter Drexler at Potsdam and Maurizio Ascari at Bologna, and attend specialist conferences and workshops that welcomed the kind of detailed, narrow-focus, high-concept papers I was beginning to produce as ways in to the actual processes by which crime fiction developed and spread in the 19th century. My Euro-colleagues approved the plan, and often offered searching comments about previously-ignored features, like the very early police stories of the yet unidentified "William Russell" or the complicated gender politics of the male-authored and usually misdated "Mrs Paschal" of the 1864 *Revelations of a Lady Detective.*

Research thrived, with special munificence from a range of Bologna-based Europe-wide activities—we thought the name of our leader, Professor Vita Fortunati, described our own lives. Back at Cardiff, work on my papers to become chapters continued, if at times overshadowed by the next meeting of the Professorial Board (the latter word was not always spelt that way), and more positively by my plans for substantial research books, like *The Mysteries of the Cities* (McFarland, 2012), the kind of thing that professors used to be expected to write in the days before they were, as now, governmentally summoned to enhance and expedite international post-industrial profitabilities.

When I retired in 2011 and returned to the benign weather and ambient vineyards of Melbourne, I had drafted and delivered some papers related to the project, and decided to spend time continuing what now seemed like a worthwhile, close-detail, book-length study, un-banalized by the curse of surveyitis. I was generously appointed an honorary research professor back at the University of Melbourne, a body distinguished both by long academic achievement and by being the major tram-terminus in the city. Access was excellent there, including that so valued by retired academics—to the photocopier and the inter-library loan system. The latter is in Australia by far the most efficient and diverse I have encountered—local service is within a week, and books from Canada and South Africa routinely arrive in my pigeon-hole. Then with typical Australian generosity I was made a vice-chancellor's fellow, with both salary and research funding again, and the task, I was told by Glyn Davis, a VC who deserves a medal, was just to busy myself in research and public intellectual activity. With the funds now available I could gather in ancient original state, or modern reprint, or electronic form a substantial number of the older sources I needed to consult, especially the manifold works of G. W. M. Reynolds, and to employ the high-order bibliophilic skills of Anna Kay on finding those texts and many other references. So I was able to complete this series of studies as they are now, not formally subdued into any single historically or conventionally dominated order, but as the Introduction argues, a set of thematically-focused essays exploring major unexamined areas in the development of crime fiction, consistently reaching into secondary areas of social and cultural formations, and interacting with the other essays in ways that are both inherently intriguing and also inevitably generate a substantial number of cross-references.

These have been made as lucidly and economically as has seemed credible, and in the same way referencing itself has aimed at making reading easy, but data-recovery possible. In each chapter a book or story is given a note when it is first cited, and after that page numbers of quotations from it are located in the text. Scholars and critics who are quoted are identified on each occasion in the notes, but secondary materials which are merely mentioned and creative texts that are not specifically quoted from are to save space and possible confusion not included in the notes, but, except the most familiar or trivial of them, they are all referred to in the separate Bibliography for the whole book.

One of the chapters, that on Conan Doyle and empire, was published in a shorter and preliminary form in an Italian journal in 2006, and the title "Sherlock Holmes' Grandmother" has, as a favorite, itself been used for a quite different, genre-analyzing essay that was published in Denmark in 2008. The other material appears here for the first time.

As in all my work, personal thanks go to learned friends who have provided generous and expert help: Maurizio Ascari, Anna Kay, Stuart Macintyre, Grace Moore, Lucy Sussex and Sean Thompson. Special thanks to Rachel Franks for her expert search for illustrations, as well as to my electronic muse Elizabeth Knight and as always Margaret for her judicious mixture of interest and forbearance.

Introduction

Books on crime fiction have in the last 20 years settled into a predictable form. Aware of the existence of a sizeable body of intelligent readers dedicated to the genre, who engage with specialist bookshops and websites devoted to publicizing and selling crime titles, and also aware of the steadily growing number of undergraduates who take at least one course on some form of crime fiction, especially in North America, authors and publishers have ventured into providing material for both categories. But publishers are cautious, and the tendency has been for the books, whether single-authored or edited collections, to be nervous of becoming too specialized: the norm has become an extensive survey. This has had the advantage of implicitly advocating the genre's identity and importance, and both crime buffs and crime students have seemed gratified at this single-volume form of self-validation. That mix of information and assertion was behind the ground-breaker in the crime history form, Julian Symons' *Bloody Murder* (1972)—which was, revealing that the genre could stimulate forces other than mere narrative revelation, in the United States renamed *Mortal Consequences*.

The historicizing of murder as the dominant mode of criminographical critical discourse has had other consequences, more limiting and negative than confidence and self-justification among the committed. The routine pattern in the surveys is for a major author to have three or perhaps four pages, a routine contributor about half a page, and the minor figures receive just a passing mention with a title, a date, and a blandly-selected adjective, or perhaps two. Equally restrictive and concealing has been the inevitable historicist shaping of the book-length surveys, so that they progress from whenever the scholarship of the author permits a beginning—all too often with Poe, but sometimes, and beneficially, rather earlier than that—and move through major locations and periods in convenient chapter-length units. This brings serious misrepresentation of the complexity of the form's development. For a start, the French input in both the 19th and the 20th century is usually overlooked, including its major influence in America; the modal changes in the so-called "Golden Age" are obscured, from the usually omitted early American woman like Carolyn Wells and Mary Roberts Rinehart to the late thirties radicalizers of the form like Anthony Berkeley Cox, Maurice Richardson and Eric Ambler. The national segmentations of the survey mode can themselves be naïve, even self-validating, such as ignoring the fact that the finest-tuned of the "Golden Age" writers was not an English unrealist but the New Yorker Willard Huntington Wright, as "S. S. Van Dine," and the best-selling of the English 1940s writers, even out-doing Christie, was the home-grown quasi–American tough-guy exponent Peter Cheyney.

But if the histories worked by concealing, as well as, in an often stultified and pre-organized form, conventionalizing the development of the genre, their largest failing has been their influence in offering a wide coverage in itself as a valid and complete account. The study of literature has not, for over a century now, been based on a process of sorting, summarizing, making quick movement through a neatly organized quasi-history to the self-privileging present. Whether it is Bradley's analysis of Shakespeare, Leavisite close reading of the classic novel, or more recent theory-based explorations of texts for their deeper and at times more disturbing meanings, literary criticism, like art criticism, has for long worked in close, slow-moving, well-informed, and often very revealing detail.

Except in the mode of crime fiction. This has begun to an extent to change—the very major authors Christie and Chandler have in recent years been the subjects of at least essay-collections, though the chapters themselves have often been survey-oriented and it is noticeable that even a full-length book on Chandler like that by Sean McCann repeats the nationalist political simplicities of the American summarizings, even making Chandler, surely to his notional irritation, a New Deal Democrat. The other dominant modern mode of literary criticism, the journal essay, has in itself only begun to scratch the surface of the crime fiction mountain of inviting creative ore—just one academic magazine *Clues* has been operating in the last 20 years: it had a break from publication in 2001 for nearly three years and its continuing survival may depend on being supported by a publisher with a large list of crime fiction studies, namely McFarland. There is recent talk of another journal, but it is remarkable how weak the periodical provision has been in the field, even against science fiction or popular romance.

This situation, with naïve historicism and its counterpart, brief descriptivism, as the dominant form of modern-day crime fiction criticism, poses two separate requirements on any new and serious contribution devoted to exploring and explaining this most popular, and so potentially most influential, of all fictional genres. One is to deal with carefully selected novels in considerable detail—to let them exist, and stand scrutiny, in their own fully examined terms—to be just what literary criticism has long called a text. The other requirement is to avoid the simplistic historicist sorting and ordering of the material and work in terms of theme-oriented categories—which may well also enlighten historical elements and processes, but will not be simplified into naivety or oblivion by hurrying along to the next decade or the new genre.

The present collection of essays sets itself to fulfill both these requirements, studying major texts in considerable detail, and also in awareness of their literary and sociohistorical context: the book is divided into topics that focus on areas of considerable interest and importance which, it appears from a long familiarity with reading, writing, teaching and supervising in the genre, have not yet been given due attention.

These topic areas have themselves arisen in principle from the process of looking closely at particular texts, in most cases through the process of selecting them for study on courses with senior students, rather than the speedy run-through which is the early-year teaching parallel of the cursory historical survey. This process of detailed scrutiny has drawn attention to recurrent issues that deserve fuller exploration, found in references deep in the texts—for example the first chapter arose in large part from the curious way in which Wilkie Collins seems to connect being a detective with coming from the Americas, in his novels *Hide and Seek* (1854) and *The Woman in White* (1860) and also his story "The Diary of Anne Rodway" (1856). The American connection Collins made seemed to link to the French interest in the energetic and innovative detection they sourced in "Cooperisme," and suggested American crime fiction was in fact a force older and wider than the narrow brilliance of Poe—a fact curiously not recognized in its strength and persistent 19th-century development in its own country, which became the overarching theme that developed for that chapter. The reflex of the need for an American analysis presented itself through looking closely at early French material. The French themselves had in a series of studies connected and examined their own tradition, and the French-Canadian Régis Messac produced in 1929 a book on the whole genre so far, which gave the French tradition a full presence: but it has, astonishingly, never been translated. Anglophone commentators have broadly failed to recognize the value of French material to Edgar Allan Poe, Anna

Katharine Green and Arthur Conan Doyle, nor the generally world-influencing achievements of the important writers Paul Féval and Émile Gaboriau.

The third chapter also developed in a way parallel to the American one, from reading the very rarely examined, and often not even cited, English short stories from the 1830s to the 1850s which present narratives of crime as observed by, in series, a Physician, a Barrister, an Attorney and then a Police Officer, who soon became a Detective Police Officer. These stories often involve not only matters of crime and malpractice, as seen by professional disciplinary specialists, but also, it seems because of that socially separated viewpoint, are also notable for representing a varying, and variously developing set of positions on social class—and it appeared odd that in England, a country still concerned, even obsessed, with varieties and variations in class matters, this topic and its complexities had never been explored. For Chapter Four, gender joined the earlier absences, national and social, in identifying the lack of an account of female detectives and female authors of detective fiction—by no means always the same—which gave fully-detailed attention to the texts, rather than the somewhat cursory early feminist studies by authors like Kathleen Klein, Maureen Reddy and Mary Craig/Patricia Cadogan, and the much more limited attention paid to gender by the crime fiction surveys.

The fifth chapter in a substantial way arose from the previous four separately theme-focused ones. In them there continually arose the issue of major 19th-century writers, notably Collins and Braddon, who had produced novels in which crime, and some kind of investigation and resolution of crime, were central, yet were not limited to the emergent form of the mystery or detective novel as such. These writers handled the themes of the first four chapters. They included American references; they were clearly aware of the French traditions; their views were often shaped by matters of class—notably the upper-class and middle-class distaste for police intervention—and they were especially given to using women as agents, victims and even investigators of crime. It seemed that this topic of the interface between the mainstream novel and crime fiction had never been explored properly, as if critics of crime and critics of the novel, with the honorable exception of Anthea Trodd, had passed each other, gazes averted, on opposite sides of the street. Therefore a chapter emerged exploring the extent to which the mainstream novelists moved towards the developing crime novel, an area in which, like the conscious critique of conservative attitudes, Collins is senior to Dickens.

In the two remaining chapters late–19th-century topics are explored which focus on similarly noticeable and notable absences from crime fiction criticism. It is a truism that Fergus Hume's *The Mystery of a Hansom Cab* (1886) was the first best-seller in the genre. Not only is this wrong—Anna Katharine Green's *The Leavenworth Case* (1878), nearly a decade earlier, certainly outsold it—but the alleged fact has never inspired anyone to write on the qualities of the novel itself or why it might have suddenly done so well in London in very late 1887 and then through 1888. Literary scholars in Australia, where the action is located, have not deigned to fill the gap, and Hume has attracted even less interest elsewhere, so it seemed right to explore and explain the phenomenon in some detail and in international terms. Hume's novel appeared in London at almost exactly the same time as Conan Doyle's *A Study in Scarlet,* and this and the fact that the patterns in most of the previous chapters lead up to the genre-dominating Sherlock Holmes stories, even including the American emphasis that Conan Doyle so much valued (he hoped for a re-union of the two countries), made it seem appropriate that the last chapter of the book would offer analysis of an element of Conan Doyle's work that seems inexplicably without coherent study, namely his treatment of the impact of imperial experience, both on innocent English stay-at-homes and in the notable number of his earlier villains who have been variously damaged by their experience of empire.

Selecting these topics as matters yet waiting to be handled by crime criticism, and planning to deal with them in terms of detailed analysis of the texts themselves, has meant a series of decisions have had to be taken about which particular texts to foreground, and how far to explore them. As will be evident from this and other work, I am a strong believer in the value of making and examining synopses of texts, as a process of permitting the work itself to reveal its concerns and patterns, as well as its omissions. I have pursued this process here, often overtly, but with some variation. When texts are likely to be very little-known or examined, like Crowe's *Susan Hopley,* Féval's *Les Habits Noirs,* Gaboriau's *Monsieur Lecoq,* or Hume's *The Mystery of a Hansom Cab* itself, they have been described in some detail; others which are less elusive, like Collins' *Hide and Seek,* Wood's *East Lynne,* or Green's *The Leavenworth Case,* are given a more summary treatment, while texts like *Bleak House, The Woman in White,* or *The Hound of the Baskervilles* are assumed to be familiar enough to not need anything as extensive as a synopsis or summary.

Though the chapters are varied in their thematic focus, there emerge a series of overlaps in the case of some texts and so at times locational decisions have had to be made—for instance, *Susan Hopley,* because of the actual restriction of its handling of the female detective theme, which it has occasionally been thought to initiate, is in fact discussed in Chapter Five before and as part of the work of the "mainstream novelists" who use crime as a focal but not total theme. Then while Dickens' writing in *Household Words* about police seems to belong also in that chapter, the strongly class-linked nature of the material is necessarily also referred to in Chapter Three, and in the same way the stories by "Andrew Forrester" about Miss Gladden the 1864 "Female Detective" have clear relevance both in Chapter 3 on class and Chapter 4 on women inquirers. As a sign of, in this context at least, Collins' continuing high importance, he is referred to even more frequently across the chapters than Dickens, and though the main discussion of his novels is located in the "mainstream novelists" chapter, cross-references to his novels are recurrent in almost all the other chapters— even as a structural source for Hume's novel.

While a historical approach tends to suggest a steady and even remorseless growth of a subject towards the somewhat self-satisfied present, a thematically-based account of the kind offered here reveals the development of 19th-century crime fiction as a more multi-sited and more variously-constructed set of intermittent formations, with changing patterns across, rather than through, time. Underlying those developments are varying non-literary structures of audience and medium, like the growth of a lower-class readership, especially among young women, and the steadily falling price of magazines through tax cuts, reduced paper costs and efficiencies of scale in the growing industry. But not all is so readily contextually comprehensible—puzzles remain, like the fairly short-lived boom in short crime stories in magazines and book-collections through the 1850s and 1860s, including another notable enigma in the brief appearance of the male-authored female detective in 1864, a figure which did not recur for some 30 years. Other developments can seem less mysterious by being very extended: the early crime-related mainstream novelists only slowly disengage with the domesticated Gothic that was 1860s sensationalism, and when Braddon eventually produced something in structure much like a mystery novel in *Wyllard's Weird* in 1885, that book has been hardly celebrated by her readers then or since—but appears to have been picked up as a source by Hume from the Melbourne *Leader* when he landed there early in May 1885.

The processes of exposing and explaining crime varied substantially over the century, with the early semi-disciplinary professionals, doctor, lawyer and clerk, appearing in popular short stories, while the police were realized as operating with some restraint. Detection in the mainstream novels tended to be divided among occasional professionals, usually lawyers, as well as knowledgeable servants, the latter almost always women, and also there were inquiring amateurs of both genders. After their often negative early appearances, private detectives only very late in the century emerged in professional, and at times female, form as Conan Doyle gave his potent *imprimatur* to that mode of analysis. Forms of professional policing had come to authority in France and America, but took much longer in England to return to their brief and restricted position of the 1850s and 1860s. All the time much of the mainstream novel, and very notably the highly popular G. W. M. Reynolds style of dramatic and democratic fiction, had managed with very limited instances of professional detection, usually exposing malpractice through a mix of events, coincidence, curiosity and confession.

In the 20th century crime fiction would expand around the world, and in the later part of that period has worked newly through many ethnic and social structures to make it genuinely an investigatory world discourse. In the same radical way in the 19th century the emerging genre dealt with the fears to be faced by the new urban populace, fears about just what horrors their unknown fellow-citizens, their neighbors, and even themselves, might be capable of perpetrating, was both energetic, volatile and open to many influences and constraints.

What was most consistently evident was the energy and the success of the genre. Though 19th-century moralists and social conservatives—including many who would claim to be liberals—often in the authoritative and authoritarian journals criticized the form for its unseemly vulgarity and its exposure of real, therefore disturbing, passions, their contemporaries among fiction writers, and very noticeably among readers, responded strongly to this wide-ranging, ground-breaking fictional realization of the new world of cities, and equally modern forms of flexibility and mobility—personal, social and, crucially, moral.

The crimes and their exposures are signs through which the century explores and experiences its challenges to convention and tradition, and also expresses its own desires for new forms of social and moral control. When Wilkie Collins, who grasped the meaning of the new genre better and deeper than any other major writer, named his first serious crime-linked novel *Hide and Seek* he found verbs to epitomize the conventions and the challenges of crime fiction; commentators will do well to seek what lies hidden in these rich and engrossing 19th-century pages, popular in every sense.

CHAPTER 1

Before the Tough Guys: The Traditions of 19th-Century American Crime Fiction

A Missing Tradition

In the New York-based *Oxford Companion to Crime and Mystery* (1999) there is no entry for American crime fiction, though there is one for Canadian, Australian, New Zealand and Japanese crime fiction.[1] This might be an assumption of major-country effortless superiority, suggesting that America, France and England are too important to be nationally pigeon-holed; perhaps the absences are based on a feeling that the entries would be too long—though the presence of essays on major cities in the overlooked countries suggests a distaste for national scrutiny could be the underlying reason. Whatever the cause, or causes, of this curious treatment, the result is that the special natures, successes and even oddities of those major areas of crime fiction are not considered in this major resource. That is unlike the treatment in this present collection of 19th-century focused essays, with one on America, one on France and several on England—the term Britain is not employed because a self-aware crime fiction in Ireland, Scotland and Wales is only a feature of the late 20th century.

The *Oxford Companion* and its editor Rosemary Herbert are far from alone in their lack of transatlantic big-country scrutiny. It is striking that unlike the French and English careful national curation, even exaggeration, of their own patterns of crime fiction history, there is almost no sense, even in usually highly self-conscious America, of the very substantial part played by that country in the formation of crime fiction, and little apparent interest in speculating on a specific American-ness in the genre. Or at least not in identifying it before the between-wars Californian private eyes, whose image seems to have been taken over as an emblem not just of American crime fiction, but of what it is to be an American guy—and more recently an American feminist as well. This is odd enough: even the English do not offer Sherlock Holmes or Lord Peter Wimsey as national ideals, or at least not consciously nor in significant numbers. But odder yet is that reading 19th-century European texts in some detail has turned up a striking number of instances where it seems that America played a major developmental role in early crime fiction, and where that leadership is also related to identifiable concepts of Americanness, and indeed concepts that in democratic and human terms have rather more value than being a mutely moralistic hard-ass with a faux-sensitive streak—which seems a fair translation of tough-guy detective identity and its meaning. So it seems appropriate to look back to an earlier, mysteriously overlooked, and thoroughly interesting American contribution to crime fiction.

It has been curiously under-recognized even in Larry Landrum's *American Mystery and Detective Novels: A Reference Guide* (also 1999).[2] His "Early Writers," covered in no more than one and half pages, are Charles Brockden Brown, Louisa Alcott, "Seeley Regester" and Anna Katharine Green. Two of those, Brown and Green, are especially important, though still under-examined by crime fiction historians on both sides of the Atlantic, but I would want to add to such a list a number of productive names and contexts to be explored in this chapter, which is essentially a preliminary discussion of a topic that deserves much fuller analysis, especially in the rich archives of American libraries. This chapter will discuss writers and works that can easily be seen as part of the identifiable genre of crime fiction: there is another topic in the way in which American crime narratives are re-used in major fiction, American as in English, and strikingly also in French literature. But though Melville's *The Confidence Man* and Hawthorne's *The Scarlet Letter* can be read as potent intensifications of criminographical forms, that is not a topic that can be undertaken here, though the English connections between mainstream fiction and emerging crime fiction will be dealt with in Chapter 5: rather, this is a first cut through the rich deposits of early American crime fiction to identify their patterns, their developments and their implicit relation to American self-consciousness.

The chapter does not deal in any detail with the only early American crime writer who has received substantial and appropriate consideration, Edgar Allan Poe. The innovative brilliance and wide-ranging influence of his stories have been considered by many critics. The three Dupin stories of 1841–45 are correctly taken as the first instance of the genius detective which will be basic to the development of Sherlock Holmes and many later figures, American like Jacques Futrelle's "Thinking Machine" Professor S.F.X. Van Dusen, or English like Christie's Marple and Poirot, and spreading into the international insightful police detective as embodied by Simenon's Maigret. The existing emphasis on Poe has in fact itself obscured other forces, like the earlier elements of disciplinary detection, both the London "Physician" in Samuel Warren's stories (see Chapter 3, pp. 78–80) and the American "Philadelphia Lawyer" stories, to be discussed below. Indeed there has been a general and much-disseminated lazy assumption that Poe simply invented detective fiction. Much less well considered has been Poe's impact in France itself—which will be considered later in the chapter—and his impact in raising the prestige of crime fiction in America, so there was both a rich interest in overseas versions of the form and a strong productivity in the country itself, with the result that clue-based mystery novels, largely by women writers, and action-focused thrillers as foregrounded in the dime novel mode all preceded the rest of the world and had considerable influence in the 20th century. Poe's imaginative flair and resultant authority have had both a well-publicized and an obscurantist impact in writing about crime fiction in America, but if a focal interest is the development of an American national consciousness in the genre, as Poe's three Dupin stories are all set in Paris (though one, "Marie Rogêt," reworks a real New York story) then they are not of primary relevance to this study.

Founding Figure

Charles Brockden Brown's short but remarkable career saw him publish between 1798 and 1800 three separate novels which take related but different approaches to issues of crime, detection and identity. As is often noted, he was influenced by the English William Godwin's 1794 novel *Things as They Are*, later known by its original sub-title, *Caleb Williams*. Caleb is a scholarly young man of lower–middle-class origins who, working as secretary for a wealthy nobleman named Falkland, comes to suspect, rightly, that his master has committed a murder. But far from being a triumphant detective, Caleb becomes hunted and finally destroyed by the wide-ranging social power Falkland can wield. Godwin intended to represent the oppressions of class power, but could not ultimately see a way of imaginatively disabling them simply through knowledge and inquiry.

In 1798 Brown published *Wieland, or The Transformation*, often called the first American Gothic novel, but one which has a range of complexities that look forward to crime fiction, and even the 20th-century psychothriller. Clara Wieland narrates a story about her weak brother Theodore's obsession with voices. Some of these—perhaps all—come from "Carwin the biloquist," who is also obsessed with Clara. Theodore kills his children, claiming the voices instructed him: Carwin says he should not have listened to them, and Theodore kills himself in guilt. Clara's house burns down, she travels overseas and eventually marries the dull, practical Henry Pleyal—and Carwin becomes a farmer. This exotic story realizes a mix of obsession, guilt and manipulation in a brilliant psychologization of the forces of Gothic fiction; Brown would manage from now on to contain his multiple instincts, first diluting his version of the Gothic and after that moving towards crime fiction.

Arthur Mervyn, or Memoirs of the Year 1793 (1799) is like a hyperactive Caleb Williams story set in the Philadelphia plague, or yellow fever year, in which the central figure, a naïve farm boy, is in a sequence of disastrous encounters with urban malice cheated out of all his money by a forger, imprisoned, becomes involved with a criminal, catches the plague, meets the forger again, is left to die, and then fortunately meets a good man, who is a doctor. He recovers and returns home to find most of his family dead: then begins a series of events where Arthur tries to help women in severe difficulties—as if, having settled into his now secure masculine identity, he can make a positive contribution to the other gender. Apparently in reward for his noble efforts, late in the novel he meets, loves and finally marries a generous young widow.

This is not really a crime story—though it does work rather like a future psychothriller, if one of highly melodramatic form, and its general effect is to provide a male version of the already developed Gothic female-in-peril narrative: as Arthur slowly struggles his way to recognition as a man to be valued, and eventually a man to be loved. The explorations of this essentially "male Gothic" melodrama were to be elaborated and made much more complex, in the context of self-consciously crime- and detection-focused narrative, in *Edgar Huntly* (1800).

This last and the best-focused of Brown's three major novels is also the most clearly predictive of the pattern of crime fiction. Edgar does finally trace the cause of the death of his friend Waldegrave, but it is a casual act of revenge by a single Native American outraged by settler mistreatment, not a motivated betrayal by one of the American characters, as we have been led to expect. The same mix of inexplicability and unfocussed threat emerges from the complex interaction of Huntly and his highly volatile friend Clithero Edny—they are the most prominent pair of several near-doubles in the story. Clithero has loved a girl in New York: his employer, her aunt, approves their love but then he is attacked by the aunt's returned twin, and shoots him in self-defense. Feeling the sister will mourn too much for her twin, he distractedly attempts to stab her at night. Stopped from fulfilling this crazy scheme, he then flees to the area north of Philadelphia where Edgar lives with his uncle. Clithero spends time among the Native Americans—Edgar himself gets stranded among them and escapes with difficulty. Finally Clithero returns to New York and, when he is being taken by boat to an asylum by the strong-minded husband of his former employer, jumps into the water to his death. Full of disturbance, mental and locational, and matching the indigenous threats with immigrant instabilities, this is a story of considerable power.

Brown's central figures are men like Caleb Williams, on the rise, skilled, insightful, suspicious of crimes about them, but the American novelist's characters are defeated not by social class, rather by power which rests on often dubious and immigrant wealth. This sounds as if Brown is already wielding with confidence the rationality-explains-the-mystery pattern that was later to be enshrined in the generic structure of the detective story. But although his narratives do resolve crimes, and his central figures are discoverers, these quasi-detectives also experience much of the bafflement, frustration and, especially, self-doubt of Caleb Williams. Indeed the final moment of Godwin's novel, when Caleb feels it is really all his fault for not helping Falkland in his problems, is narrativized in various ways throughout Brown's stories. *Edgar Huntly* is sub-titled *Memoirs of a Sleep-Walker* and, in a decidedly Gothic moment, Edgar comes to wonder if he might have himself done the terrible deed while not awake; *Arthur Mervyn* is inculpated in the crimes of the many-sided urban immigrant American Welbeck: in *Wieland* the hero is by the villain Carwin ventriloqually turned to real and self-destructive criminality.

Brown, as an American, does not fear the oppressions of class as such, merely the manipulations that the rich can use to protect themselves; but this lack of the social anxiety that runs right through English crime fiction does not leave an area of confidence. Rather, Brown explores the dark possibilities of the self and the concept of the double in a way fully familiar from the Gothic fiction of Ann Radcliffe and, more darkly, "Monk" Lewis, and while the complexities of his novels require Gothic-trained reading—especially *Wieland*—they repay that, and romantics like Shelley and Hazlitt were definite admirers. The French scholar Régis Messac has linked Brown's

work forward to that of Poe: "les donneés essentielles sur lesquelles tra-
vaillera Poe sont dejà amenées par lui à pied d'oeuvre"[3] ("the essential points
on which Poe would work are already established by him [i.e. Brown] as a
basis of his work"). Yet Brown is both an initiator in crime friction and
also a distinctly American writer. *Arthur Mervyn*, with its brilliant beginning in the Philadelphia yellow fever epidemic and *Edgar Huntly*, with its
powerful excursus into wild America and its dangerous denizens, native
and settler alike, both consciously create a vigorous, but also troubled and
questioned, American reality.

More generally it could be argued that the Americanness of Brown's
emphasis on the strains of identity, not class, liberates him as a Gothic
writer: he shapes whole novels that focus on the dark possibilities of the
self, as doubt and terror are magnified by the capacity to reason, whereas
in the slightly later British *Blackwood's* magazine such anxious narratives
were restricted to the short and single-focus "Tales of Terror," which themselves operate within the confines of a confident bourgeois world of knowledge and curiosity, in that the comfortable, and essentially conservative
readers are invited to experience and enjoy sensations directly suffered by
the unfortunate protagonists, or described in dramatic detail by a narrator
as curious, and as untroubled, as themselves. From Brown on the American
pattern feels very different. From him flows much of the vertiginous and
compulsive quality of Poe's work and indeed it is even possible to see in
Brown's heroes Edgar Huntly and Arthur Mervyn the special mix of nervous sentiment and restrained heroism that will enrich the image of the
future Californian private eye—discovering value in the self through their
criminal inquiries, but also consistently seeing the possibility of the cher-
ished self being or becoming criminal.

Early Sources

If Brown sets up a structure for future possibilities, his work was by
no means the only characteristically American discussion of crime. While
it is clear that the English *Newgate Calendar* was available in America—
like so much other English crime literature there are many copies donated
to American libraries by readers, often lawyers—only two versions published in America are recorded, both from well into the 19th century.[4] Early
American criminography did flourish however, and scholars have begun to
trace this material. Daniel A. Cohen has written on the quasi-factual literature of crime in New England from the 17th century onwards, and a

slightly later period has been studied by Karen Halttunen.[5] Both show a range of factual genres which present the threats of crime and more or less optimistic ways of dealing with it, as in the 18th-century pamphlets Cohen describes, which are like American versions of the *Newgate Calendar* entries,[6] and also through the church, notably in the powerful execution sermons. The press also contributed: Halttunen describes at some length the related genres of news and police reports (both of which show their influence in Poe) and what she calls "the new murder mystery" created "as murder-as-mystery spilled over from legal narratives of the crime into the larger popular literature."[7]

As Cohen indicates in a lengthy analysis of a real murder case and its fictional representation,[8] the conflicting and multiple narratives of a court room could operate just like a complex mystery plot, especially when a powerful defender was at work, like Rufus Choate in the 1845 trial of John Tirrell for the murder of Marian Bickford. While it seems obvious that he was the killer, Choate got him off both murder and arson charges by blackening the girl's reputation, claiming she had cut her throat in despair and then Tirrell accidentally set fire to the house in his innocent panic—even claiming that like several characters in Brown's *Edgar Huntly*, he was a sleepwalker. While he shares the surname of an important figure in both Godwin's *Caleb Williams* and Lytton's *Pelham* this can hardly have influenced the fact that fiction was quick to recirculate these "murder-mystery" elements. The murder occurred in October 1845, and Osgood Bradbury's novel *Julia Bicknell, or Love and Murder: Founded on a Recent Terrible Domestic Tragedy* was out by mid–December. The novel at least convicted the man, and makes it clear how vigorously the American press could develop lengthy fiction from the pamphlet tradition—the novel's sub-title connects directly to the sensational pamphlet tradition.

But there were also imported models. Eugène Sue's *Les Mystères de Paris* appeared from 1842 to 1843 and was rapidly translated in the U.S.—there were two editions out in New York in 1843, while London only saw a translation in 1844. There are five other early undated American editions, so others might have been at least as early. The "Mysteries of the Cities" format, an encyclopedic urban narrative focused on crime and usually having a redemptive hero, was quickly used by popular writers—*The Mysteries of Boston* by Osgood Bradbury appeared in 1844, while a more powerful and more innately American response to Sue's work was George Lippard's *The Quaker City, or The Monks of Monk Hall: A Romance of Philadelphia Life*, published in ten installments in 1844–45.[9] This was a strong indictment of corruption and hypocrisy as well as crime, Lippard being more radical than the liberal Sue, more like Sue's follower G.W.M. Reynolds whose first *The Mysteries of London* installments appeared just two months after Lippard's.

  The Quaker City assembles many of its characters in a rambling old house called Monk Hall—Lippard's first title, and continuing sub-title, was *The Monks of Monk Hall*, and the character who does most to link the strands of action is "Devil-Bug," the door-keeper of Monk Hall. He is a poor man who avenges what he sees as crimes and occasionally rewards good people—this makes him seem like a reversal of Prince Rodolphe, the master of narrative ceremonies in Sue's *Les Mystères de Paris* and Devil-Bug even has a lost but rediscovered daughter, as does Rodolphe, though Lippard lets her be saved for a happy marriage. Apart from this melodramatic moralism, Lippard includes a strong account of contemporary American urban life, with tough gamblers and corrupt businessmen who exploit the poor and the foolish, and a range of men who prey on women—Albert Livingstone operates in all those categories. The final scene shows how Byrnewood Arlington, himself weak and somewhat corrupt, is revenged on the tall, distinguished businessman Gus Lorrimer for his mistreatment of his sister Mary Arlington: he melodramatically shoots him on the ferry across the Delaware. This frames the novel—in the opening scene Lorrimer is off on the town—and also shows how corruption and interpersonal crime are, as is usual in the Mysteries of the Cities tradition, resolved by human interaction, not by police or detective intervention. Nevertheless Michael Denning argues for the standing of Lippard's work as an American radical use of this crime fiction tradition and also sees a connection forward to the moral rectitude of the early dime novel, where the earlier cowboy heroes were re-used as models for avengers in the cities, a theme outlined by Gary Hoppenstand.[10]

  Another major contribution to the American city mysteries was by "Ned Buntline" (Edward Zane Carroll Judson). He was later best-known for his creation of the myth of Buffalo Bill, but strongly in the tradition of Lippard he produced *The Mysteries and Miseries of New York* in 1847–48.[11] He combines two of Lippard's malign men's names in his worst criminal, Gus Livingstone, who in the opening pages strides through New York in search of victims. Also as in Lippard, there are maltreated innocent women like the respectable Isabel Meadows, whose brother is a weak gambler, and the seamstress Angelina, who will not survive her betrayals. Judson gives women a major role: Big Lize, a tough prostitute, can stand up for herself, but most of them cannot, like Mary Sheffield, a version of Mary Rogers the real 1841 "cigar girl," on whom Poe had based his Paris-set story of Marie Rogêt—she like others ends up in Greenwich Street, home of brothels and abortionists.

Judson pays close attention to the streets and the realities of the city, including the plethora of gambling-dens run by major criminals like Henry Carlton, a crime boss who nevertheless, and ironically, feels socially inferior to the urban gentry. There are some police, but as with Lippard the characters tend to resolve the challenges themselves, including a generous and morally admirable retired businessman named Peter Precise, but many of the harassed people, especially the women, fail before the criminal menaces of the darkly imagined city—Judson is unusual and negative in adding "Miseries" to the "Mysteries" of his title.[12]

If Lippard and Judson were the major early American figures in the Mysteries of the Cities form, it was a substantial and continuing American tradition—at least 13 versions were variously located there by 1860—and its energy lasted. Cohen shows how authors like Osgood Bradbury went on from his 1844 *Mysteries of Boston* to work on "close forerunners of the famous 'dime novels'"[13]; Henry Llewellyn Williams, the publisher of *Julia Bicknell*, started in pamphlets and his son, with the same name (see note 41) ended up in dime novels, with some Mysteries along the way. *The Quaker City*'s dedication to Charles Brockden Brown clearly links it back to the American moral criminographical tradition but it is also strongly populist in both politics and appeal: Daniel S. Reynolds calls it a mix of "fierce social satire and suggestive eroticism."[14] This is also the pattern of G.W.M. Reynolds' *The Mysteries of London*: the erotic is hardly found in Sue. But it is striking not only that Lippard is writing before Reynolds in this mode, but also that Reynolds' work seems not to have interested Americans nearly as much as Sue's. There are no U.S. editions of Reynolds' *Mysteries* until two versions were put out in 1849 of the socially much more elevated *The Mysteries of the Court of London*, Reynold's successor to his *Mysteries*—and by then many U.S. editions of Sue were available. The anti-royal stress of the attacks on the Prince Regent in the first four volumes of *The Mysteries of the Court of London* (though they stop when he became king and Reynolds turns on aristocrats instead) may well have given it special appeal in the U.S., but it is evident in the context of the *Mysteries* form that the European, rather than English, connection is strong as part of the developing criminographical energy of America.

Disciplinary Beginnings

There was another path forward from the early records of criminal cases, one which placed stress on the professionals who observed these dramatic events, and essentially led to the detective. Heather Worthington has charted this development in the British periodicals in the early–mid 19th century, where medical memoirs gave way in 1849 to legal case studies (both will be discussed in Chapter 3), but a lawyer was realized as a quasi-detective even earlier in America.[15] A set of stories appear in the American *Gentleman's Magazine* from 1838, shortly before Poe edited it, under the series title "Pages from The Diary of a Philadelphia Lawyer."[16] *The Quaker City*, Lippard claims, is based on the papers of a dying "profound lawyer" which reveal "a full and terrible development of the Secret Life of Philadelphia," suggesting a link to this recent city tradition.[17] The "Philadelphia Lawyer" stories seem startlingly modern against the clumsy *Calendar*-style narratives borrowed from English magazines that precede them, and they were probably written by William Evans Burton, the magazine's proprietor, a scholarly man of English origin who also wrote for the stage (as well as acting and managing in theatre), and is known to have contributed to the magazine he started in 1837.[18] Much as in the *Blackwood's Magazine* "Tales of Terror," the interest is in intensity of feeling, not in detection, though items of evidence may be used by the police or in the lawyer's final explanation. In the most fully developed and dramatically credible of these cases, "The Murderess," a woman has been charged with killing her baby, but claims it accidentally fell against the wall. Medical speculation and interrogation take the officers of the law nowhere, and the lawyer, who is drafted in to represent her, is rather relieved when, without his assistance in any substantial way, she is found not guilty. But as in many early crime stories, the narrative exposes the truth—or fate takes a hand: later she is herself killed by her brutal lover and leaves a written confession. This is basically a fictional imitation of a printed criminal history, but it is firmly related in several ways to its present time and place: born in America, the woman is led astray first morally by a Frenchman and then criminally by an Italian. Ethnicity is one area of strain, place another: she distractedly drifts across the American continent, ending up dead in a Territory. In this way she charts the wandering American quest for certainty and identity found from Brown to Twain and beyond, but gender joins the uncertainties of race and place. Rather than these authors' novelistic masculine triumphs, here is female defeat: she ends in despair and hysteria, beating out her baby's brains against the wall of her slum room. The story explores the limits of the possibility of the individual in crisis, as does so much in American fiction, whether crime or not.

There are seven "Lawyer" stories. One, the third, is merely a discussion, "A Chapter on Aristocracy," but the others deal, in less detail and depth than "The Murderess," with personal descents from respectability to crime. The second, "The Counterfeiter," shows a well-educated man trick a girl into a relationship and then, when short of money, forge credit notes in her father's name. He serves a short sentence, becomes a professional forger and ends up with a long jail term. The following stories are more simply melodramatic. In "The Unnatural Prosecution" a girl has, for her seducer, stolen family papers that bring income: her mother sues for their return through the lawyer, but after they are regained she will die in misery: the lawyer sees the daughter a year later, poor and disgraced. Simpler forms of emotivity appear in "The Will" where a man is separated from his parents, finds his mother dying years later and, himself dying, leaves his money to his long-lost beloved, who was with the mother; "The Fatal Shot" tells of a brave young naval officer who, in a duel with a man whose sister he loved, fires too soon and kills the man. In disgrace, he descends to criminality, but is finally captured when he realizes he is robbing the original girl and her father. A *Blackwoods' Magazine* style overburden of feeling is central to these stories; a little more like the traditional detective story of the future is "The Reprieve," in which an immigrant (of unstated origin, but probably Irish) is, to him mysteriously, jailed for murder. The lawyer is consulted by the man's sister who realizes it was his twin brother who did it—she has sent him home beyond the law, and the jailed twin is released.

Poe will bring both imaginative depth and rational analysis to the situations dealt with by the "Philadelphia Lawyer," whose stories seem essentially to mirror the observational style of the "case study" London-based stories by Samuel Warren, *Passages from the Diary of a Late Physician* (1830–37),[19] some of which were available in pirated form in the U.S. in 1831, before they were collected in Britain.[20] The "Philadelphia Lawyer" stories appeared well before the legal professional cases of "The Experiences of a Barrister" and "The Confessions of an Attorney," discussed in Chapter 3, pp. 80–85, in *Chambers's Edinburgh Journal* from 1849 to 1952, and there are differences other than time and location. The British stories are strongly class-oriented and seem to be consistently envisaging, and then deferring, a place for a critical and self-confident skilled middle class to operate, as is discussed in Chapter 3. Such anxiety is quite absent from the "Philadelphia Lawyer" stories, where the lawyer pontificates with confidence about all kinds of people and their habits. Without any aristocracy to threaten his status or provide a level of ambition for the public in general—consistent problems for the "London Physician" in Warren's stories—the lawyer is full of confidence; he inspects and reports on the puzzles and misdeeds of his contacts with a calm sense of judgment.

Not only *The Gentleman's Magazine* and its editorship look towards Poe. "The Murderess" and all but the third story (the discourse on "Aristocracy") are notable for their structure, opening with a pompous statement of general truths (in "The Murderess" about women and violence); then will come a press news report about a crime; then a lengthy and personalized report on how the matter was eventually explained. The pattern is exactly the one Poe uses in "The Murders in the Rue Morgue," except that all his elements are superior: the opening harangue is not pompous and sexist as in *The Gentleman's Magazine*, but witty, allusive and genuinely interesting (on chess, draughts and the analytic imagination); Poe's news report is both melodramatic and also an intriguing puzzle—the mysterious voice and the horrible details of death; his exposition is consistently original—the window detail, the solution to the voice problem and the final sensational production of the orang-outang as criminal. His main addition is of course Dupin's perceptive, even inspired, process of detection. The "Philadelphia Lawyer" is not involved in any real processes of that kind: he delivers a series of interested but rather distant socio-psychological observations. That Poe worked at the highest level is hardly news: that he had a clear model in American crime fiction is something apparently unknown.

America in France

Not all early criminographical paths in America led to Poe. In a sense even more interesting than the perhaps predictable shape of a highly localized, largely classless, Gothic-oriented crime fiction is the fact that early developments in American fiction were of profound impact in French popular literature and helped to stimulate a strain that would return strongly to America itself. One of the characteristics of American literature and thought which is most surprising to the English is the ease with which American intellectuals can deal with continental European traditions—often because these are their own personal traditions, through the multinational origins of America, but not only because of that. Whether it is Chaucer scholarship or critical theory, the facility with which Americans adopt European rather than English connections is notable. Poe's own very fruitful reception in France—not many Anglophone writers have had the privilege of being translated by someone of the class of Baudelaire—was preceded by a strong connection between French writers of mystery and adventure and the work of James Fenimore Cooper.

This has been explored in substantial detail and with considerable subtlety by the French-Canadian scholar Régis Messac, who codified crime fiction, its tendencies and its possible ancient origins just before Dorothy L. Sayers much more famously did those things, apparently without his influence.[21] He was familiar with the scholarship of 19th-century crime fiction in three countries, France, America, and Britain, as apparently nobody has been since. In his account, French readers of Cooper interpreted the relationship between Natty Bumppo, the Pathfinder or Leatherstocking or Long Rifle, and his native American friends and models as being very much like the relationship between a bourgeois reformist French social inquirer and the tough working class whose values and skills he respected, and yet whose actual position he implicitly undermined: real colonialism provided a model for class colonization. Messac discusses Cooper in some detail as the last of his "Pathfinders."[22]

The idea of a brave and clever criminal-conscious detective was located early in French crime writing with the real-life case and the biographical elaborations of Eugène François Vidocq: his *Mémoires* came out in 1827–28. There was French contribution to this tradition, especially from Balzac (see pp. 49–50), but it was the model of Cooper which enabled French writers to focus crime writing on a central character, whether positive or villainous. By displacing such a figure into colonial romance, Cooper used its raw energy to drive the plot, and he also romanticized the vigor of his inherently hostile companions—the Native American parallels of the energetic but alarming criminal classes who were kept off-stage as potential embarrassments in the first wave of French metropolitan fictions, even in the relative realism of early Balzac, but would notably emerge in *Les Mohicans de Paris* (1854) by Dumas. Cooper gives the hero a romantic power not found in the self-doubting Gothic heroes of Godwin and Brown, nor the tough part-criminal early French detectors like Vidocq or Balzac's version of him, Vautrin. The way to the hero detective, romanticizing the realistic conflict of Vidocq's world, is open, and where the English found the Newgate Novel sensationalized heroes too antique for continuing contemporary interest (p. 128), and the tough police detectives of French fiction and London reality were too lower-class for fictional heroism (see pp. 137–40), America, like France, could conceive an active hero against crime.

From Cooper's dark pastorals the French writers re-imagined their city as a threateningly trackless waste—a new norm of urban vision—and imagined those capable of charting it as Europeanized versions of the noble pioneer and his native assistants. For Eugène Sue in his extremely successful and influential *Les Mystères de Paris* (1842–43), it was Prince Rodolphe and a cast of aberrant natives and criminal grotesques won by his purity to the service of law: Messac speaks of the way Sue admired how Cooper had presented "les moeurs féroces des sauvages," ("the fierce attitudes of savages.")[23] In the title of the very long *Les Mohicans de Paris* Dumas made a direct claim on Cooper's translated inheritance and the novel was set in 1827, the year after Cooper's *The Last of the Mohicans* appeared. The lordly Salvator—with his "manly beauty seen in all its strength"[24]—was supported by the professional policeman animalized as Le Jackal. The pair represented Natty and Chingachook, downmarket Parisians being the Native Americans in this story. To flesh out that reading, in a form of reverse post-colonialism, the leading pair had a supporting cast of feral trackers, Native Americans Gallicized, who were to leave their mark in the music and misbehavior of the Parisian Apache tradition. There was more than Cooper in this festival of Dumaserie, but as Messac says, he was very important: he calls it a mix of "la féerée, le picaresque, et l'influence de Cooper"[25] ("the magical, the picaresque, and Cooper's influence"). Messac ultimately sees beyond the French material, feeling that Dumas's Salvator in fact "présage Sherlock Holmes"[26]: this view has been ignored by English commentators.

Messac does not only explain Poe's influence on France through the earlier interest in American writers; in another book he has argued that Poe himself drew heavily on French material, mostly a mixture of Balzac—for romantic Gothic narratives in a realistic context—and the 18th century fabulists, notably Voltaire, for the weird voyages of self-discovery and self-destruction his characters undertake.[27] While Messac may be overstating his case somewhat in that argument, the role of French material mediating between Poe and his Gothic sources in E.T.A. Hoffman is certainly credible, and it is interesting to note that, as a French scholar working at Montreal's Anglo McGill university, Messac as a French-Canadian had a European-American agenda as a basis for his insistence on the international, and ultimately extra–American status of Poe.

American Policing

The French tradition will return importantly to America, as will be discussed below in the context of Anna Katharine Green. But before looking at that, it is appropriate to consider another kind of information about what sorts of crime fiction Americans were reading, when and how, and what does this tell us about the nature, intensity and disposition of the

American criminographical experience in the 19th century. In the 1830s American publishers were remarkably quick to republish the beginnings of crime fiction in British journals, and also to make of them in terms of authorship what they felt like, to fuel their market success. Just as Warren's *Passages from a Diary of a Late Physician* appeared in book form in America before they did in Britain, the legal case stories similar to the "Philadelphia Lawyer" cases which appeared in *Chambers's Edinburgh Journal* in 1849–51 were both pirated in America in 1852 as The *Experiences of a Barrister* and *The Confessions of an Attorney* by Cornish Lamport of New York. The *Experiences* were credited to Gustavus Sharp, who is the central figure; for the *Confessions* the publisher invented the name Warren Warner Esq of the Inner Temple. These did not appear in book form in London until 1856, when the two sets of stories appeared under the title *Experiences of a Barrister*, the author being given as Sxxx Xxxxxx Xxxxxx D.C.L.— which the British Library catalogue translates as Samuel Warren—it would seem in spite of the number of Xes that "Sir Samuel" is implied, though he never attained that status.[28] The invented name Warren Warner for the American double editions (in at least some versions the overall titles were allotted to the wrong set of stories) is surely intended to associate the stories in America with Warren's fame—he had by then also published the very successful *Ten Thousand a Year* (1841), a comic social melodrama which challenged the success of the young Dickens and had the honor of being mocked by Thackeray in *Fraser's Magazine* in 1841 in *The Great Hoggarty Diamond.*

The productive energy of the American crime fiction market is also evident in the fact that when "William Russell" started publishing his influential series focused on the police detective Thomas Waters, starting in 1849 in *Chambers's,* it was America that first anthologized them—Cornish Lamport again certainly had a collection out in 1853, and the "Ellery Queen" records indicate a previous edition in 1852. Eric Osborne doubts the existence of this,[29] suggesting there was a confusion with the 1852 "Warren Warner" *Experiences,* but both the authority of "Ellery Queen" and the fact that the two titles they cite for 1852 and 1853 are quite different make a confusion less likely and give the idea of an 1852 edition some credit: it is certainly listed in the U.S. National Union catalogue. The most striking fact is that it was not until 1856 that a London publisher put out the same collection: England lagged behind America in making its own stories widely available in collections.

As the influence of the Waters stories grew and many English authors produced versions of this calm, methodical style of police detecting, America added its voice in the still under-discussed "Jem Brampton" stories. John Babbington Williams, a doctor, claims to have edited *Leaves from the Note-book of a New York Detective* (1865) from the case-notes of James Bramp-ton.[30] The title pays tribute to the London tradition and its 1857 *Leaves from the Diary of a Law Clerk* (see Chapter 3, pp. 85, 89), but the content is strikingly American—so much so it seems very strange that the series is not mentioned in Landrum's "Reference Guide." James (known as Jem) Brampton received medical training and has a range of disciplinary skills, but was left alone in the world after his father was accidentally burned to death—and turned out in any case to be financially ruined. As he tells Dr. Williams, his first case came to him soon after his father's death when a school friend asked him to look into his fiancée being accused of murder. In investigating, he, like many early detectives, noticed a button—it was on the floor of the murder room; with considerable care he found the shop which sold it on a waistcoat to the dead man's servant, who is convicted. This led to his becoming a detective police officer in New York, which, as in London, could include practice as a paid consulting, so effectively private, detective.

In both modes Brampton's work can be at a higher level than in his first outing: in the second case "The Silver Pin," after another school-friend invites him to investigate the mysterious death of his employer, he achieves success through attention to both medical observational detail and some quite sophisticated research, and finally exposes his over-confident friend as the criminal. He has a confidence about his social position which avoids the negative class anxiety of the English detectives, but Brampton's comfortable social status does not lead him to be a gentleman amateur as occurs in novels by Mary Braddon, Wilkie Collins and Ellen Wood, discussed in Chapter 5, and which ultimately underlies the role of Sherlock Holmes. The fact that the stories are introduced by a doctor and drawn from the hero's case-book (though actually almost all are narrated by him) may even suggest an influence on the stories of Conan Doyle, who knew very well the American story tradition.

Brampton's work is heavily involved with American city and business life and he uses a mixture of astuteness, powerful observation and physical courage to resolve his cases, which are quite often short and energetic. Poe's influence is clear in his close analysis of a scene, but this is a much more modern and active world than Dupin's Paris—travel across the country, usually by train, is recurrent. Though Brampton says he is connected to the official police, the stories give very little sign of any real link, and in the first story he is paid $500.

He is involved in cases ranging from widespread forgery in "The Coiners" to violent murder and a long dangerous pursuit in "The Struggle for Life." The usual pattern is for someone to be wrongly suspected; Brampton visits, looks very carefully at the details of the murder scene or, especially early on, the contested will. He will notice something, such as in the first two cases the button or the tiny mark of the silver pin over the dead man's heart. In the third story, "The Club Foot," he sees that a signature on a will is, though evidently real, quite frail compared to another by the same man: then he finds the paper is too new for the date, and discovers the alleged will-writer imprisoned by the exploitative heir. The people he clears are usually honest young men with faithful girl-friends, and the villains are recurrently acquisitive older men. Underlying the stories is a sense of discomfort with the cunning exploitations of modern money-seeking society, and a dedicated support of old-style honesty and family values.

The way ahead is clear to the Allan J. Pinkerton stories. A Scottish immigrant who had started a detective agency as early as 1850, in 1874 he published his first crime novel, *The Expressman and the Detective*. In his preface he insists that "this, like the other works announced by the publishers are all *true stories*, transcribed from the Records in my office."[31] Locating the brisk approach of the Brampton stories in the real world of private detection, he, much like the earlier English short stories, operates in a world of theft and fraud rather than murder. The first story—or case, as he calls it—is set in Montgomery, Alabama, in 1858–60 and concerns mail theft, amounting in the main instance to $40,000. As is common in real detection, not the elaborate processes of mystery writing, the initial suspect is the real criminal, and finally confesses when faced with an associate who is about to give evidence against him in court—he gets ten years in jail and they recover almost all the money. The story is told in the first person by Pinkerton, but the detection has been handled by one of his operatives—and in a curious way the story switches whenever it needs to into third-person accounts of events and dialog at which neither the narrator nor the detective were present. The first edition is a handsome single-volume book, by no means a dime novel, and apparently did well—15,000 copies were recorded as being sold in two months, and it was followed quickly by *Claude Melnotte as a Detective and Other Stories* (1875), with the lead story set in Chicago. Pinkerton went on to publish more crime fiction titles and his name has long been used as a pseudonym for the private eye in America.

Much more popular in tone, and selling in very large numbers, were the dime novel versions of urban crime fiction, such as Harlan Page Halsey's very well-known series beginning in 1872 about "Old Sleuth"—which was often used as the author's name. They could be fairly short novels like *Brant Adams, the Emperor of Detection*, a 200-page paperback selling for 25 cents in 1887, which began the publishers' *The Secret Service Series* for Christmas 1887—curiously, just when the two major titles Arthur Conan Doyle's *A Study in Scarlet* and Fergus Hume's *The Mystery of a Hansom Cab* appeared in London. The sleuth is not in fact old: he is a young active man who, like Vidocq before him, often uses disguises—an old man is a favorite, with both author and audience. He could also appear in true dime novel format, with some hundred pages for ten cents. Number 111 in the "semi-monthly" series *Old Sleuth's Own* of April 13, 1898, is *A Mystery of One Night or Detective Murray's Single Clue, a Tale of Genuine Detective Strategy*. The title, mixing as it does simplicity of night and clue with the complicated concept of "strategy," is more elaborate than the text, which is uniformly simple in vocabulary and style, melodramatic in action and colloquial in dialogue.

The publisher was offering two other *Old Sleuth* series, and asserts, "These stories are moral, instructive, and dramatic."[32] There was also a "Young Sleuth" series by "Police Captain Howard" (Harry Fenton and Walter Fenton Mott), starting in 1877 in the *Boys of New York* journal, as Cox records.[33] The dime novel thrived strongly in the market-place: in hundreds of titles, an appealing, direct and young American responded to the conflicts of the busily growing cities, often with some with vigor and naivety, even racism. The form has its own complexities: Michael Denning has written in detail on the often right-wing politics involved, but Pamela Bedore has argued for a range of more insightful viewpoints being located, if less than consciously at times, in the form.[34] In the following years Nick Carter especially thrived as a vigorous action hero; he was in a way developed from "Old Sleuth," as he first appeared in an 1886 serial in the *New York Weekly*, named "The Old Detective's Pupil" and written by Ormond G. Smith. This led to *Nick Carter's Weekly*, which ran till 1915, but he continued to appear—in 1929 Messac wrote about him enthusiastically as a mainstream, detective figure,[35] and after the James Bond success in the 1960s he reappeared as *Nick Carter, Killmaster* with more than a hundred titles. The stories have always appeared anonymously, or by "Nicholas Carter," even "Sergeant Ryan." In fact John R. Coryell wrote many of the Nick Carter titles, and the form had wide and lasting influence through being an early and widespread representation of a tough detective bravely facing "the mean streets"—the image that Hammett was to realize with some complexity and Chandler to elaborate consciously.

American Women Writers

The 1887 pulp *Secret Service* series advertises many other novels: the titles often feature women, and a number are by women authors, who, like Mrs. Alex McVeigh Miller and Mrs. Sumner Hayden are only known by their husbands' names. In spite of that continuing evidence of masculine orientation, a marked feature of American crime fiction in the later 19th century is the activity of women writers. They were not the first American women crime writers. While in Britain women like Mary Braddon and Ellen Wood made major contributions to sensational fiction, they rarely used detection techniques as central to their plotting, but American women quite early made a conscious condensation of the Poe tradition and the European-style police detectives. Harriet Prescott Spofford was apparently the first to do this. Her long story "In a Cellar," published early in 1859 in *Atlantic Monthly*, uses an aristocratic detective in fashionable Paris: the world is that of Poe, but it is a diamond theft, close to standard 19th-century crime fiction interests and the detective is less isolated from social reality than Dupin. He is an unnamed English diplomat who agrees to investigate the theft of a Marquis's jewel; however, though he recovers the diamond, it is then stolen from him, and he does not realize, as readers do, that his valet is the criminal.

Later Spofford published two consciously American crime stories, perhaps after reading the "Jem Brampton" stories published in the same year as her first. Here she moves decisively further from Poe, using a police detective named Mr. Furbush. Like Jem Brampton he is connected loosely to the New York police, and the stories localize crime fiction to America in a less masculinist way than the Brampton stories—Furbush is quite sensitive in his reactions to his ambience and to people, especially women. "Mr Furbush" (1865) involves a murder of a young woman in a hotel, which he solves through studying a photographer's output, and so identifying the victim's ring on the hand of her female guardian—who dies of shock when she is identified. "In the Maguerriwock" (1868) relates how Furbush solves the mystery of a man long missing in a rural area when he realizes that a woman who has been treated as mad, repeating a sentence about a cellar, is in fact fixated on having seen the murder committed by her husband. Not very complex in terms of detection, with each story relying on a single clue, and still looking back to Poe for the atmospherics which are central to the overall effect, these are important efforts in terms of locating stories which are generically crime fiction in an American setting, and also, though still using a male detective, increasingly involving a female viewpoint.[36]

It would seem that "Mr Furbush" was noted by Metta Fuller Victor, who was already working as an editor for the dime novel company Beadles and had published novels on a wide range of topics, adventure, romance and politics,[37] when she produced, under the pseudonym "Seeley Regester" *The Dead Letter* (1867), which appears to be the first formal American mystery novel. Mr. Burton is in a position not unlike Furbush and Brampton, a police detective who is commissioned privately to work on a case, a family murder, but his thoughtfulness resembles Furbush. More technically skilled than Waters or the amateur detectives Wilkie Collins had deployed in *Hide and Seek* (1854) and *The Woman in White* (1860), and clearly drawing in some way on the insightful approach of Poe's Dupin, Burton travels the country—including a steamship trip to California—to solve a mystery raised when the narrator finds, in the "dead letter office" where he works, a letter that has been ignored for two years.

The case that is revealed started when Henry Moreland, a banker, was stabbed to death in rural Blankville, with a lancet, by a doctor—a dubious English immigrant hired to kill by Moreland's nephew, James Argyll, whose motive is jealousy: he loves Moreland's fiancée Eleanor, daughter of a rich lawyer. The narrator, Richard Redfield, works in Argyll's office and also admires Eleanor. It is a complex case, with Burton being helped by the narrator, including deciphering the cryptic letter and observing the suspects from up a tree (Figure 1). The narrator has himself been framed as the murderer by Argyll, so loses his legal job and ends up in the "dead letter office"—with eventually fateful results for Argyll. This makes the story seem very male-oriented, but female characters do play a part. A seamstress, Leesy Sullivan, is pursued by Burton as she was on the same train as Moreland, and seems suspicious. She is merely clumsy, also in love with Moreland, and is eventually cleared. A less conventional deployment of a female character focuses on Burton's daughter Laura—she helps him with his detective work, and while he claims to have some far-sighted skills, and is remarkably prescient in interpreting handwriting, she is a fully-functioning clairvoyant and uses her powers to help him pinpoint the criminal.

This approach has been treated by Catherine Ross Nickerson as merely a recycling of Gothic approaches, but Kate Watson sees Victor as consciously foregrounding female capabilities, a view compatible with the pressures put on Laura by her father and other male characters, as well as the pains suffered by Leesy before and after Moreland's death.[38] The novel is dense in narrative and implications, with a good deal of romance and interaction between characters, as well as many suspicions. Most surprising of all, Burton himself finally dies of poison, but its source is not indicated

Figure 1. The amateur detective at work in *The Dead Letter*. Illustration by N. Orr in "Seeley Regester," *The Dead Letter* (New York: Beadles, 1867), p. 223.

other than being an unnamed criminal. This in itself may suggest Victor's inherent unease with a heroic male detective—and she provides for his daughter. She is finally adopted by the narrator, who has married Eleanor's sister Mary. The murderer is allowed to remain in Mexico where Burton has pursued him for a confession, and his murderous employer Argyll himself is also banished—his father not wanting the publicity of a trial. This repeats the common pattern in English crime fiction, where rather than involving the police the higher classes arrange the punishment of their own criminals, often sending them abroad.

The novel did well, and Victor went on to write *Too True* (1868), though it was published anonymously, perhaps because with a different publisher. This is not a murder story but deals with the mysterious jilting of a girl, and the characters are interested in some valuable jewels. Sussex calls the novel "a Gothic-influenced psychothriller,"[39] and such investigation as occurs is by a boy and a young female artist. This suggests Victor is still resisting the male dominance of the detective, and that pattern is also present in *The Figure Eight* (1869), a lively if over-complicated mystery about a doctor's murder after the theft of gold: its most striking feature is that it does without a detective entirely. The young male narrator is suspected of the crime, then another innocent man is shot dead by police, and finally the doctor's young Spanish wife is revealed as the culprit.

Apart from her other fiction-publishing energies, Victor has substantial significance as the creator of the first formal mystery novel by an American woman (not by a world writer—Ellen Davitt's *Force and Fraud* of 1865 is narrowly an Australian predecessor[40]). In Furbush and Burton the sturdily independent if less than confident pioneer inquirer of Charles Brockden Brown becomes a fully demoticized and professional, police-based version of the focused analyst Dupin, if not quite as active or business-oriented as the contemporary Brampton.

There are signs from London as early as the 1850s of the idea that this kind of modern detection of mysterious crimes was in some way an American kind of activity. Collins certainly knew Poe's work—in 1854 he produced a moderately successful pastiche of "The Purloined Letter" under the lackluster title "The Stolen Letter," but it seems the impact went deeper with him. Also in 1854 his *Hide and Seek* depends on the detective energy of an Englishman who has returned after frontier adventures, which include success in the gold-diggings and being scalped, a sort of compendium of American pioneer heroism: born Matthew Grice he has adopted the Cooperesque name Mat Marksman. Just to show this is not a one-off, in Collins' short story "The Diary of Anne Rodway" (1856), sometimes cited as proto-feminist, the tentative inquiries of the young seamstress are only resolved when her boy-friend returns from America and acts as an amateur transatlantic detective. There may even be a shadow of this in *The Woman in White*: the timid drawing master Walter Hartwright is a stronger person and a decisive detective, albeit again Englishly amateur, when he returns from his dangerous visit to South America.

American Leader

The strongest single formation of American women's crime writing, developing the moves of Spofford and Victor, was made possible in substantial part because the Franco-American connection remained strong. The success of Dumas and his *feuilleton* follower Paul Féval put crime and detection into the center of the mainstream of popular French writing, but if Poe located his detective in Paris, presumably out of deference to Vidocq and Balzac (Poe's Dupin preceded Sue, though he seems so much more sophisticated than Prince Rodolphe), it could be argued that Émile Gaboriau returned the compliment, creating in the brisk, fearless tracker Lecoq an inherently American detective who was very active in Paris. The Americans certainly recognized his vigor very quickly: both the intense interest American publishing had in overseas crime fiction and also its piratical habits are clear from what appears to be the earliest transplantation of Gaboriau, a very prompt reworking of *Le Dossier no. 113* retitled *The Steel Safe*, fully relocated in America and credited as authored by Henry Llewellyn Williams, Jr.[41] A genuine translation of *Le Dossier no. 113*, as *File no. 113*, appeared by 1875 and there would an American-only sequel, *File no. 114* by Ernest A. Young in 1886. Within a few years of their first Paris appearances, *The Mystery of Orcival* appeared in 1871, *The Widow Lerouge* in 1873 and two different versions of *M. Lecoq* (1869) were available in America before 1879: issues of these novels often carry no dates, and it is likely there are some earlier examples. If America, now mostly New York, though sometimes Boston and occasionally still Philadelphia, responded quickly to what was happening in France, London was much more sluggish: it appears that *File no. 113* did not appear there until 1884, and neither *The Widow Lerouge* nor *M. Lecoq* until 1881. In fact it seems that though the French texts had been occasionally reviewed in London, the books had been read in French.[42] There was little real knowledge of his work until Vizetelly launched a series of Gaboriau translations in 1881, the books Conan Doyle certainly read and in 1885 Hume was told were selling well in Melbourne—and both decided they could use, and improve on, them as models.

America had not needed to wait that long. It seems clear, as will appear in the discussion below, that Anna Katharine Green was familiar with Gaboriau and that her influential *The Leavenworth Case* (1878) is in many ways a powerful Americanization of his kind of urban detection. She may also have been generally influenced by Fortuné du Boisgobey. At least two du Boisgobey titles were available for Green to read in English: *The Chevalier Casse-Cou* appeared in America 1875 and *The Golden Tress* in 1876, but as she is said to have rewritten her first novel several times, his *La Vieillesse de Monsieur Lecoq* (1878), later translated as *The Old Age of Monsieur Lecoq*, was probably not an influence. Green was well-educated—in 1866 one of the first women in the world to graduate from college, Ripley, in Vermont[43]—and she could probably have read other crime novels in French. However, it appears likely that while much in Gaboriau's structure is borrowed and adapted by Green, like his map of the murder scene (Figure 5), which she also uses, du Boisgobey's greater interest in character and his calmer style may well have influenced her more: she appears to be the first to use an in-text representation of the scraps of letter that are discovered (Figure 2).

Whatever were the precise lines of influence from France, Green's stories had substantial innovative strength. With her well-developed sense of a specific desirable genre, and well-organized plots about well-organized policing, she appears to have led in the conscious construction of the genre of detective fiction at a time when London was still mixing up sensation, plain policing and the slowly emerging amateur gentleman detectives.

She was born Anna Catherine Green—the K and the second a in "Katharine" were mysterious changes in the first book—and brought up in Buffalo, but her father became a well-known New York trial attorney. She started as a poet, but then used her legal knowledge in transplanting the pattern of Gaboriau and du Boisgobey to America. *The Leavenworth Case* draws on knowledge of police procedures, as Mr. Gryce,[44] the mild-mannered and rheumatic detective, slowly and methodically thinks about things: there is about him more of Gaboriau's retired Tabaret than his vigorous and still young Lecoq. But the novel also draws on New York life, largely through its narrator, the young lawyer Everett Raymond, who acts as an independent investigator—especially towards the end—and is also highly vulnerable to the charms of the Leavenworth girls, Mary and Eleanore. He ends up with Eleanore in the type of romantic sub-plot that runs right through the story, parallel to the mystery, and survived into the Christie novels.

THE LEAVENWORTH CASE.

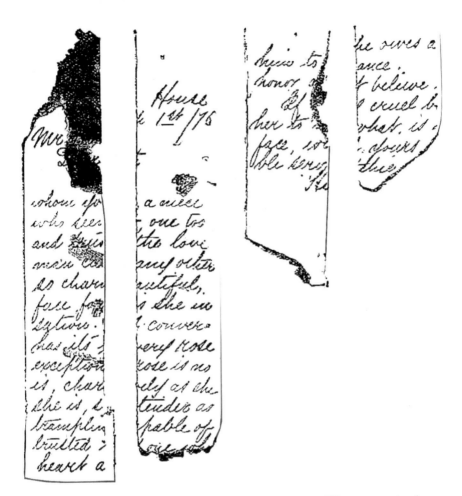

Figure 2. The torn letter in *The Leavenworth Case.* **Illustration in Anna Katharine Green,** *The Leavenworth Case* **(London: Routledge, 1884), p. 81.**

The Leavenworth Case, as a fine mystery, deserves to have its sudden surprise ending concealed here from people who have so far not read it. Horatio Leavenworth, a wealthy New York banker, is found shot dead in the library in his Madison Avenue mansion—both house and room appear to have been locked, and Green is the first to explore the hermetic mystery puzzle. She also assembles an impressive range of other major motifs of the genre: a key, letter and weapon which are all missing, but soon discovered and the torn letter illustrated in the text; ballistic evidence; a sketch-plan of the murder scene; a hectic amount of activity around the murder site; a disappeared or abducted person; suspicious actions by family members; overheard and misunderstood conversations; mysterious activities in the past emerging in the present; dramatic concealments and disclosures; a second murder; lengthy detective visits to the country where important things have happened in the recent past; a final confrontation of the main characters, organized by the detective; confession and explanation by a genuinely surprising criminal. Many of these features appear before in Poe, Victor, Gaboriau, and du Boisgobey, but Green is the first to organize them smoothly into a narrative of disorder among a socially powerful class where improper desires and personal obsessions can cause disorder and death. New York and its society are at once both celebrated and represented as at risk—the central mechanism of the classic clue-puzzle to come. The influences on the American author are mostly non–English: though Messac felt Green approached English authors in "son amour de la réserve et du decorum" ("her love of reserve and decorum"),[45] this is really only a matter of tone. The detective method, combining central, dedicated inquiry with some romance, is much closer to Gaboriau than its intermittent appearance in either Collins or Braddon.

These is also an element of nationalism, which is itself questioned. One of the suspects, Henry Clavering, has been hated and mistreated by the dead man, simply because Clavering is an Englishman: the bad treatment suffered by Mr. Leavenworth's first wife at the hands of an Englishman made him hate them all and forbid his adopted daughter Mary marrying one of them (curiously, Clavering is also the name of a romantic Englishman in *Arthur Mervyn*). Far from a motif for murder, this is represented as an improper interference with natural love and natural interaction between the two countries. At the same time Green is no Europe-lover, unlike her near contemporary Edith Wharton, and in a fascinating link with past American tradition that goes beyond literary patterns she actually set one novel, *Miss Hurd: an Enigma* (1894), at Coopertown, New York State, the home of James Fenimore Cooper.

Although Green retains a male detective he is far from the intellectual masculinism of Dupin or the macho vigor of Lecoq, and women play major roles. The sisters, in a probably deliberate reference, share the names of the two sisters in Victor's *The Dead Letter*—Green adds a final e to Eleanore. They play major and independent roles in the story, both seeming capable of murder and also involve themselves firmly in the detection as well as leading active romantic lives; a minor but finally tragic part is played by the servant Hannah, whose absence from the house on the night of the murder is the first element of mysterious complication in the plotting.

With its multiple qualities of plotting skill, outcomes both startling and satisfying, innovative gender position, and confident American location, *The Leavenworth Case* did very well, selling three-quarters of a million copies in 15 years: it, not *The Mystery of a Hansom Cab*, was in fact the first true best-seller in crime fiction, though it was not published in London until 1884 and only by the mid-eighties were Green's books appearing with some speed across the Atlantic. But it was not only the novel's success that made Green the developed leader of the early American tradition: she became a steady producer with a reliable format, something Gaboriau and du Boisgobey had not achieved or even sought. The second novel, *A Strange Disappearance* (1880), harked back at the start to the disappearance and eventual death of Hannah the maid in *The Leavenworth Case,* but developed its story in a different part of America. Green wrote on steadily, and, again not unlike Christie, developed interesting variants to her initial detective, who, like Poirot was too passive and malingering to be felt a hero. In a proto-feminist touch developed by later authors, Amelia Butterworth, a wealthy middle-aged single woman, first appears in *That Affair Next Door* (1897), where she helps Gryce and does the same, with varying degrees of independence in two other novels, *Last Man's Lane* (1898) and the very popular *The Circular Study* (1900). Later Green let a woman detective have greater freedom in lively short stories about the inquiries of Violet Strange, a young society woman who seems in part based on her own daughter Rosamund: they were collected as *The Golden Slipper and Other Problems for Violet Strange* (1915). It is one of the most interesting features of Green's work that having started, like Regester and Fortune, with models that were fully masculine in position, and only at first varying those by having an older, feebler detective and a romantic interest for the narrator, she, unlike the other two, over time shifted towards a female-dominated version of the genre, a formation which is in itself a little recognized feature of early American crime fiction and was no doubt influenced by her work.

After Green

The woman-oriented mystery had sources in America beyond Green. One of the surprises of the recent past was to discover that as well as producing anodyne schoolgirl fiction that has become sancrosanct in Anglophone moralized culture, Louisa May Alcott had also produced pseudonymously a number of sensational thrillers which realized active women in full awareness of the dangers they could both face and, in part consciously, excite.[46] The double heroines of *The Leavenworth Case* are women of this volatile and intriguing kind, though they are more ladylike than, for example, the exotic heroine of Alcott's *V.V.* (1863). Alcott's dates suggest both that she was a source for these lively women in Green and also that she was drawing on the dangerous and intriguing women realized in Ellen Wood's *East Lynne* (1861) and Mary Braddon's *Lady Audley's Secret* (1862). Green's women were never quite as vertiginous or indeed exciting as Alcott's form of American sensationalism, but the heiresses Mary and Eleanore Leavenworth were to have a long and productive after-life.

One of the features of past crime fiction forgotten in the present is the distinct "New Woman" element in a group of writers around the turn of the 20th century. There were women detectives in the short-story form in Britain, some by male writers (see Chapter 4, pp. 121–25), but the Americans were ahead in female authorship of novel-length exploration of family strains. Green is of course one of them, with her Violet Strange stories offering young and spirited femininity, but fuller and more complex achievements were made by Green's younger contemporaries. Carolyn Wells seems largely forgotten even in America, though she was an influential crafter of mysteries and the author of an innovative and predictively potent book on the form, *The Technique of the Mystery Story*, as early as 1913. She established herself with *The Clue* in 1909 but took even longer than Green to rate in London, the book not being produced there until 1920. There is a conservative element in Wells: she sets her fiction in comfortable rural areas and country towns, but also at a distance from the conventional male detective story. In *The Clue* the murder of a wealthy young woman just before her wedding—by, it turns out, her inheritance-seeking male cousin—is investigated largely by her bridesmaid-to-be, along with the unused and non-macho best man: only very late in the story is there recourse to a patriarchal, and somewhat patronizing, detective Fleming Stone, called, it seems a little ironically, "The Great Man." Wells's plots are not simply criminal-oriented, emphasizing as they do the fractures and strains that can rend apart the most conventional-seeming of comfortable, conservative American families. The way is clear for Christie to adapt this to the apparent certainties of English life: Christie's father was American, but it is not often realized how transatlantic was her criminographical inheritance.

A more bravura version of American family explorations appears in the work of Mary Roberts Rinehart, who adds in the kind of emotional drama and nervous suspense that Alcott had skillfully adapted from the

European sensationalists. Rinehart's first, *The Circular Staircase* (1908), which seems to pay in title a tribute to Green's *The Circular Study*, uses strong-minded spinster Rachel Quinn as narrator. She is to a substantial degree involved in the inquiry into the crime, though Rinehart always makes male detection ultimately crucial, even in the later novels starring Nurse Hilda Evans—known as "Miss Pinkerton." As Douglas Greene reports,[47] her first novel sold very well and Rinehart because the acknowledged leader of a group of writers who formalized female involvement in a more affective and self-conscious way than Green had permitted to Amelia Butterworth or Violet Strange: Wells's study of the genre mentions a number of women writers from the period who are now forgotten (see Chapter 4, note 45). A less impressive result of this female emergence was that this sub-genre was dismissed by some later male critics and authors, with Ogden Nash calling it in a 1940 ironic poem the "Had I But Known" school. It was never clear what these men objected to about the reflective element of the stories, apart from its firmly female gendering of speculative intelligence. Unlike Wells, Rinehart was an immediate international success, perhaps because of her bravura tone and the somewhat touristic treatment she gives of America, but it is clear that while her sales might have stimulated English women as authors, it was the cooler, more technically skillful model of Wells that appealed most to Christie and, beneath their elaborations of the genre, Sayers and Allingham.

Towards Modernity

To say that the classically English clue-puzzle had some substantial American input is to draw vivid attention to the need, emphasized throughout this chapter, to rewrite the geohistorical map of crime fiction. As Green shows in her first novel, commentators do not need to look to Israel Zangwill's *The Big Bow Mystery* (1892) or Gaston Leroux's *Le Mystère de la Chambre Jaune* (1907) for the locked room, and Green, Wells and Rinehart show a calm, rational approach that is more effectively imitable than the unstable, ironic style of E.C. Bentley's *Trent's Last Case*, published in 1913, which is often cited as the harbinger of the alleged English "golden age."

That age in itself was not only English. The American male critics usually follow Chandler as he rejected his own educational roots to denigrate the English between-wars mystery as artificial and trivial—and fail to see its class tensions, personality-based uncertainty, and its subtle, probably crucial, national displacement of generational fatality in the war. They also ignore the fact that the model shaped by Christie, the now forgotten H.C. Bailey and the perhaps better forgotten Monsignor Ronald Knox was given its richest and most elaborate achievement in America in the very elaborate novels of Willard Huntington Wright, writing as "S.S. Van Dine," and the equally pseudonymous but even more illusionary cousins Frederick Dannay and Manfred B. Lee who made up "Ellery Queen," author, detective, and brand-name in the scholarship of the genre.

The American clue-puzzlers were of course displaced, though not as quickly as the tough guy critics would have us think, by the new wave of Hammett and Chandler. But was it a new wave? A historicist study interested in the Americanicity of crime fiction can see the lines of inheritance going back to Jem Brampton, mobile, moral, and tough, and his transatlantic localization of the London police detectives. That tradition was continued in the cool rigor of the Pinkerton stories, the moralized street wisdom of the dime-novel detectives in the "Old Sleuth" tradition, and the hectic adventures of Nick Carter, which seized readers from 1886 on (Figure 3),[48] to such an extent that from his rational French-Canadian distance Messac saw the 1890s as, the age of, to quote the title of his Book Six, "Sherlock Holmes et Nick Carter," an idea sure to affront English literary patriots and, the more interesting feature, surprise American crime critics.

Hammett, according to Chandler, seized crime for a democratic no-nonsense America, but it was not in fact an international victory; it was a palace revolution in American publishing that gave power to a realistic and street-level form of policing against a formal and socially elevated type of crime writing that was identified with England. The tough guys turned away from Green's socially distinguished and female-friendly mode of mystery—though they blamed its features on the English—and opted for the demotic urban sainthood of "Old Sleuth," "Old King Brady" and their like (whom Denning calls "the proletarians of detection"[49]), as well as some of the manic moralism of Nick Carter and the realistic detecting methods Pinkerton had put into his novels—and Hammett had learnt on the job with the same agency.

So there are many surprises in thinking about American crime fiction in terms of what actually happened, in terms of real writing and real publishing, not just what has been refracted through the ideologies and ignorances (the two are symbiotic) of reception over time. In view of the length, the breadth, the vigor and the national relevance of the varied traditions of American crime fiction, it becomes easier to understand why in the period after the Second World War American crime fiction has been so dynamic. Not only is there a massive publishing and film industry to realize

Figure 3. Nick Carter shooting a society thief. Cover illustration, *Nick Carter Weekly*, no. 261, December 28, 1901.

the genre, but emergent crime fiction had a century before established itself, from Brown and Cooper, on as a medium of American national identity. Film noir and the tough guys confirmed that, but the wealth, in all senses, of feminist, ethnic and gender-conscious crime fiction that has flowed from America in the last 20 years has shown that the dynamic forces of identity politics have been able to continue to channel themselves—even identify and express themselves—through this genre. But that too is not new. As soon as America become an independent nation, crime fiction was available for debates about the individual seeking freedom and certainty in an environment—personal and gendered as well as social and urban—always in some way one of disputed identity and ownership. Like all other fiction in touch with its times, and with a genuinely modern feel to its processes, crime fiction in early America could answer real threats with credible inquiries and consoling resolutions.

The question remains why a country like America that is usually so assertively self-aware, and that celebrates its popular achievements so much, seems not to have noticed, or wanted to notice, the way in which the narratives of crime fiction have been homologous with the narratives of the establishing of American identity. Perhaps an overseas inquirer ought not to hope, or even perhaps try, to resolve this conundrum, but at least it seems appropriate, even important, to draw attention to this long-established mystery of American crime fiction.

CHAPTER 2

Sherlock Holmes' Grandmother:
French Contributions to
the Formation of Crime Fiction

Art in the Blood

Nineteenth-century fiction is, in that world of social change and personal self-creation, naturally interested in the personal origins of central figures. So it is hardly surprising when Sherlock Holmes sets at rest on this matter Watson's mind—and no doubt that of his massive audience. At the beginning of the *Memoirs* story "The Greek Interpreter," Watson has been asking about the sources of his skills in observation and analysis, and he explains:

> "My ancestors were country squires, who appear to have led the same life as is natural to their class. But none the less, my turn that way is in my veins and may have come with my grandmother, who was the sister of Vernet, the French artist. Art in the blood is liable to take the strangest forms."[1]

As he was establishing Holmes early in *A Study in Scarlet* (1887), Conan Doyle referenced the French crime fiction tradition with deliberate negativity, when Holmes responds to Watson's mention of Gaboriau by saying "Leocq was a miserable bungler,"[2] but his account of his origins implies a fairer recognition of the way in which French writers had shaped the tradition of detective analysis. They had produced the first effectual detective, Vidocq, then the first extended sequence of crime stories, by Féval, and then the first heroic police detective, Lecoq. Poe's choice of Paris for the home of his genius detector was both an early response to, and a potent prediction of, the originality and the energy of the French initiative in shaping the new genre in its new world.

From Criminal Arras to the Surêté

The first substantial French engagement with the policing of crime was made in a primarily factual mode in the *Mémoires* of Eugène François Vidocq (1827–28), which became very popular in France, and did well in English in 1829 in both Britain and America. Though the *Mémoires* purports to be the four-volume autobiography of a criminal turned police spy and then senior police officer in Paris, its style is very like a first-person novel and it also underwent a range of ghost-writing that effectively made it a work of fiction—and it was certainly welcomed as such, notably in the many stage versions and edited selections that were popular for decades.

The text of the *Mémoires* offers puzzles and problems. The account usually given is that the publisher wanted four volumes: Vidocq managed the first and did at least correct the second, but then a ghost-writer took over, Louis François L'Héritier de l'Ain, who extended the series to four volumes, elaborating Vidocq's notes substantially and even including parts of a novel of his own. Vidocq disavowed the later material in a note to the first volume, but this did not in any way weaken the effect or success of the whole—indeed this whole multiple self-presentation is much like the way Vidocq as police agent would involve himself with the criminals he was seeking, with its mixture of confidence and invention.

The shape of the story is like a confessional picaresque narrative, far from the single-case focused stories into which the detective novel will evolve in France. Vidocq tells in leisurely mode how he was born in Arras in 1775, drifted through poverty into crime—first by raiding his baker parents' till and stealing their silver-plate dinner settings. After legal detainment he engaged in that boom industry of the period, the army. He did well, being both large and aggressive, but soon, through weakness for money and also for a series of inveigling women, he merged into the mobile semi-criminal semi-military population that were the underbelly of Napoleonic France, known as "L'Armée Roulante" ("The Roving Army"), sizeable groups of ex-soldiers who wore uniform, pretended to be officially active, and actually engaged in wandering malpractice.

Vidocq's criminality occupies the *Mémoires* for a substantial period. It is not until half-way through the second of the four volumes that he takes a crucial step when he is denounced in Lyon to the police by fellow-criminals—simply because he is now trying to be less active with them and "they counted on the fact that once I was recognized by the police, having no other refuge than with the gang, I would decide to take sides with them."[3] Typically, Vidocq seizes the situation and contacts the local commissioner of police. He denounces a number of local criminals, with a complicated series of pretenses and double-dealing, and also faces with some courage and skill a range of real dangers to himself—this is a more heroic narrative than the intellect- or method-based detective processes of the future.

Vidocq's move towards legality is by no means simple or straightforward. Released from both criminal and police pressures, he returns to Arras, finds his father is dead and stays with his mother for a while. With his local criminal record expunged he wears heavy disguise, and takes up work as a lace-seller, including spending ten months in Paris. He is betrayed by a girl to the police, escapes, and opens a shop in Rouen with another woman, but she is unfaithful: they separate and after more problems he moves to Boulogne, becomes a pirate for a year, then ends up in Paris again, with his mother, and works for a while as "an itinerant dealer in novelties" (164).

He feels that criminals are surrounding him once more and finds this distasteful—"the more I read into the souls of the criminals, the more they showed themselves to me, the more sympathy I felt for society which nourished such a breed in its bosom" (184). So, in Chapter 16, which Rich's translation entitles "My Début with the Police," he makes contact with Monsieur Henry, "chief of the division of safety in the Prefecture of Police" (174), and is put in touch with the Baron de Pasquier, the Prefect of Police. They cautiously withdraw him from the criminal world—with several intermediary jail terms. He says "These two generous men were my liberators," they "guided my first steps" and "I was installed as a secret agent" (192).

This was in 1809, and Vidocq immediately became busy. Relying on his substantial knowledge of criminals from jails, but often disguising his memorably large physique, he consistently contacts minor members and female hangers-on of gangs planning a crime, finds out the details, and offers himself as a participant. He will tell the authorities where and when to intervene, and will frequently himself be jailed, then permitted to escape. Throughout the process he will constantly be on the watch for someone, especially a woman, who will know him too well to be fooled by the disguises. This is dangerous work and he fears for his safety; equally he is often violent, both in defending himself and in arresting serious criminals. He is very successful, and not always popular as a result:

M. Henry was astonished by my activity and my omnipresence, while several of the officers of the regular police did not blush to complain. The inspectors were little used to being up several nights in a week and found the service I occasioned them too arduous when it was in some ways permanent; they complained. Some were even so indiscreet, or so cowardly, as to reveal the *incognito* by which I manoeuvred so successfully [205].

These events are dated 1812 and Vidocq has become not just a secret agent but as he puts it "the principal agent of the Sûreté" (237). In this role he is extremely busy—he records that in 1817 he was responsible for 772 arrests and 39 recoveries of stolen goods. Such intensity of business impacts on the narrative—there are cases running into each other, characters apparently dealt with will later re-appear, assistants become targets, convicted people turn into informants, all in a helter-skelter mix. But the story does at times settle into what will become the familiar pattern of the case study. For example, Chapter 19, "I Lodge with the Enemy," tells a single, unified story about Vidocq hunting down a criminal nexus focused on a quasi-lady piano teacher Madame Noël, whose son is a highwayman. Vidocq meets and admires her; he becomes familiar, deploys a secret agent as their confidential messenger, shows her his key-making skills, manages to avoid a woman who knows him too well, suddenly realizes that his agent has changed sides, and nevertheless manages to arrest his targets and also the delightful Madame Noël. A 5,000-word chapter, it could easily be expanded into a novel, and there are a number of others with this focus and coherence: Chapter 23, which Rich entitles "The Clue of the Two Footprints," involves bad weather, suspicions and urban crime—the villain steals lead from roofs—and with its effective clues could be taken as an archetype of modern urban crime fiction.

In Chapter 25 Vidocq switches from an elaborate presence as a Jewish peddler to a continuing role as a German servant—with appropriate dialog for both roles—and manages to regain for a wealthy jeweler what are assessed as 100,000 crowns worth of diamonds. He is also familiar with women, having both a disaffected wife and a series of passing and for a while supportive partners—there are more women criminals and near-criminals in this story than in most 19th-century crime fiction. Some are genuinely tough—Sophie and La Belle Lise laugh when Vidocq says they will serve about six months each. But they can also be tragic: when he manages to arrest the elusive recurrent thief Sablin, his heavily pregnant wife is on the scene: Vidocq delivers her child, she makes him the godfather, but he later hears that after serving her five-year sentence, she has hanged herself. Similar is the story of Adèle—though this is from the novel that L'Héritier de l'Ain inserted, it is developed and moving, not out of keeping with the grim but also sentimental process of Vidocq's narrative. A young and beautiful crook, she eventually serves six years. She sees the error of her ways and goes straight as a needlewoman—but her past prevents her gaining enough business. Close to starvation, she gives herself up for other crimes and is reported as the first French woman to receive a life sentence: she is in jail lamenting as the story is written.

Vidocq's rich mix of urban drama, picaresque criminality and ultimate legitimacy was enormously successful, especially on the stage—the disguises were a great hit, and apart from all the disguises and masquerades, it was widely reported Vidocq could change his height from his natural, and then very tall, 5' 10" to a good deal smaller. Editions and magazines soon began to make Vidocq's own handsome image prominent (Figure 4). If in that way, and in their development of chapter-long case-studies, the *Mémoires* showed a future model for a brave and focused investigator, they also showed that crime narratives could really sell copies.

Figure 4. A popular picture of Vidocq. Title page illustration, Eugène-François Vidocq, *Mémoires*, illustrated edition (Paris: Tenon, 1830).

Vidocq's position at work had not proved simple or stable. As he himself predicted there were opponents inside the system, and he came under examination for corruption and was threatened with dismissal and disgrace. As a result he opened in 1833 "Le Bureau des Renseignements Universels pour le Commerce et l'Industrie" ("The Office for Universal Information for Commerce and Industry"), the first private detective agency.[4] He also produced fiction, though without great success, as noted below.

There were two notable after-lives for *Les Mémoires de Vidocq*. One was the rich French treatment of detection and crime in the decades ahead: the other, which in itself no doubt in part validated that development, was the fascination of major French novelists with the figure of the highly sophisticated criminal who was also capable of being on the side of good. Balzac and Hugo, two of the greatest names in recent European fiction, both read Vidocq with interest and profit.

Balzac deployed him in several novels, first in *Le Père Goriot* (1835) as

Vautrin, also known to the police as Collin: he operates in Vidocq fashion both as a major criminal and a para-detective. He returns under his real name of Jacques Collin (but mostly masquerading as Abbé Herrera) in *Illusions Perdues* (1843). In *Splendeurs et Misères des Courtisanes* (1844) he, again like Vidocq, turns to helping the police and finally becomes chief of the Sûreté. Though Balzac relished re-creating the power of the figure's power, he never made him the central communicator of the novels' emotions and meanings—rather he is a crucial secondary figure. Hugo made a parallel response to Vidocq's ambiguous identity and values—he split the figure into both Javert, the dedicated policeman of *Les Misérables* (1862) and his target, the former criminal Jean Valjean.

Féval and the Crime Novel

Crime is a substantial element of the 1840s Mysteries of the Cities genre, initiated by Eugène Sue in his 1842–43 *Les Mystères de Paris* and G.W.M. Reynolds in his even fuller and more radical *The Mysteries of London* (1844–46). Sue's *Mystères* did very well as a daily *feuilleton* on the front page of *Le Journal des Débats*, and Anténor Joly, looking for something to match it for *Le Courrier français*, turned to the Breton lawyer turned novelist Paul Féval, who had just done well with *Le Club des Phoques*, "The Seals' Club." By December 1843 the paper was printing Féval's *Les Mystères de Londres* as by Sir Francis Trolopp, a change of spelling and gender from Frances Trollope, well-known in Britain and France as a travel-writer and novelist, not yet as mother of the prolific novelist Anthony Trollope.[5]

A less positive response to Sue's initiative was by the persistent Vidocq, who in 1844 published, as usual with the help of ghost-writers, *Les Vrais Mystères de Paris*, in seven volumes. Laying claim as their title indicates to his authority in this domain, the Vidocq-focused volumes mixed real and fictional events, with moderate success in the busy fictional market. He had already responded to the new audience for crime fiction with a two-volume novel, with memoir elements, *Les Voleurs* (1837), and followed up both that and the *Vrais Mystères* with the five-volume *Les Chauffeurs du Nord* (1845) set back in revolutionary times: the sub-title is *Souvenirs de l'An IV a l'An VI* ("Memories from 1795 to 1798"): the "chauffeurs" ("heaters") are criminals who torture people over fires until they reveal the location of their money and valuables.

In *Les Mystères de Londres,* his first major novel, Féval offered a massive fantasy version of crime, well beyond any possibility of detection and relying on events in the narrative itself to defeat the scheme. It is focused on hostility to England: the Marquis of Rio Tinto plans to rob the Bank of England (via a tunnel), blow up the Houses of Parliament, execute the King (William IV), and with an army of 100,000 Irishmen take over London. Sue's Rodolphe had battled against the professional criminals of Paris, but the Marquis has enlisted London's "gentlemen of the night," and allows them little liberty for personal criminality. This Marquis is Fergus O'Brian, an Irishman representing distinctly French interests in the decades after Waterloo, namely the destruction of English power. His massive plot is brought down by a mix of Scottish and English aristocrats and gentry, higher-class ultra-patriots, not police or ordinary citizens.

Féval followed his adventure into political fantasy with a more criminally realistic account of events French and English. After *Les Mystères de Londres* he published regularly and *Le Bossu* (1857) was the most successful, a Europe-wide disguise-based melodrama set around 1700, combining historical fiction in the tradition of Scott and Hugo with a melodramatic, hyperbolic narrative style that became known as "le roman de cape et epée," "the novel of cape and sword." The story appeared in the mainstream newspaper *Le Siècle* in 1857 and was a popular success. Its hero Lagardère seeks to restore to her true status Aurore, daughter of the dubious Duc de Nevers: this sounds like a reworking of the plot of Prince Rodolphe and his daughter Fleur de Marie from *Les Mystères de Paris*, but this version is weirder: it turns out that Aurore, her identity unknown, has been married to her own father. This exciting narrative did very well, including over time: Féval's son, also Paul, wrote sequels to it, the last being *La Jeunesse du Bossu*, published in 1934, the year after he died, and the series is now in print again, in response to the success of the 2003 French television series *Lagardère*.[6]

Féval then turned to crime fiction, in an elaborate form. *Jean Diable* appeared as a serial in 1862–63: Brian Stableford, its translator and a Féval scholar, calls its central investigating figure "the first fictional mystery-solver who is formally identified as a *detective*."[7] That is technically true, as the earlier English material which deployed that mode was all in short stories (see Chapter 3), but though it does have a main character who is a detective the novel is not focused on him and his investigations: in any case its structure was not imitated, as it is itself somewhat historical and is also set in both France and England.

Jean Diable starts in Paris 1863, its year of publication, but looks back to London, in 1817—when Napoléon was still active in St Helena. Gregory Temple is Scotland Yard's leading detective—over 20 years before they existed, and even more surprisingly he has been there since 1790. He has written a major book on the art of detection entitled *The Art of Discovering the Guilty*, stressing—well ahead of Sherlock Holmes—that an apparent impossibility offers a way in to solutions. He has an assistant, James Davy and their major current case is the murder of Constance Bartolozzi, in London, which may involve the mysterious and polymorphous master criminal Jean Diable, John Devil. There are sudden problems: Gregory drafts his resignation and stalks out. James Davy remains behind. He goes through the files and destroys some: his initials seem suggestive.

The story relocates to France where it will stay, though it does have a range of international adventures, mostly in back-stories. Central, if also multiple, in identity is Henri de Belcamp, son of the Marquis de Belcamp, and so Comte de Belcamp. The father lives in a castle in a peaceful part of the Oise valley—Féval favors these rural settings not far from Paris. But Henri has been away for a long time. His mother was an English beauty called Helen Brown, the daughter of a rich brewer, whose two fellow-brewers both became the fiancés of Constance Bartolozzi, recently murdered in London, who also came from Miremont-sur-l'Oise. There is too much riotous elaboration of plot to bother with, either here or in general, but what we do need to know is that the Marquise Helen moved on, and started drinking and stealing, but she also supported her son Henri when he studied—very energetically. He started at Edinburgh, and by now, in 1817, has gathered five doctorates, from Edinburgh, Cambridge Tübingen, Prague and Jena. He returns home to the castle and seems to like the local beauty Jeanne, inheritor of nine million francs. Money floats around Féval novels in huge amounts, sometimes, though not here, in forged banknotes.

Henri has friends who look like him, do not sound like him, but seem to cross his tracks. One is the English Percy Balcombe (note the resemblance to Belcamp). Another is Henri's mother Helen Brown's other son Tom, who is apparently the same age as Henri. Then there is John Davy. By the end it is pretty clear that Henri and Percy are the same and it is hard to believe that Jeanne, to marry Percy but also saved from death by Henri, does not know this. The plot seems to make it clear that Henry and John Davy are the same as well, and that he, or they, are probably also John Devil. The Tom Brown issue remains a puzzle: after Henri dies at the end, by his own hand, Tom Brown is said to be executed in London. Perhaps Féval meant that: or perhaps he ran out of time or room to explain how Henri arranged a substitute, which is what he frequently does. Even more than in the *Mystères de Londres* the characters assume identities and cross nationalities as part of their criminal or indeed anti-criminal identities.

There are some other familiar events. One is the Australian adventure.

Helen and Tom were, it seems, transported. Percy was also in jail in Newcastle Penitentiary, whatever that was. But Henri was out there to make money in mining, well before the gold-rushes. He helped Percy out of jail and they took off across the country, towards Adelaide, were bailed up by fierce aborigines near the Lachlan River, and narrowly escaped, to find some German missionaries, one of them very beautiful. Henri looks very like her fiancé, but he then turns up.

If that excitement reminds us of the Marquis of Rio Tinto, we are also locked into his politics. There is throughout not only a criminal class led by John Devil, whoever he may be at any given time. There is also "The Knights of Deliverance," who are like a freemasonry with the code word "For the Best." With many high and also low confederates, their role is to plan the escape and re-establishment of the emperor—the novel's start in 1817 now bears patriotic fruit. But it is not just a retrospective dream. Led by Henri, they are planning to deploy the new steam-driven ships which are being built by an Englishman named Perkins—Henri met him in Australia. With them they will make the restored Emperor invincible and in particular establish a French international empire based on what the English currently call India. It is a positive futuristic reflex of Fergus O'Brian's plan to destroy England.

Like Fergus's plans, all goes fine until very late on, when one ship is destroyed in a riot in an African dock and the other just sinks, full of conspirators: Féval often gets out of dead ends by just jumping the wall. Henri shoots himself after his long-lost mother turns up and dies, and his father is fatally hurt. They all seem simply to fade away, but that happens in Féval: it is all plot not morality. If the international and the multi-personal are imagined, it is mostly on the criminal side—but Gregory Temple, who is largely off-stage through the story, is nearly as multiform as Henri. The detective matches the criminal, as in Poe and many others. The only positive uniformity is the lost identity of France, but that itself is not aristocratic or bourgeois, and certainly not rural—there is lively satire of village idiocy throughout. Multiplicity is envisaged, across nations and identities, but that innovative possibility is only a threat or at best a counter-threat. Essentially, *Jean Diable* is a French fantasy of nation, and of identity-changing. It does recognize English leadership in engines, detection, public order, and gentleman's tailoring, but is a good deal more French in its focus than *Les Mystères de Londres* had been, though, rather like Sue's use of Prince Rodolphe's noble German background, there is attention paid to that region as well.

After this, Féval tended to restrain his efflorescent plotting to France, and in 1863 he launched a long series of novels under the overall title *Les Habits Noirs*. These "Black Coats" are the criminal organization that is shown to be running France at all levels, and attention is paid to both high and low. The first novel is *Le Forêt Parisien* ("The Parisian Forest"),[8] and central to it is M. Lecoq, the arch-villain. Féval's editorial assistant at the time was Émile Gaboriau and he would famously redeem this name for his great detective, and indeed Féval's wicked Lecoq does a lot of detective-like things, not unlike Gregory Temple. The Habits Noirs also have international force: both their head, the Colonel, and the enduring victim-turned-avenger André Maynotte have Italian identity—André and his beautiful wife Julie are Corsicans, but without any evident Napoleonic connection: it is later now.

In 1825 Lecoq has arranged on behalf of a man from Germany named Schwartz a safe-robbery: 400,000 francs is stolen. As is a Habit Noir custom, an innocent is framed for the crime, André Maynotte, a Corsican metal worker. He, his wife and child run for it: he is caught and jailed, she escapes and meets Schwartz on the coach to Paris. Maynotte breaks out with a criminal named Lambert, who knows Lecoq, but he is killed as a rope breaks and Maynotte takes his identity. It is assumed Maynotte is dead, and his wife marries Schwartz. In Paris Lecoq sees Maynotte, who is then taken ill: Lecoq and the "Colonel" who runs the Habits Noirs leave him to die, but the colonel's grand-daughter Fanchette, later known as "La Comtesse," helps him and he recovers and leaves for London, with his son. Time passes and there are many complications around the senior Habits Noirs personnel, including Schwartz, now revealed as a Baron with family.

In Paris a man called "Trois Pattes" ("Three Paws") appears, seriously crippled, without the use of his legs: he crawls up and down stairs and through the streets. He and many others are involved in plots which usually center on Lecoq. Trois Pattes lives next to a Norman named Bruneau. He is also friendly with Michel, a romantic young man whom Schwartz would like to marry his daughter, but the Baroness Schwartz (formerly Madame Maynotte) refuses permission. Michel, described in a chapter titled "Our Hero," lives with two poets who are writing a play, *Les Habits Noirs*. Paris is said to be a forest, hence the subtitle, and there is a reference to Vautrin (195). In other literary references Paris is said to be filled with "savages" as found in the work of Cooper (257), Vautrin is referred to again as linked to the Habits Noirs (284–85) and Lecoq is described as "a Vidocq and a half" (287).

The poet-playwrights work out Maynotte is Trois Pattes. Lecoq has a sign on his door reading, Agence Lecoq: it handles all kinds of business. He is friendly with Michel, who is the Baron Schwartz's son, and has been saved from jail by Lecoq and has borrowed money from him. Lecoq (like Vidocq) has started a *bureau des renseignements*; he knows a highly placed Marquis, who wants to be Prefect of Police, and Lecoq may become a Minister. Lecoq now is head of the Habits Noirs and offers the Marquis control of the organization.

Trois Pattes brings a forged banknote for Lecoq's approval: they will run four million of them. Lecoq knows that the Baroness Schwartz's first husband is alive, and he also knows Michel is Maynotte's son. But Lecoq thinks Maynotte is an enemy of his named Bruneau. Trois Pattes agrees to check on Bruneau, then Fanchette speaks of Bruneau as Maynotte, and says his vengeance is approaching.

In a dramatic climax at Baron Schwartz's house, the Baroness recognizes Trois Pattes as Maynotte—her former husband. Schwartz attacks him and Maynotte's wig comes off—he is also Bruneau. Then Maynotte has Lecoq trapped at Schwartz's safe by the armband Lecoq used in the very beginning to frame Maynotte for the safe robbery. Lecoq confesses, then shoots at Julie, but Schwartz takes the bullet and dies. Even more spectacularly, Maynotte beheads Lecoq with a safe door. The conclusion is a light-hearted round-up commentary during a play, where Julie and Maynotte are once again together.

This is grand melodrama, but identity is also a grandly melodramatic theme. Féval takes the urban fluidity that is the first context of self-aware crime fiction and lets it effloresce in terms of both its human and its national powers of re-formation. Where Balzac and Dickens stuck to humanist morality and class separation, where Reynolds and Sue had overriding if differing political accounts of their world, Féval is just letting urban European modernity run riot, and all of his plots have the same vertiginous characteristics.

Émile Gaboriau and the Detective Novel

The success of Dumas and his *feuilleton*-producing follower Paul Féval put crime and detection into the center of the mainstream of popular French writing, but Féval's most important donation to the present was that while he was writing *Jean Diable* in 1862, he had just started to employ as secretary a young man born in 1832 in Charente, named Émile Gaboriau. He edited Féval's magazines, probably ghosted some of his work, picked up his techniques and focused them better. Féval's worst villain, Lecoq in *Les Habits Noirs: Le Forêt Parisien* is, presumably deliberately, revived in Gaboriau's work and becomes the first major police detective in crime fiction—Yves Olivier-Martin calls him "the prototype."[9]

Gaboriau was already writing non-fiction commentaries and historical material, and his interest was soon engaged in the popular French form which Bleiler calls "factual crime."[10] Early in 1866 his first crime novel, *L'Affaire Lerouge*, appeared as a weekly serial in *Le Petit Journal*. The novel starts with a grisly murder, and the police under Gévrol, "The General," get everything wrong, focusing on a wrongly-suspected man. An elderly bookish amateur, Tabaret, becomes involved, and through him the past of other characters is explored and finally the criminal is identified—as is common in French fiction at this time, the malefactor is a corrupt and vengeful aristocrat. Tabaret is a low-level, unassuming version of Dupin, thinking things out rather than engaging in action, and there also appears a young policeman named Lecoq, a reformed criminal, but all he really does is refer the case to Tabaret—and he seems too young to have any reference to Féval's master-criminal of the same name.

Gaboriau evidently saw the force of combining an insightful Dupin-like inquirer with the honorable but limited active police figures who had come from Vidocq through Dumas. It would seem that an interest in professional policing, probably derived from the "Waters" London-based short-stories (see Chapter 3, pp. 85–89) which appeared in French by 1858, made Gaboriau turn away from his elderly version of Dupin to a vigorous Paris detective named Monsieur Lecoq. This was also the title of a novel he was already working on when *L'Affaire Lerouge* was published, but according to Bonniot,[11] the length of that book, especially its extensive second volume going back into the history of the duke who is involved in the initial murder, led him to write, for publishers demanding material on the basis of the success of *L'Affaire Lerouge*, three brisker novels which all involved Lecoq and appeared before the major, and ultimately the best-developed one, *Monsieur Lecoq* was published in 1869—in which as a result the hero is about five years younger than he had been in the earlier-published novels.

In *Le Crime d'Orcival* (1867), Lecoq's first full appearance, he is an intense and vigorous detective, master of disguise, insight and moral energy, who dominates the whole story with the exception of that Gaboriau characteristic, a long historical and explanatory narrative, which is read to him by the judge with whom he is working. The story begins dramatically—it is summer 1862 and two poachers out at night find at the edge of the river the bloodstained body of the Comtesse de Trémorel. The mayor and

Plantat, the local *juge de paix*—more or less justice of the peace—visit the chateau early, but find no one there, as the count gave the servants time off to go to a wedding in Paris overnight. The house is severely disarranged, with bloodstains everywhere, but no sign of the count or his body.

Lecoq is sent to deal with the case. He inspects the house and its disorder with great care, observing that the five overturned wine glasses actually contained vinegar. Marks he examines near the river make him realize the countess was carried there. He thinks, and the doctor confirms, that most of the stab-wounds on her body were made well after death. Then Lecoq goes to stay at Plantat's house, and they and the doctor continue to discuss the case. The servants suspect one of themselves, Guespin, who disappeared in Paris and knew the count had just received a large sum of money. He is arrested by M. Domini, the *juge d'instruction* in charge of inquiries. The two poachers are also arrested, for no good reason, just as some sort of precaution.

Lecoq and Plantat suspect the count killed his wife and then searched the house for a document of great importance. A complication emerges as the mayor's wife and daughter are distraught and ill because the older daughter has written to say she will kill herself as she is pregnant to the Comte de Trémorel. Then another event occurs: Lecoq hears a man in the garden and restrains him: it is the doctor's assistant Robelot. He has come with the intention of killing Plantat, who will he thinks discover that he supplied the poison used to kill de Sauvresy, the former owner of the chateau, and the first husband of the countess. They restrain Robelot and arrange to have de Sauvresy's body exhumed. In the morning they find Robelot has killed himself and they find some 18,000 francs hidden in his house, no doubt the payment for the poison.

Plantat has by now read Lecoq a long document which gives a detailed history of de Sauvresy's marriage to the beautiful village girl Bertha, how she become involved with her husband's close friend de Trémorel, and how she began to poison her husband. He becomes aware of this, writes about it, and how he believes that in future she will be punished by de Trémorel, who loves Laurence, the mayor's daughter, but accepts Bertha for the money she can bring him. Plantat concludes that having killed his wife, and found the crucial document—presumably to do with income, as he has always been short of money through gambling—de Trémorel has now gone to Paris to be with Laurence.

Lecoq, not having after the opening scenes done much in the way of detecting, agrees with this assessment and sets his men to look for the pair in Paris. He also interrogates the suspected servant Guespin and is satisfied that the count sent him on the night of the murder to Paris on a meaning-less mission, in order to make him seem the murderer. The fugitive couple are found through Lecoq guessing the count will have re-furnished a house expensively: his men tour the appropriate shops and find he is posing as an American, and Laurence is with him. The detective and the judge meet her first and explain it all; then de Trémorel appears. He wants to flee again but Laurence insists on a suicide pact—but he fails to act: so she shoots him dead, and is about to kill herself when Lecoq grabs her gun. She is to be even luckier. Just before this climax, Plantat has revealed a further point of complication, telling Lecoq that after his wife and sons died a few years ago he fell in love with the mayor's beautiful daughter Laurence, in spite of being some 30 years older. This tendency towards banal romance recurs in much of Gaboriau's work, and here has the startling outcome that Lecoq advises her to reject suicide and take up a happy life with Plantat. She does, they marry in a couple of weeks and leave for Italy. Finally in a lower-level parallel to the aristocratic interest in property, Plantat makes a present to Lecoq of the house he owns in Orcival.

This novel never had the success in America of its successor, no doubt because the details of aristocratic life and misbehavior were not as inter-esting there as urban bank robbery, the subject of *Le Dossier no. 113*, or *File no. 113* as it was known in translation. There was a version set entirely in America, *The Steel Safe*, produced as early as 1868 by Henry Llewellyn Williams, an energetic activist for French crime fiction in America (see Chapter 1, note 41 on him). The first American translation of the novel appeared in 1875 and others followed, including the very successful Scrib-ner's version of 1900. Lecoq is a good deal more active here, both in detec-tion and in his disguises—in *Le Crime d'Orcival* he told Plantat that only three people, one of them his lover, knew his real face, but this capacity was not activated in the novel. As usual with Gaboriau and the new mystery novel genre, the story of *Le Dossier no. 113* starts with a bold crime—at the Fauvel bank one morning the safe is found to be without the 350,000 francs that the owner had ordered be made available that day. Only he and the cashier, Prosper Bertomy, know the combination. (Bertomy was re-named Jasper in the Scribner's edition and that has persisted through new translations.) Prosper had, against orders, had the money brought to the bank the previous day—he thought he might be late in the morning. This and his knowing the safe's password lead to his arrest by the investigating police officer, known as "Squirrel"—but he does not get far and his superior Lecoq will soon take over.

Lecoq persuades the judge to bail Prosper, who has been living for a while with Nina Gypsy, a charming if rather casual young woman, since about two years ago M. Fauvel's niece Madeleine (in English translations, Magdalene) broke off her engagement to Prosper. Nina left their apartment while he was in jail: she is occasionally questioned, and now has a male friend named Caldas. Prosper is met by a large man with fair whiskers named Verduret, who says he is a friend of his father and is going to prove him innocent. Verduret looks into a range of matters, and states his suspicions of the Marquis de Clameran, who has made it his business to get to know Prosper, also knows Madeleine, and has a friend Raoul de Lagors, who claims to be another aristocrat from Tarascon in the far south-west.

The long second part of the novel goes back some 20 years to 1841 and tells a complex story about the de Clameran family. Gaston the marquis's heir kills a man and escapes: he is thought to have then drowned. His father dies of shock, and his brother Louis takes the title. Unknown to Louis, Gaston's beloved, Valentine de Verberie, from an enemy family, leaves for England, where she has a son Raoul—Gaston did not know she was pregnant. Valentine eventually marries the banker Fauvel, who is befriended by Louis, Marquis de Clameran, and by Raoul de Lagors—the latter lives with the Fauvels. He is a spendthrift, and under Clameran's control: Clameran wants money, bothers Valentine, and also says he loves Madeleine: to ease her aunt's grief she drops Prosper for him.

Verduret has been away in Tarascon researching, and when he returns to Paris Prosper has become very bothered by an announcement of the marriage of Madeleine to Clameran, and has sent an anonymous letter to Fauvel denouncing Raoul as his wife's lover and having sold her jewels for money. The outcome is a major revelation scene—a novel-size version of Poe's explanatory conclusions, in which it is revealed Raoul, set on by Clameran, stole the money, with Mme Fauvel's help—but she tried to stop him, hence the scratch on the safe door that interested Lecoq. Nina had got the password for Clameran from Prosper when he was drunk. Verduret recovers most of the money, still hidden in the house, but lets Raoul escape with 50,000 francs as the scandal in court would be too great for the Fauvels. He also reveals that the real Raoul died very young and Clameran enlisted an English jockey's son to be Raoul. Clameran is found dancing semi-naked on a roof and is institutionalized as insane. Madeleine is reconciled to Prosper, and he becomes a director of the bank. But that is not all. As the reader may well have suspected would happen, Verduret pulls off his large wig to reveal none other than Lecoq, the ultimate in inquirers—but he is also a Frenchman, and to the now somewhat subdued Nina he reveals he is also none but Caldas, though it is not clear if he was acting as a detective when disguised as her lover.

Le Dossier no. 113 is a very effective mystery novel, working up to a fairly evident, but well melodramatized, solution, and including a number of high-quality entertaining vignettes. It is in fact a good deal livelier than *Monsieur Lecoq*, and gives the hero-detective a full and vigorous part, or indeed parts, to play. That is not at all the case in *Les Esclaves de Paris* (1868), where, while he is known as "this celebrated detective,"[12] Lecoq only appears towards the end. The "Slaves" of the title are mostly aristocrats in Paris who have come under the malign power of Mascarot, a very learned but seriously evil man—Bonniot suggests the name is meant to remind readers of Balzac's "Z. Marcas" the villainous central figure of an 1840 novella.[13] He has two major assistants, Catenac, a lawyer, and Hortebize, a homeopath, who use their access to vulnerable people to find details they then use for blackmail, as much to humiliate the gentry as to make money for themselves. The central story is the disruption of the marriage of an all-round fine gentleman, de Breulh, with a very grand and rich young woman, Sabine de Mussidan. The villains develop a poor young musician into a fake lost heir and attempt to force a union between the two, but in the end it turns out that Sabine's original love André, an impoverished painter, is the true lost Duc de Champdoce, and all ends very happily, under Lecoq's benevolent gaze. This urban melodrama is more sympathetic to the aristocracy than most of Gaboriau's work, but has some links to other novels—even overlapping in some characters with the later non–Lecoq story *L'Argent des Autres* (1874). A characteristic 19th-century lost heir narrative meshed with an urban villainy frame, *Les Esclaves de Paris* shows the range of material of interest to readers and also to writers—as with Féval, Gaboriau's style of novel can wander substantially across the popular field of the period.

But Gaboriau did return to and complete his plan for a major, uniformly active detective mystery. The novels after *L'Affaire Lerouge* had done well, and set the scene for a major publicity blitz in spring 1868 in the magazine *Le Petit Journal*, detailed by Bonniot,[14] for his best-known novel: *Monsieur Lecoq* started as a serial in 1868 and appeared as a book in 1869. It immediately dominated the other fiction and was widely accepted as the strongest novel so far in the tradition of detecting mysterious crime. The energetic young policeman (no explanation is offered of this story preceding in time the already published adventures of Lecoq) has the Mohican-like ability to read a scene—the novel opens with an aria of forensic detection mostly to do with footprints, followed by tremendous doggedness on the chase. He also offers a youthful rejection of the corrupt confidence of an old world, whether that of senior police, his informal adviser Tabaret or, as the second (historical and largely Lecoq-free) part of the novel shows, the authority of the aristocracy.

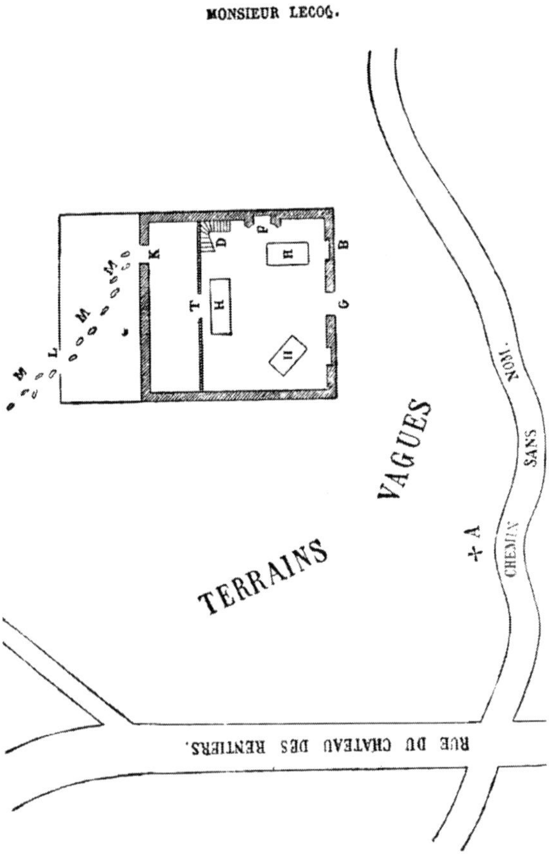

From the start *Monsieur Lecoq* is more detailed than Gaboriau's previous novels in its social and urban observations and its presentation of Lecoq's technique: in this mode it is ground-breaking in presenting a detailed map of the investigations around the bar where the murders occur (Figure 5). It is also quite searching in its account of national events of 1816 and their aftermath—in this way more sophisticated than Féval's unfocussed romantic patriotism. The novel has two volumes, which in English have at times appeared separately, with volume 1 "The Inquiry" published as *Monsieur Lecoq*, and volume 2 appearing under its original

Figure 5. The detective activities map in *Monsieur Lecoq*. Illustration in Emile Gaboriau, *Monsieur Lecoq* (Paris: Dentu, 1869), p. 74.

sub-title as *The Honour of the Name*. Many English readers of the 1917 Hodder and Stoughton edition of *Monsieur Lecoq* must have been baffled to come to the end of what they thought was the novel, to find only a suggestion who the criminal might be, and Lecoq's promised future investigation. Differently puzzling is the Dover reprint of 1975 which has the last few pages of volume 2 simply tacked on to the end of volume 1, without any indication of this in the "Introduction" by E.F. Bleiler, just a word on the cover that he has also "Edited" the book.

The story through which Monsieur Lecoq establishes himself as a major detective is set in about 1830 and starts almost casually when a police patrol, on a February night at 11 pm, leaves the station at the Barrière d'Italie and moves through a very rough area towards the Seine: Gévrol, still known as "The General," is in charge. They hear shots from a bar called "La Poivrière" ("The Pepperpot"). Two men are dead, and one soon dies, but before that he manages to say that "Lacheneur" enticed him there. A man who has been wounded in the face and neck tries to escape but is caught by a young policeman, who is praised by Gévrol. Widow Chupin, the bar-owner, says the three attacked the arrested man, and were shot by him. Gévrol arrests her and the "murderer"; the young policeman expresses doubts about this, and Gévrol leaves him to investigate.

A small, energetic man of Norman origin, Lecoq is at most 26 years old. He studied law, but when his parents died he did not continue into a profession but became a law clerk, then an astronomer's calculating-assistant. He fantasized about lucrative crimes to the astronomer, who said he should become a thief or a policeman. He has found police work dis-enchanting, but is excited by the possibilities of this situation and with the elderly and distinctly limited policeman, Father Absinthe, he decides to investigate. He recalls that as the police arrived, the "murderer" made the battle of Waterloo statement, "It is the Prussians who are coming"[15]; Lecoq believes this indicates that he had let his accomplices escape. He then examines the scene outside and finds women's footprints in the snow: he deduces that they met a man waiting there, and after further examination of the scene, clearly following Dupin, Lecoq concludes the waiting man was tall, middle-aged, in a cap and a brown wool coat, and wore a ring. He sees that the women took a carriage, makes a plaster mold of their foot-prints, and decides he will try to trace the cab-driver. Back in the bar he establishes that the women were not drinking with the arrested man and someone came back for something. Lecoq finds a diamond earring on the floor: a map of the scene and the women's movements is provided in the text.

At the police station where Gévrol took the arrested people, a man, apparently drunk, has turned up and was also arrested. Lecoq calls him the "accomplice": he has had access in prison to the widow and the "murderer." Lecoq thinks the "murderer" is a gentleman—he suspects he has used mud in jail to conceal the fine white skin of his feet. Judge d'Escorval praises Lecoq's report but also seems rather distant: he too has visited the "mur-derer." Lecoq finds the coachman who picked up the women, but they ran from the house where he dropped them. At the mortuary, no-one identifies the dead men, but Father Absinthe follows some people who seemed to recognize one of them. The initial judge, d'Escorval, is reported as having had an accident, and is replaced by Judge Segmuller, who interrogates the widow, shows she contradicts herself and sees in her "the senseless obstinacy of the brute" (145). The "murderer," now called "May," seems born again after meeting the new judge and gives some account of himself. He speaks three languages and says he is a fairground worker recently come from Germany: when interrogated he weakens a few times, but does not reveal any more.

Lecoq then locates May's trunk at a hotel—it did, as he said, come from Leipzig. Madame Milner, in charge there, denies knowing May, or his name. Absinthe was followed, got drunk, and interrogated, all by May's accomplice. Lecoq interviews the daughter-in-law of the bar-owner Mme Chupin, who knows a man named Lacheneur, as mentioned by the third man to die. Her husband said Lacheneur would make their fortune. Lecoq hunts for him, but time passes and the crime is nearly forgotten, and most accept May's account of himself—only Lecoq and Segmuller disagree.

Lecoq starts to watch May from in the roof above his cell. After several days, he sees bread thrown in and realizes May's song is a signal: he obtains the bread that has been thrown out, with tissue-paper in it bearing a coded message that he manages to decipher. Then Lecoq throws in a message in a piece of bread, but May gives it to the police, as if innocent—evidently aware he is being watched. The other police think Lecoq is wrong to suspect May, and even the judge is having doubts. Lecoq suggests May be allowed to escape, and followed. When this happens, May gets money from Mme Milner, buys clothes, then takes a cab and climbs a high wall into a large house belonging to the Duc de Sairmeuse. When they search the house, there is no sign of May; Lecoq has the sudden idea that perhaps May is the duke, and he goes to consult Tabaret (whose career is briefly summarized). He praises Lecoq but says the original judge was not in an accident, and May is indeed the duke, and he has acted "to save his name and his honour intact." Lecoq says if that is so, "I shall have my revenge" (366).

Volume 2, "The Honour of the Name," begins in the past, in 1815 at Sairmeuse. The duke returns from political exile to find his house has been bought by Lacheneur, a former servant. Lacheneur's daughter Marie-Anne insists her father return it and when he does the duke is not grateful but eventually gives Lacheneur some money. Marie-Anne is admired by Maurice, son of the Baron d'Escorval, a supporter of Napoleon, who is helped to keep his position by the Marquis de Sairmeuse, the duke's son—who also admires Marie-Anne. The duke wants his son to marry Blanche, daughter of the very conservative Marquis de Courtornieu.

Lacheneur develops a plot against the duke with some help from Maurice, which turns into a peasant rising and an attack on the nearby town of Montaignac. This is easily beaten by soldiers led by the duke, and after a long trial, in which he is very bullying, 20 men, some innocent, are executed. Under pressure from Marie-Anne, d'Éscorval is helped escape by the marquis, but d`Éscorval is badly hurt in the escape. Lacheneur also escapes but is caught and executed. Marie-Anne and Maurice marry, she returns home, and Maurice disappears into an Italian jail. The marquis has married Blanche de Courtornieu, but has separated from her. She thinks he is still seeing Marie-Anne, but in fact Marie-Anne has had Maurice's child. Blanche employs the duke's agent Chupin to watch the marquis, who has ruined her father's standing with the king; her father has also been attacked by Lacheneur's son Jean, and is now insane. Under pressure from Marie-Anne, and through his continuing feeling for her, the marquis has agreed to save d'Éscorval's reputation.

Through Chupin, Blanche finds Marie-Anne, goes to her house and poisons her: the dying Marie-Anne tells Blanche she is married to Maurice, has a child, and asks her to look after it. As Blanche leaves, Chupin is killed by Jean Lacheneur but survives long enough to tell his own son about Blanche's guilt. Later the same night the marquis arrives with a letter of freedom for the Baron d'Éscorval. Even later that night d'Éscorval himself is brought to Marie-Anne's house, but is sent away again by a priest, and does not know she is dead. The next night Maurice arrives at the house, back from Italy: he is stunned by Marie-Anne's death, but then meets the marquis, who swears to avenge her.

After all this hectic action and reaction, Blanche and the marquis are reconciled, basically through her pretense of continued love. The duke dies, apparently in a fall from a horse, but probably he was killed by Jean Lacheneur, who now leaves for Paris, as does Chupin's son—but the family cannot find Chupin's hidden money. Blanche is haunted by her murder of Marie-Anne, and when her aunt threatens her with exposure, Blanche agrees to take her to Paris and pay for everything for her. Complexities continue: in Paris with the new duke, formerly the marquis, Blanche hires a detective, Chelteux, to find Marie-Anne's son: later he looks for Jean Lacheneur and is killed by him. Young Chupin is married and has a son Polyte, but is then killed in prison; Blanche's aunt also dies.

The new duke has been overseas for four years, and now has grey hair—it must be about 1830, at the latest. Chupin's son and widow know nothing, but Lacheneur begins a plot against Blanche, using the widow Chupin as an agent. Finally, Blanche goes on the fatal night with her servant Camille and meets Lacheneur's three thugs, one of whom is to be presented as her son. Lacheneur is not there—he has fallen in a quarry and hurt himself. Blanche is disguised, but has forgotten to take off her earrings. The duke, disguised as May, arrives: his faithful servant Otto has followed him. The thugs go for the earrings, the duke shoots two and fatally wounds the third. The police arrive: the women run away and meet Otto outside. The duke tries to leave the back way, is trapped by Lecoq and says, "It is the Prussians who are coming." Otto is the "accomplice" and his lady-friend Mme Milner helps him with the "May as fairground worker" story. The repentant Blanche kills herself with poison.

In the Epilogue, a mere ten pages, Maurice's son is returned to him by a repentant Lacheneur. Lecoq recalls Mme Milner's bird said "Camille" and seeks someone at the duke's house with that name—she is Blanche's servant. In red-haired disguise (perhaps the Verduret costume from *Le Dossier no. 113*?), Lecoq visits the duke with a letter he has forged as coming from Judge d'Éscorval asking for money in return for his secrecy. The duke writes his agreement, and Lecoq reveals himself. Soon afterwards the duke is found not guilty of murder, and the story ends.

Gaboriau's novels brought a new structure and attitude to the developing genre of crime fiction. These were stories entirely focused on the puzzling nature of a single crime—not merely, like so many 19th-century novels, French and English (major examples of the latter category are discussed in Chapter 5), using a series of crimes or some past wrong as motives for human interaction, manipulative and emotive. Gaboriau's new crime-focused and steadily-developed mystery structure was authorized through a single detective presence, and now false leads and puzzling confusions would amplify what had been in short stories a single case-structure into the ramified plot of a novel. The French creation of the newly central detective in an extended narrative combined the capacity for perceptions that Poe had perfected with the street-level action that the English police detectives had brought into the form. This combination of puzzle and authority itself meshed with the long-held interest the French found in Cooper's stories. As Bonniot notes, the young Gaboriau admired Cooper greatly,[16] and also read eagerly dilutions and popularizations of Cooper like those by the Anglo-Irish America-based author Mayne Reid—who was also to be part of the young Conan Doyle's reading.

Most of these writers, in France and England, used the city for the basis of their innovative fictions, charting the multiple activities, the mystifying differences, and above all the sense of isolation, alienation and possible hostility of this new phenomenon, the megalopolis. But Gaboriau was the first to link this rich, troubling context to the techniques and above all the explanatory mechanism of the detective novel. Messac insists that

Balzac is in many ways the father of Gaboriau's work, with his interweaving of social and locational tensions in the newly potent and newly volatile city, and at basis he suggests that they both intend to reveal "non seulement le drame retentissant qui se joue en cour d`assises, mais aussi les drames plus secret dont celui-là n'ést que la dénouement" ("not only the resounding drama which is played out in the court, but also the more secret dramas of which that is only the conclusion").[17]

As with Collins, selling both in cheap serial form and in relatively expensive complete novels, the new material appealed to a socially wide audience, and while Gaboriau certainly thrived on the streets, he was also admired by the great—Disraeli, novelist and prime minister, spoke highly of his work, and he was famously admired by two rather different, power-rich figures, Bismarck, the mighty German Chancellor, and the more pacific Woodrow Wilson who led America in the crucial post–1918 period. This suggests a real combination in Gaboriau of low-level credibility among a mass audience with some higher attainment of admirable authority, as sensed by social leaders.

Two elements shape this unusual combination of democracy and elitism. Unlike most crime fiction before and after, Gaboriau locates true heroism, both physical and intellectual, in a serving policeman. The police-procedural as a sub-genre will not be properly born until the 1960s work of "Ed McBain," and even then, and in its many television versions and dilutions, the police heroes, increasingly of both genders, will need to show that they are also deeply, and even fallibly, human. But none of those immediate successors who accepted Gaboriau's shape of the crime-focused puzzle would accept a hero policeman, especially Conan Doyle and Anna Katharine Green, the most immediate transmitters of his heroic detective structure into the Anglophone mass market.

What empowers the special, supersocial heroism of Gaboriau's detective is that he is also a representative of that other new 19th-century force, outlined in general by Michel Foucault and linked to crime fiction by both D.A. Miller generally and Heather Worthington in the early period (see Chapter 3, pp. 78–79)—the hero who deploys disciplinary expertise in the identification and control of social disturbances and aberrances: it is Lecoq who firmly and convincingly locates such powers in the police.

There is one other crucial feature of Gaboriau and Lecoq. The previous investigators, from Vidocq to Dupin, all had wonderful successes in baffling contexts, but they never faced a criminal who was consciously their rival, who sought to twist and turn the evidence against detection, as does the Marquis de Clamaran in *Le Dossier no. 113*, for his own purpose, and the

Duc de Sairmeuse in *Monsieur Lecoq*, for the "honour of the name." Gaboriau seems the first to imagine the dual narrative, the challenge of the criminal against the detective, that Todorov saw at the core of the classic mystery[18]: Poe's ourang-utan or Collins' Godfrey Ablewhite never consciously confronted and sought by inventing evidence to outwit the detective who was their only possible nemesis. Poe imagines the criminal/detective encounter in "The Purloined Letter," but at an ideal, almost playful level. Gaboriau for the first time imagines this elemental disciplinary battle of conflicting narratives, danger and detection face to face shaping the central challenging conflict at the heart of what can now be called legitimately a "whodunit."

As well as these deep-laid urban, disciplinary and narratological powers, Gaboriau gives Lecoq all the traditional detective skills. He can track a footprint in the snow like Cooper's hero; he can wait for days and surveill a prisoner like a jailer in a Foucauldian Panopticon; he can scour the city for evidence like Vidocq; and also like Vidocq he is theatrically formidable in disguise. This brave, active, polymorphous, ever-inquiring police disciplinarian was surely enough to catch readers' attention around the world. But in France there was an additional element: in the 19th century the national self-concept was recurrently troubled. The country's glorious past was compromised by being royal, aristocratic, exploitative; the different grandeur of the Napoleonic period had been defeated by its enemies, and even traduced by its own excesses. It is not surprising that historical fictions and fantasy adventures gripped French audiences, from the Musketeers to Monte Cristo.

Less easily distracted writers confronted the situation—Balzac by imagining an awkward new world of bourgeois values; Sue by inventing a non–French lord who supervised the Mysteries of modern Paris; Zola would ignore the past and plunge into the conflicts of the socially mobile present. Gaboriau recurrently finds the problems of the present in the inheritance of the corrupt past, but after *Le Crime d'Orcival* he is not simply anti-aristocrat (and even there the lady is worse than the lord). In *Dossier no. 113* it is only a fake aristocrat who causes the trouble; and in *Monsieur Lecoq* the Duc de Sairmeuse as a young man acted with decency when his father raged back from exile, and in the time of the action, inheriting the threats in the present, he behaves with courage and skill in a world of brutish aristocrats and corrupt *arrivistes* to defend his family's name and eventually earn the statement "Not Guilty" for himself—and by implication at least, some of the aristocrats.

What is internationally and historically most notable is the way

Gaboriau established, for others to copy and develop, the familiar form of the mystery novel. It is clear that Anna Katharine Green before 1878 had been reading Gaboriau: Fergus Hume was specific about following him in seeking to establish himself in Melbourne in 1885 (see p. 159); Conan Doyle makes Holmes early in *A Study in Scarlet* speak with revealing aggression to disavow any possible connection with Gaboriau: after saying "Lecoq was a miserable bungler"[19] he asserts it took him six months to identity a criminal he, Holmes, would have nailed in 24 hours. In fact, apart from the police affiliation, as Bleiler comments "much of Sherlock Holmes is based on this very Lecoq" (v), and Conan Doyle in his first two novellas also uses Gaboriau's historical explanation of the present disorders, though in the first two his inspiration comes primarily from Stevenson and Collins, see Chapter 7, pp. 196–95. The posthumously-published short narrative *Le Petit Vieux de Batignolles* (1876—*The Little Old Man of Batignolles*) may well, as Bleiler noted (xv), have directly influenced Conan Doyle: it has a medical student narrator, an austere detective (admittedly rather more like Maigret than Holmes), uses in evidence letters written in blood, and crucially identifies a left-handed man and a dog that does not bark.

Gaboriau died early in 1873 and was recognized in his time as a master of the form, with a special power of human realization: his contemporary Marius Topin saw him as "a logician of the first order,"[20] and "a dialectician as rigorous and neat as Poe" (336), but one who also added the novelist's gifts of "vivacity of writing, natural dialogue and the creation of vividly alive characters" (336). There was something mythic about the detective's name (his motto *semper vigilans*, "always vigilant," traditionally belongs to the Gallic cockerel), though it does also link back to Vidocq, and Bonniot suggests it may also refer to the Lecoq who was a major operative among the Paris police under La Reynie in the time of Louis XIV.[21] French literary tradition has seen him as generating Maigret and the modern heroes of the *romans policiers*—even patriotically claiming Hercule Poirot as a descendant.

The strongest inheritance this gifted writer left was that a mystery novel can be self-standing in generic terms as an intriguing and satisfying puzzle, and it can attract audiences that are both large and also extremely loyal. It was not yet a dominant form—as noted above, several of Gaboriau's later novels do not use the hero at all. The compulsory presence of the detective would only emerge later, through the person of Sherlock Holmes, but Gaboriau did much to make possible the strength and, in each story where he appears, the dominance of this figure.

After Gaboriau

Du Boisgobey is best known in criminographical circles for having continued, perhaps exploited, Monsieur Lecoq after Gaboriau's death in his *La Vieillesse de M. Lecoq* of 1878. Like Féval and Gaboriau he by no means concentrated on detective fiction and the novels always had a strong romance element. A classic instance is *Le Crime d'un Omnibus* from 1881, soon translated into English and quite possibly the inspiration for the title of Fergus Hume's *The Mystery of a Hansom Cab* (see Chapter 6, p. 159).

As in Gaboriau, the novel has a brisk and arresting opening. In Paris, in about 1860, an artist, Paul Freneuse, going home late on the horse-drawn omnibus, observes a man give the last seat to a woman—he goes up onto the open top, though it is a cold night. The woman, heavily veiled, squeezes in next to a girl, who is very quiet. Soon the man upstairs leaves, having stamped his foot first, and the women gets off at the next stop, leaving the girl leaning against Paul. At the terminus he realizes she is dead, and reports this—he goes back for his umbrella, sees some paper with a gold pin in it, and assumes it was hers.

At his studio next day he is painting, using as model Pia, a young and beautiful Italian girl. His clumsy friend Binos, "a mediocre artist,"[22] appears. They discuss the event on the omnibus and Binos insists it is "a murder, cleverly set-up and masterly executed" (18). Binos scratches the cat with the pin and it dies at once. He does not trust the police so will investigate with the wise friend he knows from his favorite bar, Piédouche—who mentions Gaboriau and Lecoq in discussion and then confirms through a druggist that the pin is poisoned. This strong opening is framed in two long chapters, and then the story develops.

Paul seeks fame as an artist, and is interested in both the connections and the beauty of Marguerite Paulet, only child of a very wealthy banker. He plans to paint her, and visits the theater with them—but outside he sees the man from the bus, who is, with a pock-marked woman, studying him. Paulet knows the man as a "business agent" (63), and the man and woman leave—Paul also sees the fruit-seller who was on the bus and she confirms the man was the upstairs passenger. Paul takes a fiacre to follow theirs, but the vehicle is empty when it stops.

In an unfashionable Paris whose streets and bars are very well, if succinctly, described, Binos meets Piédouche. They trace where the dead girl lived from a clue on the scrap of letter found with the pin—she was an Italian singer called Bianca. Paulet is visited by the business agent, whom he has been employing to find out if his half-brother, who long ago left

Paris, has as he has heard rumored, any children. Blanchelaine, the agent, tells him the girl has just died, a day before her father—it is his will Paulet is concerned with. Next day Paulet and Marguerite visit Paul—she is not quite sure of him, though her father would accept him as a son-in-law. They find Paul painting Pia, who talks about her sister Bianca Astrodi. Paulet is told by his brother's lawyer that the will mentions a girl named Pia as well as Bianca. Marguerite thinks Paul loves Pia—who has also inherited money.

Blanchelaine and his wife become prominent in the story. Paulet agrees to offer him 10,000 francs if he resolves the problem, and his wife persuades Pia that Paul loves Marguerite and she should go away with her and her husband. They do not plan to kill her yet, as this would be suspicious, but to get her to renounce the bequest and later kill her—they still have a poisoned pin. His wife gets her to leave her lodgings with her, and the real surprise is revealed—Blanchelaine is also Piédouche.

Bonis and Paul are searching for Pia with the help an old deaf man from the bar, Père Pigache—who sometimes seems to move surprisingly quickly. They all go to the Blanchelaines and he enters alone, seems unable to hear anything, but alarms them by his report of police at the bar, and they discuss Pia and their plans with him. He leaves, and runs to the waiting fiacre—he is "a senior agent of the Sûreté police" (231). They regain Pia, who realizes Paul loves her. Blanchelaine is arrested, Madame Blanchelaine kills herself with the pin: Pia rejects the inheritance and will live happily with Paul. Perhaps unfairly, the novel ends by saying Marguerite, though rich, is lonely and "has been blamed for the omnibus crime" (234).

Pacy, with a good mix of detection, feeling and context, like Gaboriau's stories this has a very narrow range of characters, and it might seem improbable that the two Astrodi girls are doubly linked to Paulet through his half-brother, their father, and also his daughter's interest in Paul. This may well look to the common theatrical context of these melodramas, with casts small and mysteriously interconnected—and the doubling of Piédouche and Blanchemain is a further, more strained version of that deployment of improbable links. The novel was reasonably successful and is a fair average example of du Boisgobey's work.

He was a very active producer up till his death in 1891. His appeal was very strong in America, with some 50 of his titles translated from 1880 to the early 1890s. In London they came more slowly, and mostly through the publisher Vizetelly after he had done well from 1881 with Gaboriau: in 1885 he produced a two-title publication including *The Omnibus Crime*—there would be many du Boisgobey titles in the "Sensational Novels" series.

The American success of du Boisgobey continues the transatlantic interest in Sue and Gaboriau (see Chapter 1, p. 19, 35), and also links to his continuation, in varied and sometimes diluted form, of the detective tradition that was now becoming established in American and English crime fiction. The Anglpohone readers were far less interested in the flamboyant rhetoric of du Boisgobey's very succcessful but essentially fanciful contemporary Ponson du Terrail (whom Messac discusses at great length). He was rarely translated in English at the time, and then in a few historical novels. The Library of Congress and British Library catalogs record no translations at all from this period of du Terrail's late Gothic melodramatic stories about the fantastic adventurer Rocambole, who appears from 1857 to 1869, at times siding opportunistically with the forces of order.

Du Boisgobey is not as concerned as Gaboriau was—at least in *Le Dossier no. 113* and *Monsieur Lecoq* to give the detective full power to unveil the mystery, and that is no doubt why his work fell away from favor after the American writers who followed Anna Katharine Green had projected a complete focus on the mystery into new forms, and the English, following Conan Doyle, had done the same. The French were not so narrow in range. The most popular of the turn of the century French writers was Maurice Leblanc, the creator of the "gentleman-cambrioleur" ("robber-gentleman") Arsène Lupin: Leblanc openly parodied Conan Doyle—at first appearance in 1905 making his opponent simply Sherlock Holmes but when Conan Doyle complained turning him to Herlock Sholmès, then, for the English-language market, Holmlock Shears.

But if the French tradition still valued the melodramatic and the fantastic, it also retained the powers that Poe had seen long ago. The emergent mystery novel, with its focus heavily on clues and detection gained considerable strength in the new century from a new French initiative, as the journalist Gaston Leroux responded to the Anglophone developments with *La Mystère de la Chambre Jaune* (1908), a brilliant realization of the locked-room mystery, with a splendid surprise ending. The young Christie read and learned from this, and Leblanc's influence and the post-war impact of Simenon would ensure that the French contribution to the world of crime fiction continued to be substantial as the form irresistibly grew around the world through the 20th century.

CHAPTER 3

Ferret at Work:
Class and Detection in
Early English Crime Fiction

Contexts

A category so far very little explored in crime fiction is class—and the category is in general also ignored in modern literary criticism and commentary for various political, or apolitical, reasons. But in the earlier texts it is a matter of recurrent concern, even anxiety, and this chapter will consider the various representations of class and class mobility in the development of crime fiction in England. The first, and in many ways the continuing issue is how many classes? English thinking is still triune in this matter, avowing the eternity of the upper, middle and lower classes. But the idea of upper, middle and lower needs to be forgotten to reach useful conclusions: in the context of 19th-century crime fiction, especially the early to mid-century period, it will be necessary to oscillate between two and five classes, two being the traditional assumption of only high and low, five being the developed reality with medial classes recognized.

In some early crime texts like *The Newgate Calendar* (eighteenth and early nineteenth centuries), and Edward Bulwer's *Pelham* (1828) the social world is also simply binary, and crime is based either on lower-class people betraying their betters in the gentry (the dominant *Calendar* pattern), lower-class people jockeying for advantage inside their own class (the *Calendar* variant), or as time goes by the gentry not living up to their class's standards (*Pelham*). In more complex texts a medial social position can be imagined, but ultimately dismissed as impossible: *Caleb Williams* (1794) asserts strongly that a lower-class inquirer can expose the vice and self-protection of a lord—but Godwin, having finished the novel, immediately revised his radical ending to make Caleb politically capitulate; in *Eugene Aram* (1832), Bulwer imagines a potent dissenter to social and moral order, only finally to contain him in crime and execution. A different challenge to a world of only upper and lower classes is implied in novels that imagine and to some degree develop characters who actually do realize a positive and socially interstitial position in the plot and its evaluations, but these novels turn out to be distinctly hesitant about the role of these characters and they are absorbed, often by marriage or at least friendship, into the gentry—examples are Mr. Brownlow in *Oliver Twist* (1838) and John West-lock in *Martin Chuzzlewit* (1844). As late as *Bleak House* (1852), Adam Woodcourt, a capable, courageous lawyer, remains curiously offstage, despite receiving the hand of Esther, the wealth of the Jarndyces and, oddest of all, the second actual version of Bleak House to live in: his near anonymity is a classic case of how writers found it hard to create an extended and positive image of a character not clearly higher or lower class, and so without automatic evaluations readily available.

Those treatments themselves expose both the perceived limitations and the continuing power of a binary class model, and through its operations the crime fiction as a whole can seem to conduct, at least to some extent, a debate—is it possible to go beyond a binary class system? In responding to that question and pursuing this debate through the early crime fiction material, it will be helpful to have in mind what social history can tell us. The fullest account of early 19th-century social stratification and related self-consciousness is by R.S. Neale. In a study which seems not to have been replaced in over 40 years,[1] he represents not three but five social classes, and four of these distinctions will be recurrently useful.

The five are:

Upper Class—aristocratic, landholding
Middle Class—industrial and commercial property holders, senior military and established professional men, all aspiring to acceptance by the upper class
Middling Class—the petit bourgeoisie, upwards-oriented professional men, other literate people and successful artisans, collectively less deferential than middle class
Working Class A—industrial proletariat (among whom are routine artisans and urban service workers)
Working Class B—agricultural labourers

In the first three classes, in the early period the crucial distinction is between Middle and Middling: the former is clearly related with some complexity to Upper while the latter is to some extent emergent from the artisan/ service worker element of Working Class A. There is a firm gap between

Middle and Middling, and that is why Middling is better than Lower-Middle as a name, to stress the difference, even gulf, between the two positions, one that the texts themselves seem to be clearly aware of.

The last two classes listed do not provide either an audience or a set of characters of any importance for the earlier crime fiction, but this situation will change by the mid–19th-century. One developmental social force is that the rise of literacy and the change of the reading public in the early 19th century starts with the major middle-class audience, and then towards the mid-century there is development in middling- and even working-class A readership. In terms of magazines this change is visible in the movement from the conservative upper and middle-class *Blackwood's Edinburgh Magazine* (1817) to the liberal middle- and middling-class *Chambers's Edinburgh Journal* (from 1832) and the wider-ranging *Household Words* (from 1850), by which time there was a substantial expansion in literacy, in part inculcated by educational practices, often supported by charities, usually religious, and in part by the growth of service jobs for young people requiring literacy, as in large city shops. Many of the socially lower readers bought the very cheap weekly serials—usually a penny each—by which novels were slowly and very successfully disseminated through the late 1840s. Another factor in developing readership was the cheapening of books and magazines through new forms of printing equipment and paper-production, and also steady falls in tax on magazines and newspapers. A striking feature clearly visible in the popular fiction of writers like Reynolds and publishers like Lloyd is the evident appeal to a female reading audience in the middling class and working class A by the 1850s—when Reynolds published six major novels of personal memoirs, five of them with a central female character from the middling or even artisan classes, see Chapter 5, pp. 136–37. As will be argued throughout this chapter, these structural developments will have an impact on the nature and the thematic interests of crime fiction into and beyond the mid–19th century.

First Texts

Misdeeds against a character had been central to the formation of the novel itself, whether they were the removal of honorific and financial rights like those of *Tom Jones* (1749) or threats to the security and integrity of the person as in *Pamela* (1740). The Gothic novel explored less probable and more imaginatively engaging threats, usually in overseas contexts both exciting and threatening, and normally made against the person and liberty of a central female figure, who proved to be equally sensitive and brave. Godwin moved closer to a realistic social understanding of crime in *Caleb Williams* and has often been thought the ultimate founder of the crime-focused story—Julian Symons said this is where "the characteristic note of crime literature is first struck."[2] While Godwin eventually drew back from the radical anti-aristocratic originality of his story, his American admirer Charles Brockden Brown shaped in *Edgar Huntly* (1799) a powerful novel that explored behavior and morality in the new world confronting Edgar as a young American baffled by a murder, faced with both Europe-originated men willing to use their manipulative power and also a second domain of threat, the fierce but by no means unprovoked Native Americans, see Chapter 1, pp. 16–17.

The political potential of these very early mysteries would remain long untapped, perhaps because though Godwin was a Londoner and Brown lived in both Philadelphia and New York, neither made the major initiatory move of modern crime fiction, realizing the new, alarming, and multiple forces of the cities, where neighbors did not know each other, where old-style communal forces of order—as imagined in operation in *The Newgate Calendar*—were quite absent, and new forms of work and wealth themselves were often invitations to crime and the assumption of new, even threatening, identities. Those urban forces, to be so potent in the work of the major generically foundational writers, Poe, Gaboriau, Conan Doyle, took some time to emerge and be recognized and would themselves be involved in challenges to the simple two-class social concept. Another new and slowly-developing formation was what Foucault has outlined as the move towards "disciplinary" detection, the idea that only a highly skilled and professional inquirer into the nature of crimes, and especially criminals, can handle the threats of modern social urban and social complexity.[3]

In numerical terms the busiest form of early crime fiction, still looking towards the Gothic, was in what are called "Tales of Terror."[4] These were stories that appeared regularly from the start of *Blackwood's Edinburgh Magazine* in 1817, a conservative magazine, famously opposed to the liberal, even leftist, Romantic writers of the far south—especially John Keats and Leigh Hunt, to both of whom *Blackwood's* reviewers were brutal. It was aimed at a highly literate audience, essentially middle class in Neale's terms, and as well as essays lauding the qualities of traditional people and literature, it, in a notionally contradictory mode, regularly carried stories relating the excitements of adventurous, dangerous and even criminal activity. These processes were normally perceived from a highly stimulated viewpoint, usually that of the victim of the bizarre circumstances, but when the events would prove fatal an uninvolved commentator would act as mediator. The richly sensational stories would relate with both distance and amazed fascination the possibility of respectable people (from the viewpoint only of men, essentially a gendered appropriation of the Gothic) becoming through personal indiscretion, crime or—especially popular—some disastrous accident exposed to drastic forces, like being caught in a steadily shrinking iron cell, or stretched beneath the murderous noise of a mighty bell. The stories explored the alarming and enthralling negative possibilities of the sensitivities and vulnerabilities of the newly-imagined individual, the success-oriented center of bourgeois society.

Asocial and intensely personalized as this material is, it was also very rarely urban in setting—one exception is Henry Thomson's much-reprinted story "Le Revenant" (1827) about a man who escaped hanging by a prearranged series of operations. But the city very soon stamped itself on crime and crime fiction, through the very successful *Mémoires* (1828) of Eugène François Vidocq, an ex-soldier and ex-convict who became a major figure in the Parisian police force that enacted Napoleonic ideas of control. His memoirs, discussed in detail in Chapter 2, see pp. 46–50, show him acting routinely as a detective, using informers as well as his own investigations, often operating in disguise.

The Bow Street Runners, established in the mid–18th century with a curious link to fiction—their founders were the magistrates John Fielding and his brother Henry Fielding, the major novelist—were the only organized English crime-confronting force until 1829, and *Richmond: Scenes in the Life of a Bow Street Runner* appeared in 1827: it was published anonymously, but is thought to have been by the popular novelist Thomas Gaspey. Tom Richmond is without clear social context: he grows up in a comfortable rural context, is educated at private school, and is then sent to train for a career as a merchant. So he seems essentially middling class, but his position is not clarified or stressed at all: he just drifts through society as an outsider. After wandering with an itinerant theater troupe he stumbles into joining the Runners, and though he is based in London he travels substantially on his cases, which have an equally varied social meaning. He tends to confront lower-class professional criminals like London pickpockets or the mobile gang run by the Welshman Jones, which operates across the south of the country in the lower-class criminal modes of grave-robbing, smuggling, and horse-related crimes. The stories can drift into socially higher misunderstandings, but not seriously: "Richmond's Fourth Case" tells of events in the troubled marriage of a retired city merchant, Joe Banbury, living in what Richmond calls Banbury Castle, "no immeasurable distance from the metropolis."[5] Banbury feels he ought to be re-enacting the part of Petruchio in *The Taming of the Shrew* and causes a good deal of annoyance, but eventually Mrs. Banbury speaks up for him, the Runners do not detain him and he returns to a quasi-gentry fantasy peacefulness. The fifth and last story is a higher-class problem familiar in popular fiction, an account of a nobleman ruined by gambling, expressed in terms of upper-class values, which finally seem to be somehow superior to their follies.

Richmond sees a fashionable lady passing forged notes: he thinks, respecting his social betters, he should hint she is in trouble, but then decides to go for the accomplices who have in this way embarrassed her. He soon meets—indeed saves from drowning—young Percy, "the heir to a splendid title" (222), who has lost his money in high living and gambling and is set upon first by a crafty farmer, who wants his daughter to marry Percy and so gain access to the estates, and then by the glamorous lady forger. After a long and quite exciting narrative, the rich Farmer Grinstead is disposed of, and the never-named temptress poisons herself with laudanum, as gentry villains so often will. Her vicious husband is killed in a duel by Percy, who then like a true gentleman flees to Europe "to avoid the consequences of a trial" (266)—but the lower-class criminals all head for the Old Bailey. As Bleiler notes in his Introduction,[6] Richmond's cases do not fit with other early patterns whether psychological, like *Caleb Williams*, Gothic like the work of Matthew Lewis, or based on a hero defending himself like Gaspey's *The History of George Godfrey* (1828), essentially a return-from-transportation fable. *Richmond* is not unlike Vidocq in recounting criminal actuality, but without the heroic energy and with recurrent elements of mere entertainment, but its main significance is in accepting the two-class basis of social and criminal life that will long persevere in crime fiction. Probably because the Runners themselves were hardly heroic or convincing, and were seen as well out of date by 1827, the stories were not at all successful—the reprint of 1845 used original printed sheets that had not been bound up in 1827.

A contemporary piece of overt two-class crime fiction operates at a much higher literary and imaginative level and focuses positively on the gentry. Edward Bulwer (not till 1846 taking, as her will requested, his mother's surname Lytton), went on to be member of Parliament, Conservative minister for the colonies, and eventually Lord Lytton. His *Pelham* (1828) not only deals with lofty life in Paris and London, including the British Parliament, but also involves the well-born Henry Pelham in a murder mystery—he finds the body of a man known to be the enemy of his close friend Sir Reginald Glanville. As Bleiler notes,[7] the mystery is based on a real Bow Street murder case, but here asserts the possibility of noble, external detection—the novel's subtitle is "The Adventures of a Gentleman."

This first approach to a 19th-century crime and mystery novel was both early, and without generic influence—Bulwer turned after this to the past and the Gothic, and also to lower-class heroic crime, in his Newgate Novels *Paul Clifford* (1830) and *Eugene Aram* (1832), inspiring W. Harrison Ainsworth's best-selling *Jack Sheppard* (1840). *Pelham* shows clear links back to *Caleb Williams*, but Bulwer reverses Godwin's challenging politics: where Caleb exposes the lordly Falkland as a murderer, Pelham's engagement with crime is to save his excitable but true-blue friend Glanville from a malicious charge of murder. *Caleb Williams* is also reversed, it seems consciously, in that where Godwin's Falkland killed Tyrrel to protect his honor, for Bulwer the slightly differently spelt Tyrrell is behind the crime that frames Glanville. Though Pelham flourishes in Paris and London, the criminal action is rural, taking place near the racing center Newmarket in East Anglia, but urban lower-class criminality is strongly recognized in the late sequence where Pelham, usually merely curious rather than actually detecting, does eventually undertake physical inquiries, and that in the city. He goes with Job Jonson, a rough criminal guide, into one of London's East End hells to find the conclusive evidence to clear Glanville. Jerome McGann sees this idealistically as a version of the hero visiting the underworld turned into an "apocalyptic ritual" designed to prove Glanville is innocent and "Pelham is a marvel,"[8] but it is, rather, a gentrification of the Newgate world, showing Pelham's capacity as a true gentleman to traverse the dangerous world of the only other class being recognized here.

Towards Disciplinary Detection

A closer relation to class and criminality, and a firmer, wider, location in the modern city, begins to emerge in the first stories which can be generically described as professional case-studies, the mode which would develop into what Foucault has called the "disciplinary" approach to crime control. One of *Blackwood's* minor sensational writers, Samuel Warren, a man with medical training who then became a lawyer, relocated that emotive criminal discourse, in the disciplinary spirit in which he was trained, into recounting cases of the aberrant and criminal behavior a doctor saw among his respectable London patients. *Blackwood's* ran Warren's "Passages from the Diary of a Late Physician" from 1830 to 1837 and they appeared successfully in collected form, including in Germany, and also widely in America through the common practice of pirate publishing.

Warren was already studying law when he began the *Passages* and the Physician finds a good deal of crime as well as disease to be found in the stories. Worthington argues that the disciplinary viewpoint and the case structure makes these operate like crime fiction and point towards overtly criminographical patterns to come[9]: they explore modern London, viewed from a professional viewpoint, but still see its people in a two-class way. The conservative *Blackwood's* context, where the angst and error of the gentry class is often entirely personalized, even isolated, is developed by Warren by observing usually aristocratic misbehavior in a wider social context, often negatively affecting others of their own and sometimes of a different class. Though he is in fact a middling-class aspirant to the professional middle class, Warren's narrator, a young doctor of "a poor but somewhat ambitious family,"[10] has neither middle-class self-consciousness nor disciplinary self-confidence: aristocratic life is the only one to aspire to, and he feels from the start that "the great misfortune in my case was, undoubtedly, the want of introductions" (1832, 1.9).

The narrative asserts a two-class world as things improve for the doctor with an introduction. Fairly late in the first story, "Early Struggles," he sees an earl's daughter knocked down in the street, provides assistance, and her grateful father gives him the entrée to polite and lucrative society. Nevertheless the realities of Warren's fiction tell a more complex social story, at times hostile to the gentry, sometimes pitying the lower class, but remaining uncertain about any medial domain of value or social life. Typically, "The Man About Town" (1830) offers a dark prediction of the self-inflicted end of the aristocracy, as the heir to a marquisate declines into syphilitic madness and death, and the disgrace of a lower-class context.

In "Mother and Son" (1831) a fatherless gentleman falls into vice, becomes involved in dueling and ends in Newgate: acquittal saves neither him nor his mother from tragic death. Though a medial social world is visible in "The Forger" (1830) it has no positive outcome, as a fake gentleman who is the forger ends with a Calendaresque confession before execution. The same rejection of perceived middle- and middling-class self-assertion emerges in "The Rich Merchant" (1831): his vulgar wife and heedless son waste all his goods and both he and his faithful daughter die in the depths of miserable poverty. A more elaborate, even bitter, social drama is developed in "The Merchant's Clerk" (1836)—the later date may explain its socially aware theme. A sweet-natured girl marries her businessman father's clerk, not the dissolute aristocrat her father requires, and so he frames her husband for embezzlement—the husband is himself failed gentry, having left Oxford because of his father's gambling debts. The attempt to inculpate him fails, and they marry, but fate blocks their happiness: assuming she has died having their child, the clerk kills himself and she, relinquishing her quest for social independence, returns to care for her father, though still hating him. In this bleak world of social conflict, where the middle and middling classes can only seem a menace, including to themselves, all that can be contemplated calmly is the social apartheid revealed in the story.

Yet the two-class model is not necessarily pro-gentry: in "Rich and Poor" (1831) the doctor attends a dying earl, then visits a very poor Irish family whose son has just been transported. Warren's narrative can feel for the poor, but has no sense of any way forward towards reform or social change against these injustices and disparities: while the doctor-narrator's position and voice are themselves medial in class and discursive terms, the utilitarian ideas of reform and the social implications of discipline, are not found in the stories, which find no space for positive middle- or middling-class activity.

Warren wrote a few legal case studies and possibly produced at least some of a set of 11 stories published rapidly from 1849 to 1850 in *Chambers's*, known as *The Experiences of a Barrister*, though he almost certainly did not write the following series, *The Confessions of an Attorney*, and definitely did not, as some American publishers of the period claimed, produce *Adventures of an Attorney in Search of Practice* (1839), a lighter, largely non-criminal series written by Sir George Stephen. Perhaps in part because legal discipline is more intimately engaged in social action and reaction, and this discipline deals in nuances and half-truths not known to medicine, the *Experiences* are more socially investigative and less judgmental than the *Passages*; they begin to develop a view of the middle, and even the middling, class that moves towards self-consciousness and a sense of self-value for those social formations. But this apparent progress may also depend on the difference between the audiences and ideologies of Warren's conservative *Blackwood's* where the "Physician" stories were published, and the liberal *Chambers's* which presented *The Experiences of a Barrister*. The *Barrister* stories vary considerably in their social ideology: it is as if there is an uncertain debate going on about whether there can indeed be a model of social class which goes beyond the two primary classes, and what might be the values, and the threats, of the classes in between.

Warren himself never claimed the Barrister or Attorney stories, and it appears that they may have been produced in imitation of his two legally-oriented stories "Who Is the Murderer?" and "The Mystery of Murder, and Its Defence," published in *Blackwood's* in 1842 and 1850.[11] It seems quite possible that the creator of the Barrister stories in imitation of Warren was the still pseudonymous "William Russell," and that he was also responsible for *The Confessions of an Attorney*. Six of the "Attorney" stories were published as the second half of the volume entitled *Leaves from the Diary of a Law Clerk* (1857), which was attributed to "The Author of Recollections of a Detective Police Officer," namely "Russell," though a headnote to the six reprinted *Confessions* suggests a possible difference in authorship between the two sets of stories.[12]

The first *Barrister* story, "The March Assize" (1849), actually deals with rivalry among the middling classes, as a shop-keeper is framed for theft and eventually hanged because of the enmity of a shop-worker he has fired. Melodramatic in its tone and outcome, and resolved through confession, this is not a crime story of any complexity, and merely observes the middling-class as in a zoo, from a comfortable if sympathetic distance, as the poor were distantly recognized in Warren's 1831 story "Rich and Poor." The same note is sounded in a better-developed *Barrister* story, "Esther Mann" (1849), where a woman is hanged for petty theft after her husband is press-ganged into the navy. Social rise is possible here: he is an excellent sailor and will prosper after her death when he is free of the navy—but that will be in America: middling-class rise may exist on earth, but is not represented in England. Other *Barrister* stories deal with in-class conflicts at a somewhat higher level: "The Northern Circuit" (1849), the second story, and "The Accommodation Bill" (1850), the last, both deal with dissension among tenant farmers in the north, people hovering between the middling- and middle-classes and using crime as an instrument of aspiration.

Conflict at a higher-class level is the key element in "The Marriage Settlement" (1849) and "The Second Marriage" (1850): in both cases a lawyer's skill saves a mistreated young and genteel lady. The stories realize the social sexism both represented and at times deplored in much 19th-century fiction: the delicate features and soft skin of the beautiful young women will be marked with pain in the story, the villains who cause the trouble are brutal and grasping men, middle- or middling-class gone wrong, and overt in their wish to rise socially. They are, it seems, as foreign to good social order as the treacherous and inherently overseas villains of "The Mother and Son" (1849) and "Circumstantial Evidence" (1850), respectively, a Spanish mother who poisons a rich lady on behalf of her upwards-mobile son, and an army officer back home from empire who frames his own step-son for a lucrative domestic murder, an interestingly early version of the dangerous impact of empire felt back home, as discussed in Chapter 7.

In these stories the narrative identifies and resolves social disorder without any significant detective. Legal skills observe, and occasionally protect, but never really intervene, avoiding any sign of such a socially reformist disciplinary mode in operation. In "The Second Marriage" there was a little off-stage detective work by the barrister's attorney, and in two interesting stories this process provides a means of middling-class self-assertion—though still in the cause of the gentry. "The Contested Marriage" (1849) and "The Writ of Habeas Corpus" (1849) have very similar structures. In both a young upper-class lady is being deprived of rightful property—in the first her now dead husband disowned her, and so their son's title and lands have gone elsewhere, in the second story brutal relatives are trying to certify the young woman insane to seize her inheritance. The two stories deal with upper-class conflict, and the middle-class lawyer is attentive and supportive to those interests, but the key move is that the cases are resolved satisfactorily through the busy activity of the middling-class attorney, Mr. Ferret, who also appears briefly in "The Marriage Settlement." His name is clearly ironic, almost dismissive, and the barrister is called Sharpe, with unfavorable implication. These distancing names may be a form of class constraint, but the figures still function: Ferret is undeniably from the middling class, but he acts effectively on behalf of the gentry, and, to some perceivable degree, for his own success and middling-class status.

In "The Writ of Habeas Corpus" Ferret, with his "quick, gray, eye,"[13] was just the man for such a commission: "Indefatigable, resolute, sharp-witted and of a ceaseless, remorseless activity, a secret or a fact had need be very profoundly hidden for him not to reach and fish it up" (45). He has his own element of social mobility, having been for many years a mere managing clerk; but "ambition, and the increasing requirements of a considerable number of young Ferrets, determined him on commencing business on his own account" (45). He is also highly active: in "The Contested Marriage" he travels around England and finally finds proof of the original marriage, while in "The Writ of Habeas Corpus" he is more assertive and "with his habitual energy and perseverance" as well as "his usual minuteness and precision" (74 and 75) pries the heiress away from her aggressive relatives.

But Ferret can serve more than the gentry, as in "The Step-Father" (1856). This did not appear in *Chambers's* and Worthington suggests it was produced to fill out the 1856 anthology; it did not appear in the 1852 and following American editions, pirated as they originally were from *Chambers's*. The story has a progressive social politics that may relate to its slightly later date, or, conceivably, may have caused it to be held back from *Chambers's*. It deals with tensions between the son of a tax-official's widow and the rich city dealer his mother marries: it transpires that the step-father is actually ruined and is trying to frame the son so he can inherit money coming to the mother. Ferret is very active, and now has his own investigative clerk: the established middling class is now working for the honest middle class against city capitalist fraud, and the gentry are here at least not necessary as a source of value to be protected.

The *Barrister* stories, especially those featuring Ferret, both recognize and value the existence of a middle class with a middling class in general agreement with their social project. The resolution of the stories does not suggest disciplinary detection skills are available for any non-gentry power to use: Ferret's achievements are basically clerical, middling-class, and any outcomes in favor of a lower class seems derived by coincidence. This agent-free force will recur in crime fiction stories and also in the mainstream novels discussed in Chapter 5 that deal with crime: the effect is to suggest that fate and natural order intervene against improper class insurgency or un-traditional wrongs against people of all classes, including the gentry themselves.

The Experiences of a Barrister was followed later in 1850 in *Chambers's* by a series of seven stories called *Confessions of an Attorney*, which were pirated by Cornish Lamport in New York in 1852 as *Confessions of an Attorney by Gustavus Sharp*, though in some cases the cover carried the name Samuel Warren, as well as that of Charles Dickens, several of whose crime-related *Household Words* essays appeared.[14] The stories were not published together in London until 1857 when they appeared in the same collection as, and after, *Leaves from the Diary of a Law Clerk*, attributed to "William Russell."

In title the *Confessions* throw the focus onto Ferret's role, though the attorneys are now named Flint and Sharp (without an e). Though the preface to the *Confessions* honors attorneys in liberal and class-conscious terms as protecting "the humble and needy,"[15] the collection starts more negatively, and less charitably, by revealing a middling-class man involved in self-defeating dishonesty. "A Life Assurance" (1850) tells how a low-level city character pretends his son is dead to collect the insurance, but is then outwitted because a relative leaves a fortune depending on the boy's life. Yet this middling-class mischief is condoned: the attorney just returns the check to the insurers, with no explanation. Continuing the emergent middle- and middling-class sympathy of the *Barrister* stories, the erring *petit bourgeois* is not destroyed, as such troublesome social interventionists tended to be in Warren: the attorneys may have distaste for their own class's negative capacities, but, as in the late story featuring Ferret "The Step-Father," they are now not enemies of their own class nor only in service to the gentry.

This partially radical, or at least reformist, opening of this new contribution to the debate is, though, blurred immediately in "Bigamy or No Bigamy?" (1850), where the person in difficulty is a Countess, the context is definitely financial, and the skilled middling-class are shown to triumph for the gentry. Something of the same two-class concept is implied, if negatively, in "Every Man His Own Lawyer" (1850) where a pompous merchant gets into a costly legal mess by not consulting a lawyer when he buys an estate, but that folly does not blur his class identity or destroy him as might have happened in Warren. But in general, these stories privilege strongly the middle- and middling-class skills of barrister and attorney and so have an anti-two-class thrust. That can re-focus an older type of binary class story: when "Jane Eccles" (1851), like Warren's "Esther Mann," is wrongly hanged for forgery there is now a reforming lawyer's voice to be implicitly heard, and the way the attorney helps protect an honest shoe-mender from a charge of theft in "The Chest of Drawers" (1851) makes middling-class values seem heroic and in harmony with middle-class professionalism. The force of the medial classes is strong in the long and complex story "The Puzzle" (1851), where an inheritance dispute involves East Indian wealth and disputants. The familiar pretty, maltreated lady, here socially lowered to city merchant stock, is Mrs. Allerton, but her step-mother produces another Mrs. Allerton, claiming that the suffering beauty has no rights to the property—it turns out that a theatrically skilled servant is the false Mrs. Allerton. The world of mercantile money, it appears, is also the world of elusive identity, and the disciplinary skills of lawyer and attorney, middle and middling class in unison, are offered as the only secure basis for value and identity—and so wealth—in this now familiar and not unvalued mercantile world where middle class and gentry seem to have become hybridized.

The thrust of the *Experiences* and, especially, the *Confessions* is a good deal more towards middle- and middling-class value and self-consciousness than has been seen before or is seen in much contemporary fiction: it is for example normal in Reynolds' 1850s novels for the finely moral ordinary person to be rewarded by marrying an aristocrat if a young woman (*Mary Price* and *Ellen Percy*), or to be discovered to be one if male (*Joseph Wilmot*).

The fact that the *Barrister* and *Attorney* stories appear in *Chambers's*, a liberal and fairly inexpensive periodical may be a crucial element in their representation of problems and possibilities relating to class, and a sign of new class challenges being acknowledged, if also ultimately sidelined. But there can still be reservations about class transition, as is clear in the long, powerful "Attorney" story, "The Incendiary" (1852).[16] Sharp tells this about a wealthy farmer who has the mercantile skill to sell up and wait for prices to fall and then re-purchase, all with the non-mercantile ambition that "my children, if I have any, shall, if I do not, reach the class of landed gentry."[17] He does grow rich, and has a daughter. But, as both the story and the narrator stress, he fails to educate her like a lady and so—the direct connection is insisted on—she falls in love with a waster. She dies after having a daughter and her maddened father tries to get rid of the child's father by framing him for arson: the farmer turned financier is the incendiary of the title, but also represents a threat to structures of social order. Sharp predicts that the child will marry, with her wealth, into the squirearchy, and so the story participates in the familiar class-appropriation process, a process quite different from the frontal assault on class barriers that the mercantile farmer had planned.

This last story seems a dilution of the class-mobile implications of other *Barrister* and *Attorney* stories, and there is little Ferret-style detection in the *Attorney* series, nor is there in the effective successor sequence, *Leaves from the Diary of a Law-Clerk* (1857), which is attributed to "William Russell." As the *Confessions* stories were printed in the same volume after *Leaves* in 1857, produced by Brown, the publisher of *Experiences of a Barrister* in the previous year, when the *Recollections* by "Russell" were also successfully anthologized in London by a different publisher, Kent, there may be links between "Russell" and the *Confessions*. Rather than them looking back to Warren, it seems quite possible that the multi-productive "Russell" might have also written the *Attorney* stories. That view would assume that the presence of the "Attorney" stories along with the "Barrister" ones in the 1857 American edition allegedly authored by Warren and published by Wentworth of Boston was American opportunism. Whatever the authorship, it is clear that these early semi-disciplinary stories were clearly of some public interest.

Police Detectives in Action

The Experiences of a Barrister first appeared early in 1849 and later in that year, before the *Attorney* stories started, *The Recollections of a Police*

Officer by "William Russell," with whom these lawyer stories would somehow become involved, began in *Chambers's Edinburgh Journal.* An American pirated collection appeared in 1852—sometimes wrongly cited as 1853—and the first English collection, with 13 stories, and the adjective "Detective" inserted before "Police" in the title, was published in 1856, followed by a second series in 1859 with eight more stories. Both of these were attributed to "Waters," from the name of the leading character, and the brief preface was in each case signed "C.W." (in later editions "C. Waters," though the hero is Thomas Waters), but these stories were also attributed to "William Russell." This seems impossible to have been, as is sometimes claimed by people with limited familiarity with the period, the *Times* journalist William Howard Russell, well-known for his coverage of the Crimean War, who was busy overseas as a war correspondent in 1850 when the Waters stories was emerging: as William Russell Ll.D. (his old college Trinity Dublin had honored him with the doctorate), in a letter to *The Times* in October 1864 he denied being "William Russell," the author of *Eccentric Personages* (1864). Presumably this was both the author of the Waters stories and the "Russell" who produced *Extraordinary Men* (1853) and *Extraordinary Women* (1857): the British Library Catalogue describes him each time as "Miscellaneous Writer." "William Russell" is also associated with some books on maritime topics edited by "Lieutenant Warneford," and an early copy of *Tales of the Coast Guard* (1856) is in several versions described as being put together by the so far unknown C.P. Morgan. The mystery of "William Russell" still awaits detective resolution.

Naming a "police officer" and then a "detective police officer" in a title as the agent inquiring into crimes was a distinct step forward, going some way to address the negative response to police that English attitudes, and crime fiction, had so far made. A modern police force had been founded in 1829 by the Prime Minister Sir Robert Peel—hence the nicknames "Peelers" and "Bobbies" for the London police, the latter lasting to the present. A special detective force had been established in London in 1842, though it was at first very small, with two Inspectors and six Sergeants. These professionals are slow to emerge as central in English crime fiction, and that might be put down to the relative unpopularity of the police as a concept—police were early on seen as a French-style form of social surveillance, likely to disrupt traditional English citizen freedoms. But directly relevant to the present discussion is that the police, including their inspectors, were consciously recruited from the lower class, as if they were simply seen as soldiers, and officer-style activity remained in the hands of the politicians and administrators who would run the force from above.

This reality generated the view that the main task of the police was to keep control of their own originary class, and not intervene in the affairs of the middle and upper classes. This view is basic to the essentially positive account of police detectives given by Dickens in the *Household Words* essays beginning in 1850, see Chapter 5, pp. 137–38, and is clear in later illustrations of Field at work among lower-class criminals (Figure 6). The resultant class hostility to the police would last a long time, and has been suggested by Anthea Trodd as a major cause for the limited success and presence of police detectives in the work of major fiction writers.[18] As a result, the processes of inquiry into and resolution of crime above the lower-class level were long to be in the mainstream novel kept largely free of police activity: this extensive topic will be discussed in Chapter 5.

The social seclusion of police was handled with some subtlety in the first police crime fiction stories. Their author "Russell" made a crucial move in that Thomas Waters was actually a gentleman who lost all his money gambling, but instead of turning to unsuccessful crime, like one of Warren's patients, he joined the police. Waters' gentry origins seem, and were no doubt meant, to make his detection more acceptable—and it is noticeable that his engagements are not with the hard-core professional thieves of lower-class origin (the targets of Dickens' admired detectives), but more with people succumbing to weakness, who are usually not of lower-class origin, but middling- or even middle-class. Much in the Waters police detective stories is a compromise with the hostile social attitudes that prevented the police themselves as being accepted as wide-ranging and cross-class detectives of crime, and operates as a moderate dissent from the contemporary social attitudes that prevented the police in general from being accepted as wide-ranging and cross-class detectors and punishers of crime.

The opening story details Waters' change of position. "One Night in a Gaming House" (1849) is reminiscent of the fifth and last of Richmond's cases: but joining the police here is the basis of the unfortunate gentleman's rescue, where Richmond's man Percy, in old gentry style, killed the man who ruined him in a duel and fled overseas. In keeping with being a generation later, the world of Waters can no longer be seen as simply binary: the stories explore confusion and greed in the modern world, with some emphasis on the middling and middle classes, and evidently continue with a police detective guiding events, the debate developed in the *Experiences* and the *Confessions*.

One of the earliest, "XYZ" (1849), is about city clerks, both honest and dishonest, and how the police, led by Waters, are able, through work both brisk and lucky, to sort them out. Mercantile life is familiar but also

Figure 6. Inspector Field in a rough London kitchen. Illustration by E.G. Dalziel to "On duty with Inspector Field," 203–10, in *The Works of Charles Dickens*, Household Edition, *Edwin Drood and Other Stories* (London: Chapman and Hall, 1879), see p. 209.

very risky: in "The Partner" (1853) a would-be gentleman is forced to work in the city by his merchant father rather than, as he prefers, become an army officer. He loses his gentry fiancée and is accused of theft, framed by a malign merchant. But unlike Warren's *Passage* about "The Merchant's Clerk," on which this may be based, all turns out well: the mercantile world is unpleasant and dangerous but may be negotiable, even successful for the aspirational middle class. The late date of "The Partner" seems to have caused it to miss the 1852 New York edition, and it only appears in the 1857 London collection of *Leaves from the Diary of a Law-Clerk* by Russell where the stories of the *Confessions of an Attorney* also appear.

But though the Waters stories normalize, even value, the world of the middle and middling class, there are still some about higher-class people like "The Two Widows" (1850) dealing with minor gentry and their women or "The Twins" (1850) about a stolen baby heir where real lineage is restored and the gentry criminal escapes punishment, to the disgust of Waters. The second series, published in 1859 starts with "Mark Stretton," where the people are lower gentry. But most of the later stories deal with middling- or even artisan-class people—"Found Drowned" is about the murder of an inn-owner by two crooks in league with his wife, while "The Orphans" presents an urban criminal setting fire to an apartment, killing the orphans' mother in the process, to steal the savings and valuables of an artisan family. The 1859 stories can be quite long—several are over 10,000 words, and often turn on problems in marriages, which Waters observes rather than detects, but in cases of theft or murder he does conduct quite active inquiries.

The 1859 volume advertised the previous one, saying it has sold, at 1/6, 75000 copies: these stories were clearly an influential meshing of detection and the police. In a way they are police-procedurals a century before that sub-genre came to dominance, but detection in them is little more than watching and gaining information from someone who knows the criminal. The tone is restrained, the writing quite simple, and they effectively extend the form of the professional case-study into the domain of the police, and so extend the social range of the period's crime fiction, to some extent challenging the lower-class limits the police face elsewhere, both before and after.

"Russell" did not restrict himself to establishing an acceptable police detective, nor indeed, if he was also Warneford, to producing a series of maritime adventures. He absorbed patterns from other domains of middle- and middling-class inquiry in *Leaves from the Diary of a Law-Clerk* (1857), which offers stories about a Ferret-style law-clerk and a legal practice, with some police involvement. These, like other detective stories from the 1860s, do not seem to have appeared in a periodical, unlike the *Confessions of an Attorney* which follow them in the collection. Gentry issues recur in the *Law-Clerk* series: "The Diamond Necklace" sounds like a classic property case, but in fact turns out to be a lost heir story, though things have moved on somewhat: here the wealth is not landed but in substantial securities. But "Malvern and Malvern" is a traditional gentry ejectment story which is resolved by the legal professionals' discovery of a bigamous marriage. Though the stories are now recognizing and valuing the legal skills and mercantile wealth of the middling and middle class, there is still a strong and more than nostalgic emphasis on the values and mores of that upper class to which both middle and, if indirectly, middling classes aspired.

By the 1850s, crime stories in the periodicals had taken note of clerical and mercantile affairs—naturally enough, because so many of the readers of *Chambers's* were from those classes. But the notice taken of middle and middling classes is still often negative, dealing with frame-ups, conflict and the dissatisfaction of mere money relations—the shadow of the cash-nexus seems to loom over many of these stories, including the ones about gentry gamesters. There are some in-class friendships and fidelities to be found below the gentry—more among the middling than the middle class it seems—but any sense of real lasting success and unchanging security tends to lead to the restoration of old values and rights. When we see skilled work by middling-class people like Ferret or, in his socially reduced status, Waters it is often to expose the fraudulence of others of their status or to restore the rights of attractive distressed gentlewomen. This continued respect for the anxieties of the higher classes in a socially changing and challenging world should not be seen as unrealistic—Lord John Russell's government, running from 1849 to 1856, had 21 cabinet ministers in the period, and 14 were actually aristocrats; another five were heirs to baronetcies. Aristocracy still ruled, literally: this was a Liberal, not Tory, government—in Parliament, as in crime fiction, aristocratic values still had power.

The Social Development of Detection

The 1860s saw more police activity in fiction, in various forms. *A Detective's Notebook* (1860) and later in the same year *The Diary of an Ex-Detective* (1860) are by Thomas Delf, writing as "Charles Martel." The pseudonym, remarkably, is also the name of the great 8th-century hero of the Frankish kings against the insurgent Arabs: Victorian referentiality can be puzzling, as with Catherine Crowe's use of the name Gaveston for her villain, see Chapter 5, p. 130. In spite of the collection's title, the detective is still linked to the police and is at times called Inspector F---, which must suggest the famous Inspector Field, who retired from the police in 1852 and opened a private agency: he was written about by Dickens in *Household Words* and is accepted as the model for Mr. Bucket in *Bleak House* (see Chapter 5, p. 140). In these stories he is at times active and persistent in detection, almost always operates alone, and is rewarded with a £100 note in "The Lost Portfolio"—but as the Prime Minister has shared the chase and arrest, that narrative might be seen as a fantasy. The stories are miscellaneous, even random, in social focus. The detective is a plain man with "wet and muddy boots" and "a slangy voice,"[19] but his identity does not project far into the meaning and values of the stories. The first story, "The Gamester," is a sentimental version of the Richmond-Waters gentleman-gambler narrative. Other stories are miscellaneous, even random, in social focus: "Cheating the Gallows" reveals blood-stained conflict among middling-class city shop-workers, while "The Golden Haired Wig" is a joke story focusing on Bandy Bill the Welsh burglar appearing in improbable female disguise. "Moneybags and Son" is a version of the hyper-anxious stories like the *Barrister* story "The Mother and Son" and "The Partner" by "Russell": a rich grocer's son steals his father's money and betrays a middle-class girl from Russell Square, but both survive near fatalities (she from a suicide attempt, he from a fight) and actually marry happily. This unconvincing bourgeois triumph is as far as the somewhat uncertain pen of "Martel" can go to celebrate the new world.

A different path is taken by the first set of stories overtly about a private detective, *The Revelations of a Private Detective*, produced by "Andrew Forrester" in 1863. This author's identity has long been a mystery: the surname might suggest a pseudonym meant to reference the well-known Forrester brothers, John and Daniel, senior police who became security officers at a major London bank—Delf's second volume was dedicated to them—but so far this idea lacks persuasive argument. It has also been suggested the author might have been a woman because of *The Female Detective* story-collection published under this name in 1864, and the fact that novels by a "Mrs Forrester" started appearing just after the "Forrester" detective stories stopped appearing,[20] but her style is historical, romantic and quite learned, which is nothing like "The Female Detective" stories.

Kate Summerscale noted in her book on Sergeant Whicher and the Road Hill House Murder of 1860 that a pamphlet about this case by James Redding Ware of 1862 was "also published as a short story" in the 1864 "Female Detective" collection, where it was titled "A Child Found Dead: Murder or No Murder."[21] Judith Flanders in an essay in *The Times Literary Supplement* of 2010 and in her 2011 book on this basis identified Ware with "Andrew Forrester"[22] and this has been accepted by Mike Ashley in his introduction to the 2012 British Library reprint of the "Female Detective" stories, where he adds that the final story in the collection "The Mystery" appeared in 1862 in the magazine *Grave and Gay*, which "may well have been edited" by Ware, and that another story from this magazine appeared in *The Private Detective* by "Forrester" in its 1868 edition.[23] While the British Library evidently accepts the "Forrester"-Ware identification, there seem to be grounds for doubt. The "Child Found Dead" story is represented by the female detective as being a manuscript given her by a doctor, while "The Mystery" does not even mention her. Both have a coolly ironic tone, quite different from that of the female detective stories and they could well be stories simply brought in to make up the numbers, as was quite common at the time.

Whoever his author was the "Forrester" male private detective is, in traditional terms, at first employed by a solicitor, though he often works, like many of these early figures, in insurance cases. The author evidently has legal knowledge, as the cases can be frauds based on wills and trusts, and there are legal jokes like the defender Mr. Tortuous Dodge who ends in jail, and Mr. Loosetongue the divorce lawyer, as well as Police Inspector Slimy. A number of the cases are resolved because the detective extracts confessions, often after recognizing a former criminal, though he does at times closely observe doubtful people, as when in "Mrs Fitzgerald's Life Policy" he discovers the Ireland-based couple are enjoying the £3000 they have received for her death. In the final story, "Arrested on Suspicion" the resolution relies on solving a complicated cipher—this story also makes an admiring reference to Poe, and elsewhere Mr. Ferret the attorney is mentioned.

A variety of middle-class malpractice and evasion recurs in the second "Forrester" collection *Secret Service, or Recollections of a City Detective* (1864) ("Secret Service" was the title of Dickens' Chapter 38 of *Martin Chuzzlewit*, detailing the actions of Nadgett, another insurance investigator, see Chapter 5, p. 128–29). It begins with a lively election-management story where the agent manages a near-crime rather than detecting any. Basically non-detective narratives follow, both realizing and questioning bourgeois values. In "Mistaken Identity" when a respectable tradesman is summonsed for child support, the agent finds with some inquiries that a traveller who resembles the tradesman gave his card to the maid he seduced.

These stories, like those in the *Barrister*, *Attorney* and Waters series, seem imbued with a sense that crime is inherently class-linked and is often based on an attempt to change class. That may seem rational, even automatic, in England, always sharply aware of social divisions and their apparent, meaning. But it is not an approach found elsewhere in the Anglophone world. There is no trace of class hostility or even superiority in the lively criminal stories enfolded in William Burrows' *Adventures of a Mounted Trooper in the Australian Constabulary* (1859). John B. Williams's *Leaves from the Notebook of a New York Detective* (1865), featuring the exploits of Jem Brampton (see Chapter 1, pp. 28–29), operate without broad social anxiety of any visible kind. Robert Curtis's *Irish Police Officer* stories (1861) offer a different reading of the two-class system: the narratives consistently respect the status and values of ordinary people and crimes are generally instituted by the landowners and—a sensitive topic in Ireland—their agents. In another thematic variation, James M'Levy's Glasgow-based stories *Curiosities of Crime* (1861) replace the class anxiety of their English equivalents with a strongly moralized hostility to crime and violence.

A striking variation occurred in the 1860s when the detective becomes substantially altered not in class but in gender. Catherine Crowe's *Susan Hopley* (1841) had made limited moves in the direction of female inquiry (see Chapter 4, p. 100), and Wilkie Collins had developed this concept more recently, though with limitations: his short story "'The Diary of Anne Rodway" (1856) shows a lower-class girl making some headway in detection, but she is finally helped by her middling-class lover returned from America—which seems to predict the path of *The Woman in White* (1860), where Marian Halcombe does bravely well in uncovering the mystery, but the resolution is taken over by the art-teacher who is her half-sister's beloved, and has himself not long ago returned from South America.

Two versions of female detection appeared. *The Revelations of a Lady Detective* (1864), published under the pseudonym "Anonyma" was probably written by the busy hack W. Stephens Hayward, best known for his two courtesan novels, *Anonyma, or Fair but Frail* (1864) and *Skittles* (also 1864). *The Revelations* is still quite often cited as having been published in 1861, but this is an error, apparently based on a misreading of the British Library's accession stamp for 1864 on the first edition. It was actually published some six months after the innovative first female detective stories by "Andrew Forrester," *The Female Detective.* In *The Revelations* Mrs. Paschal is a capable fortyish woman who works with the police, and apart from her gender, she and her cases are essentially conservative. They are basically a familiar set of class-conservative stories, starting with a bank-robbing countess—she is foreign, which apparently explains her upper-class fallibility. Then Mrs. Paschal deals with the aristocracy and the lower classes at odds in "The Lost Diamonds," and has a fantastic foreign villains story, complete with a perilous escape by the river, in "The Secret Band." The only story that acknowledges possible gentry failings is "Mistaken Identity": the title gives away the reason why "a respectable civil engineer of gentlemanly appearance"[24] is arrested for skittle-sharping, a minor gambling crime that recurs in this period. It was his brother did it, but these familial, in-class failings are manageable: like many gentleman criminals of the period, he is let off and goes to Australia, but is not transported there, as he would have been if lower class.

A good deal more interesting and progressive in terms of social debate is the slightly earlier, and no doubt influential set of stories by "Andrew Forrester," *The Female Detective* (1864). The Ferret class position is distinctly developed here. Firmly set in the world of the middling class is the long and thoughtful story "The Judgement of Conscience," focused on a simple, good shoe-mender. His sister's fiancé kills her employer out of jealousy, and her brother feels he is responsible because he was so unsympathetic to her. There is no happy resolution—though the shoe-mender ends up in Australia as a migrant who is "doing well"[25]—but there is clearly value given to people at this social level. Yet the value is carefully contained: the shoe-mender himself early on makes a speech attacking, in somewhat outdated fashion, the Chartists for their aggressive, selfish and even "tyrannical" attitudes (147, a rare instance of conscious politics in the earlier crime fiction texts. Other *Female Detective* stories can socially extend the pro-gentry pattern. "Tenant for Life" is a story about false seizure of an inheritance and property, but it uses as an initiating frame the thoughts and affectionate life of a London cabby and his wife. "The Unknown Weapon," a long gentry-murder story which E.F. Bleiler much admired and reprinted as one of his *Three Victorian Detective Novels*,[26] focuses on the independence of a woman in service to the quite untrustworthy gentry. Those stories seem to be reworking earlier material with an additional middling-class focus and set of values, even sympathizing at the working class A level as in "Georgy," where a young London lad of that name turns to forgery and theft, is basically admired for his wit and charm, and allowed to get away with £300 of ill-gotten gains. Whoever "Forrester" might have been, he, or conceivably she, was the most radical of these writers.

Elements of innovation occur elsewhere in the work of "Forrester." Something like a prevision of the woman detective seems implied when in the first of his three collections, *The Revelations of a Private Detective* (1863) the detective is a "soft-looking, quiet, almost womanly man, with fair hair and weak, soft blue eyes,"[27] and from the start these lack the social certainties and constraints of their predecessors. The gentry can be fallible: the answer to "Who Stole the Plate?" is the earl's son, and the humble detective and the saddened earl share their distaste for him. The middle class can be calmly and judiciously inspected: in the second collection by "Forrester," *Secret Service, or Recollections of a City Detective*, another story using the popular title "Mistaken Identity" deals with "an eminently respectable city tradesman,"[28] while "Who was the Greatest Criminal?" shows the lawyer to be the worst and the banker the best in a world of bourgeois values. "A Romance of Social Life" is a complex cross-class story of women's varied fidelities. After a rich merchant marries his clerk's daughter, the wife frames a servant for theft when she herself has been stealing for her lover; the girl goes to jail, all is discovered, the wife becomes a prostitute, and the merchant will marry the freed servant. In the same almost feminist spirit "The Missing Will" is not about property at all, but about a solicitor who passes his will and his wealth on to his mistress, knowing his family would destroy such a will. Celebrating ordinary men and women of honest feeling in a world of urban complexity, the stories by "Forrester" seem quite modern, and appear to have worked their way out of the anxieties through which earlier writers have confronted social change and represented it as crime and social disorder. The class ideas in the "Forrester" stories appear to be broadly in harmony with the wider dissemination of this kind of fiction and the growing strength of middle-class, and by now especially middling-class, self-consciousness.

Detection Across the Classes

By the end of the 19th century the slow and often uncertain movement in crime fiction away from the social simplicity of a two-class system to a wider range of perceptions of class, including their varied social values, is complete. The development towards acknowledging middle- and middling-class values comes to a confident conclusion in the cases of Sherlock Holmes. The two opening novellas deal with solidly middle-class people facing threats from the past and abroad, but Holmes operates in a multi-class way, tracing their problems through the evidence of servants and proletarian onlookers—his capacity to go in disguise, so be both disciplinary middle-class and also operate in middling- or often working-class mode is striking. In the short stories this dynamic multiplicity simplifies somewhat, at least in terms of his clientele. The first *Strand Magazine* case "A Scandal in Bohemia," while its title teasingly offers urban misbehavior via the louche connections of modern "Bohemian" life, actually refers to the king of Bohemia and his problems with a former mistress. Holmes operates in his usual multiple-class way, with the validation of solidly middling-class professional Watson as his partner. But immediately after that elevated beginning, the stories pick up what will in their earlier sequences be a recurrent personnel—middling-class city workers, baffled by their mistreatment at work or in the family. In the second and third stories, "The Red-Headed League" and "A Case of Identity," a clerk and a typist face respectively professional criminals robbing a bank, and quasi-incestuous betrayal as her step-father pretends to be a fiancé to keep her money in the family.

The *petit bourgeois* of the skilled or semi-skilled middling classes, with middle-class aspirations, were the major audience for *The Strand*—classically they were commuting into London for work, often even changing trains at Baker Street itself. Their concerns are focal as the saga gathers way, and there will also be occasional ventures into the extra-urban problems of the class to which those people aspired, the wealthy professionals, who found moving to a fine rural mansion no protection from the villainous jealousies of their alleged friends and even family members.

The ways in which Holmes actually solves a case also mesh with the focus on middle- and middling-class concerns. The famous arias of analysis, where he reads a character from clothes, or personal problems from a gesture or a physical feature, are in fact never used to solve the crime—they are a hyper-disciplinary self-assertion of the detective's imaginary authority, inherently outside class. Holmes has three separate case-solving functions. He does research in archives, often his own substantial ones—when he operates as a middling-class white-collar worker. He goes off alone, investigating, usually in working-class disguise and often in dangerous locations, and after that cross-class heroism, he will report on the adventure to Watson back in the firmly middle-class professional context of the Baker Street flat. Thirdly, he will visit and examine in familiar disciplinary ways the scene of the crime usually with Watson, and sometimes also the police, in a sort of middling-class disguise. So Holmes shows his socially polymorphous potential, a Prometheus for the *petite bourgeoisie*.

Figure 7. Illustration by Sidney Paget to Arthur Morrison, "The Lenton Croft Robberies," in *Martin Hewitt, Investigator* **(London: Ward, Lock and Browne, 1894), p. 5.**

As Conan Doyle grew annoyed with his easy success in this, to him, less than dignified form (he wanted to be Sir Walter Scott for his time), he invented the middle-class master-criminal Professor Moriarty to dispose of Holmes—contrary to most opinion, he is not a regular rival, but in fact appears very rarely. But Conan Doyle's attempt to kill off the apotheosis of the middle and middling classes was rejected by both the audience, in a clear form of readerly social resistance, and, more directly and effectively, the very substantial sums of money offered by publishers to revive the great detective. There were some later quasi-espionage stories where Holmes operates on behalf of his nation, and the *petit bourgeois* characters do thin out somewhat in the later stories when Conan Doyle himself has, as a knight of the realm, ascended substantially, even into the upper class.

Conan Doyle's development of the bourgeois but also cross-class detective hero was a major move, and had immediate followers and variations, which tended to be socially more narrow-range. A striking alternative to Holmes was the realistic middling-class detective Martin Hewitt, a straightforward hard-working anti–Holmes. Arthur Morrison was a journalist born in London's East End who would become famous for the social—and socialist—realism of his revelations of slum life, *Tales of Mean Streets* (1894) and *A Child of the Jago* (1896). Described by E.F. Bleiler as "the most successful" of the Conan Doyle parallels published by *The Strand*,[29] his first adventure "The Lenton Croft Robberies" appeared in *Strand Magazine* in March 1894. Hewitt is true to the plain English crime fiction short-story tradition, being a law-clerk turned private investigator; he handles crime in a calm, methodical way (Figure 7) questions servants and works out the crime. In the first story it is simple, even ironic—the secretary's parrot has stolen the jewels—but the second, "The Case of the Dixon Torpedo," involves a national matter where his unheroic way of studying the "curious chances and coincidences,"[30] as well as some acute detailed observation, leads him to a well-concealed surprise revelation: this is the usual Martin Hewitt mode of inquiry and assertion of middling-class values.

An archetypal and lively variant of such modern and socially-grounded detection, combined with the tradition of female detection, somewhat overlooked since the 1860s, appeared in *The Experiences of Loveday Brooke, Lady Detective* (1894) by the prolific novelist Catherine L. Pirkis (see Chapter 4, pp. 112–16 for a fuller account of her significance and context). Loveday is a little over 30, and serious-minded: her eyes narrow to slits when she is thinking. Left alone and penniless when young, she worked as a detective and now has her own Fleet Street Agency: her previous employer calls her "one of the shrewdest and most clear-headed of my female detectives."[31] In the first story she picks up the literary references that reveal a secretary to be bogus, but she is also very astute—in the second story she works out that a devoted mother has substituted a sister to enable her criminal brother to escape. Using her brains and her substantial independence to rise to the level of professional middle-class activity, Loveday brings new elements of class mobility as well as gender liberation to the detective.

By the turn of the century, all classes above working-class level have been basically established as both potential criminals and also detectives—and there would in the late 20th century even emerge some successful detectives from the working-class like London's 1970s James Hazell, Edinburgh's 1990s John Rebus and more socially elusive modern figures like James Lee Burke's Dave Robicheaux of New Orleans and Peter Corris's Sydney-based Cliff Hardy. But in the early period, the story of 19th-century crime fiction from a class point of view is a long and complex struggle for values other than those of the gentry—and especially values of the police—to be established as credible against crime. Though, and because, the police were formed from the lower class, the emergent detectives were generated from other parts of the social spectrum and even a different gender: in this respect at least fiction seems more important than crime in terms of the social, developmental, class-focused nature of early crime fiction.

CHAPTER 4

"Jonathan Wild in Petticoats": Women Detectives in Victorian England

An Absence of Gendered Detectives

One of the factitious truisms arising from modern reflections on the patterns of earlier crime narrative is to be found in terms of the gendering of the detective. We assume easily that what is cultural is natural: the thoroughly gendered detective is such an entity. The deeply, inarticulately masculine tough guy like Bogart has generated his comparable challenger in the tough gal of Sara Paretsky—who has herself been criticized by a number of feminists as being effectively a tough guy in drag.[1] Such complexity as has emerged in crime fiction criticism has not really shaken the masculinism of the assumptions about the detective, or the reflex that a female detective is a challenge to the genre as well as herself.

It was not always so, in two ways. While the early detectives were almost always male, they were not always inherently, implicitly, gender-stereotypical—and there were always women inquirers around, if unevenly in both presence and in tone and success. The brave and often inquisitive Gothic heroines have aspects of the detective, and as early as 1820 in E.T.A. Hoffmann's *Das Fräulein von Scuderi* an elderly lady explains mysterious crimes in Paris and saves an innocent suspect who is the victim of circumstantial evidence. The early detectives are varied in type, amateurs like Godwin's Caleb Williams, Poe's Dupin or Collins' Anne Rodway, or professional inquirers like Warren's London Physician, Ferret the lawyer's clerk, Waters the first police detective by "William Russell" or the 1864 "female detectives"—see Chapter 3 for a discussion of these figures. Very few of them are strongly gendered in the sense that they realize and reinforce stereotypes: they undertake their inquiries without any assertively gendered approach.

That statement can be best clarified by indicating its exceptions. A couple do operate in that way. Both Tom Richmond, who becomes a Bow Street Runner, and Henry Pelham, gentleman about both Paris and London, are strongly male-gendered. They have more or less explicit sexual encounters with women when young, both throughout exercise a strong male gaze over women and, especially, wenches, they both encounter villainesses but defeat them, both settle down with an ideal little woman. Masculinism in a nutshell. In fact the Richmond-Pelham narrative has remarkable resemblance to a 1930s private eye story, down to the wavering over whether to turn in the beautiful villainess, shared by Richmond and Sam Spade. But the other early detectives, almost all of them male, do not exhibit that gender-stereotypical structure, or even any significant parts of it. Yet both a masculine and a female positioning become normal as detectives develop in the popular literature of the century.

Recent authors specializing in women detectives see as an early example of female detection Catherine Crowe's anonymously published novel of early 1841, *Susan Hopley, or Circumstantial Evidence*. From 1843 on, the sub-title changes to *the Adventures of a Maid Servant*, which might seem a domestication of what was offered as a crime story. However, the narrative does not offer any developed awareness of gender and detection interacting, in spite of Brenda Ayres calling it Crowe's "female detective novel."[2] Sussex, who has looked in detail at the text, speaks more cautiously, calling it "a major crime novel," having "three female detectives" who are "effective amateur sleuths" and she sees it as overall "the first substantial crime novel by a woman."[3] There was clearly some developing interest in the crime fiction form—Warren's stories had been published in three volumes by 1837, Poe would very soon write his Dupin stories in America, but *Susan Hopley* has many non-crime fiction elements in it, and is not the start of female detection that some feminist critics have felt it to be. The proper place for a discussion of Crowe's first novel is in Chapter 5 with other uncertain moves by the mainstream novelists towards—and often away from—crime fiction. The approaches and techniques, even conflicts, of the woman detective will emerge much more slowly.

Mid-Century Male-Created Woman Detectives

Women first appear as self-conscious detectives in the collection *The Female Detective* published in May 1864 under the name "Andrew Forrester":

the third collection of detective stories under this authorial name, after *Revelations of a Private Detective* in 1863 and *Secret Service, or Recollections of a City Detective* in January 1864. Evidently the form was doing well— "William Russell," author of the Waters "detective police officer" stories as long ago as 1849, published the collection *Leaves from the Diary of a Law Clerk* in 1857, and Thomas Delf, a long-serving hack writer, produced *Leaves from the Diary of an Ex-Detective* and a sequel to it, both in 1860 under the pseudonym of Charles Martel. The "Forrester" collections developed this process of imitation with variation and presumably this is what led the author to the idea of a "Female Detective"—there were none in the police force until the 20th century, though it appears seems women were at times used unofficially as informants and even investigators: Allan J. Pinkerton had employed Kate Warne in his American agency as early as 1856.

Whatever the authorship of the stories in *The Female Detective* (discussed in social terms Chapter 3, pp. 93–94), they make up an ill-matched collection, two stories being at novella length and the others much shorter, from little more than 3,000 words to at most 6,000. The first, "Tenant for Life," one of the two novellas, does begin with a consciously female range of activities. The detective only in this story indicates her professional name is "Miss Gladden"—to the police she works with she is just "G." It is not clear why commentators in the past have called her "Mrs Gladden," unless perhaps some copies use that form. She is not employed by the police, but is often consulted by them. At the start of this story she tells about a friendship she has with an ordinary London couple and how she goes on holiday jaunts with them—which leads one day to their discussion of two babies they adopted from women who could not manage them. The first died at nine, but the second was in a very strange way bought for £30 by a woman within 20 minutes of their receiving it.

She becomes determined to pursue the matter, not just out of interest but also professionalism—"Good as many of the cases in which I had been engaged might have been, I knew that not one had been so near my fame and, in a small way, my fortune, as this."[4] She uses her milliner's skills to gain work in the house where the baby was bought, years ago now, presenting her card as "Miss Gladden, a milliner and a dressmaker"—she has actually taken courses in these areas to be convincing. She interacts with Miss Shedleigh, who bought the child, and shows herself good at lengthy, friendly, and ultimately informative discussions with her and especially with the housekeeper. But the focus of the story does not in fact deal with issues that could be seen as female-gendered—it is yet one more of the inheritance mysteries and substitute-heir stories that populate mid–Victorian mystery

Figure 8. The Female Detective at work. Cover illustration to "Andrew Forrester," *The Female Detective* (London: Ward Lock, 1864).

fiction. The child was bought so the family can keep an entailed inheritance, but the end is male melodrama as the genial true heir Sir Nathaniel Shirley dies of a heart attack—melodramatically represented on the cover of the collection (Figure 8)—and though there is no proof that the child was not part of the family, Mr. Shedleigh nobly gives up possession of the inheritance to Sir Nathaniel's heir.

A striking number of these stories operate in this way, with a somewhat stagey female-oriented opening, and then a male-focused story which often has no real, certainly no legal, resolution. The second story, "Georgy," of barely 4,000 words, has the detective befriending a woman whose son is an amiable clerk—but he turns out to be a skillful embezzler of funds at the law firm where he works. Miss Gladden shows this with some fairly simple interviews after he disappears, and there is no trace of an arrest, only a rather whimsical sense of well-wishing for the young criminal.

The somewhat longer "The Judgement of Conscience" does start with the detective noticing John Kamp, a skillful shoemaker, when he is trying to help a woman taken ill in the street. She becomes friends with him and his sister and, much as with the couple in "Tenant for Life," a mystery emerges—but here it is starker. His sister Johanna has a soldier boy-friend, Tom Hapsy, and they expect to marry—but after not seeing them for some time Miss Gladden finds the sister has died of grief after the soldier left her: he thought she was being too friendly to her employer, a vain clothes merchant, who evidently was harassing her and she was trying to keep her job. This is in a real way woman-centered—though it is also a story told in G.W.M. Reynolds' *The Seamstress* (1851)—but then the men take over the story to its end.

Higham, the clothes merchant, is found shot; Miss Gladden thinks John Kamp did it to avenge his sister but then she notices his revolver is still fully loaded, and with the help of another woman employee Higham has bothered—but this one did not mind—she finds the soldier Tom Hapsy regretted his treatment of Johanna and avenged her. He confesses to the crime after John Kamp has turned himself in as being guilty in conscience if not in fact. Kamp is released and is now doing well as a medical assistant in Australia, "where they are not so socially particular as in England" (175).

Several other stories have a limited female viewpoint. "A Mystery" is about a girl being locked up for refusing to marry her father's choice—her boy-friend gets her out via a fire escape and they marry. This is both very short, barely 3,000 words, and also told in a distant male voice without the usual conversations and sympathies Miss Gladden brings. Equally not in her voice is the authorially interesting (see Chapter 3, p. 91) "A Child Found

Dead: Murder or No Murder." This studies in a parallel version the issues of the Road Murder case—though an opening note denies any link between the two. This was given to Miss Gladden by a "medical man" and the intelligence of the story is a barrister called Hardal, who eventually works out that "the incomprehensible acts of this murder prove that they were done in unconsciousness, in insanity, and by a woman" (198). But this somewhat distant view of womanhood is never proved, as the story simply breaks off—Miss Gladden says she will publish more if she ever receives it.

Oddly, the other story in the collection that is, in spite of its title, completely unresolved, "The Unravelled Mystery," is stimulated by the same "Medical Man." Here Miss Gladden starts with some quite full commentary on detectives, saying that in England they are not nearly as efficient as in France. She then, at the request of the doctor, investigates further his analysis of a head and some body parts recently found at a bridge over the Thames. His study of the body (principally its very dark hair) leads him to conclude the man was foreign, probably Italian, and he suggests the use of a knife to murder him suggests a gang killing. Miss Gladden decides that is all true, that he probably came from Soho, was killed there and then dumped in the Thames: and that is as far as the story goes. It is a fairly limited and stereotypical inquiry—Bleiler seems generous in likening it to Poe's "The Mystery of Marie Rogêt."[5]

This ill-assorted mix of narratives, sometimes offering a female viewpoint, but never really maintaining it, is climaxed by the novella-length "The Unknown Weapon." This was highly praised by Bleiler, and he printed it as one of the three in his *Three Victorian Detective Novels*—the other two were Wilkie Collins' *My Lady's Money* and Israel Zangwill's *The Big Bow Mystery*, so this is serious company: he also said it was "one of the small group of pioneer works that have some reason to be called the first modern detective novel."[6] In this he was noting that it is slightly earlier than *The Dead Letter* by "Seeley Regester," and was certainly praising it highly, for what is no more than a novella with a open ending—the mystery is solved, but no-one is punished in any way. Both Bleiler and Klein suggest that it has differences in style from the other stories—Bleiler says it has the brisk "style of a French feuilleton episode," while Klein sees "a deliberately experimental fictional style" with the characters showing "definite personality characteristics,"[7] but these differences, which do not in fact seem very large, may only mean it was originally written, or edited, for a different periodical than the others.

The story simply begins, with no explanation how Miss Gladden becomes involved. A young man, the heir of Squire Petleigh of Petleighcote in the north of England, has been found dead outside the family home, killed with "a rough iron barb" (218). For the lengthy first part of the story, a good quarter of it, Miss Gladden tells us what she reads of the inquest in the newspaper. The family have been away, but the housekeeper Mrs. Quinion was present, as was a very limited servant girl who, Miss Gladden discovers, is having nightmares about a large box in the house. She studies the body and clothes, finding an important-looking key and noticing a lot of fluff on the clothes. She interviews the housekeeper, who seems suspiciously keen to see the servant girl gone, and she manages to replace the servant with, surprising from such a period, a "woman police officer" (275). By sheer chance—which she acknowledges as an important element of detection—at the inn she sees the dead young man's favorite book, and it falls open at a story about a man using the delivery of a large box to enter a house unobserved.

Miss Gladden then advertises to suggest the housekeeper has inherited money, and while she is away seeking the bequest she and the policewoman search the house. They find the box, cunningly hidden as the housekeeper's bedroom table—the text refers to Poe and "audacity hiding" (294)—and they also find the strange weapon of the title—a Spanish picador's barb. They realize the youth, short of money and ostracized by his father, had smuggled himself into the house, intending to use the key to gain wealth— the fluff was from him sleeping in the box. Mrs. Quinion, realizing a man was in there and assuming he was a threatening burglar, had killed him in the box with the barb, then, seeing who he was, carried him outside in the morning.

But then Mrs. Quinion, suspicious, returns, sets fire to the house, and the detectives escape with difficulty. The housekeeper is gone for good: Miss Gladden carried the case "no farther" (303), having felt "I acknowledge that she conquered me." (302) In the destroyed house an ingot of melted gold is found, which no doubt the young squire was seeking with the special key. It is a strangely unresolved ending for a strongly-developed story that, like so much in this collection, takes some advantage of the unusual female positioning of the detective, but never makes that in any way thematic as, to at least some degree, would later crime writers using women as their central figures. Essentially, "Forrester" appears to have been a male writer creating a female detective just to vary the flow of detective-story collections—and also probably to connect with the evidently very large female reading audience of the period. As Klein comments, the author makes the female detective's status as a woman, and her motives for her activities, equally unclear—a process Klein calls "refusing to clarify her identity as a woman," and she comments that in "The Unknown Weapon" "she makes it easy for them (readers) to forget that she is a woman."[8]

Whatever its limits from a modern feminist position, *The Female Detective* was a success—the book was very soon reprinted and it evidently stimulated the appearance within six months of what seems to be a cover-version, *The Revelations of a Lady Detective.* This appeared under the name "Anonyma" which was also used for the author of a series of "Courtesan books," or fictional memoirs of women of pleasure. As Sussex reports, seven of these were published in 1864 by Vickers, a dubious publisher of long-standing—though his father George Vickers, who died in 1848, had produced the four-volume urban mystery sequence *The Mysteries of London* by G.W.M. Reynolds, 1845–48. The "Anonyma" context suggests something dubious about a lady detective—and the jacket deliberately supported that, with her smoking a cigarette, showing her extensive underskirt and looking seductively sideways at the reader.

The collection offers ten varied and in gendered terms fairly innocent stories about the detective skills of Mrs. Paschal, a widow of about 40, describing herself as "well-born and well-educated," who is employed to investigate specific cases by Colonel Warner, "head of the Detective Department of the Metropolitan Police."[9] Both date and author have been questioned. As noted above (see p. 93) the idea that the book came out in 1861 is just an error, but the author remains less than certain. Samuel Bracebridge Hemyng, a young barrister, has been suggested, but there seems little focused knowledge of or interest in legal matters through the stories, and William Stephens Hayward seems the more likely candidate—also very young, but as Ashley notes, a man who had been accused of rape (the victim did not appear in court) and, more successfully, of debt, and then wrote busily to the end of his short life of 35 years, with later attributions as the author of some of the "Anonyma" texts.[10]

The stories are more even in length than in *The Female Detective*, five being between 10,000 and 15,000 words and the others between 4,000 and 7,000 words. Mrs. Paschal, like Miss Gladden, is watchful, good at gaining information from servants and other women, and is rather more physically active and brave. In the first story, "The Mysterious Countess," she follows her target through a long difficult tunnel, then gets trapped on the way back. She wishes she had brought her Colt revolver with her, but is able to rouse people at the tunnel's end—which is in a bank—and though at first arrested, she is soon recognized. In the second story, "The Secret Band," also one of the longer ones, she becomes involved with a seriously dangerous London-based Italian gang led by a man named Zini, is finally captured by them and about to be executed, bound on a great metal water-wheel: but she is rescued by a level of melodrama well beyond Miss Gladden's experiences:

> A vivid, blinding flash of lightning darted through the open space above the wheel, and sought a victim. Zini, from his proximity to the metallic construction of the substantial part of the wheel, offered the most prominent mark, and it struck him, reducing him to a scathed mass of charred humanity [89].

In response, as she is saved, Mrs. Paschal is briefly, and less than heroically, female: she says, "When I found myself among friends and freed from the great danger which lately menaced me, I showed that I was a woman and swooned away" (89).

Most of the cases are much less melodramatic, and in a number of them Mrs. Paschal is the only woman involved—this Italian gang story is one and others are "Which is the Heir," "Stolen Letters," and "Mistaken Identity." Also distancing the stories from any positive female-oriented position is the fact that in several of them women are clearly represented negatively. In "The Mysterious Countess" the person Mrs. Paschal pursues is the countess herself, disguised as a man—a very small one, who has been robbing the bank at the end of the tunnel to fund her elaborate life style after the death of her aged husband. She is hardly represented positively by the narrative, and commits suicide when captured, with a poison pill concealed in a very beautiful ring. The following story, "The Lost Diamonds," is a calmer account of the Duke of Rusteburgh's missing jewels—he is an obsessive collector of them and his younger and somewhat ignored wife takes up gambling and soon turns to diamond-pawning. Mrs. Paschal finds it all out, embarrasses the Duchess and the money-lender, but the family returns to some sort of peace.

Two more unusual stories also stigmatize women. Evelyn St Vincent is a sensitive young heroine in "The Nun, the Will and the Abbess," a Catholic heiress whose mother is obsessively religious and is influenced by a priest who wants Evelyn to enter a convent rather than marry the cousin she admires. The priest's motive is simply devotion, but the abbess has worse intentions—she pressures and then forces Evelyn to sign over her wealth to the convent, even imprisoning and torturing her. Mrs. Paschal intervenes and Evelyn is restored to her cousin, but as in a number of these and the "Forrester" stories, and also normally in the mainstream crime-related novels discussed in Chapter 5, there is no penalty for a socially respectable criminal. The abbess in fact, having made Evelyn a nun and gained her signature for the money, makes her promise £100,000 when she is 21 before releasing her—but Evelyn will pay that gladly.

A different kind of female hostility is central to "Fifty Pounds Reward." John Eskell, a banker's clerk, has a foolish wife who makes friends with a bullying butcher's wife, who persuades her to forge a check to buy clothes. The check is found, a reward is offered, then the wife confesses. Eskell bans the butcher's wife from the house, but Mrs. Paschal arranges a penalty-free resolution where the butcher pays for the check and Eskell and his wife are reconciled.

One story does focus positively on a woman, but in an inactive and tragic mode. "Found Drowned" tells how Laura, a pretty and very capable baker's shop assistant, is admired by the baker's apprentice, but is also picked on by Sir Castle Clewer, "the foremost rake and libertine of the age" (179). She is found dead in the Serpentine, and Mrs. Paschal is employed on the case. She suspects Sir Castle but he denies it: at Scotland Yard Colonel Warner believes him, and wants her to follow up the apprentice. He has disappeared, but one evening coincidence assists detection—she sees a vagrant being driven from the Adelphi arches by the police; studying him she sees some resemblance to the apprentice and it is him. He runs from her, falls into a grave half-full of water, confesses he murdered Laura through jealousy, and—no deferral of police action for one of his class— is hanged.

This revelation of male vanity and the strength of the sense of honor of even a rake and libertine when he is aristocratic has links with the final story "Incognita," where a rich young man, Walford Wareham, has become enamored of a former actress, Fanny Williams, and Mrs. Paschal is asked by Colonel Warner, on behalf of the man's mother, to see what she can do. She meets Mrs. Wareham who, no doubt recognizing how she is getting special treatment from the police, behaves as if "she looked upon me more as a friend and ally than Jonathan Wild in petticoats" (244). Mrs. Paschal becomes maid to Fanny, admires her way of dressing up and making her hair blonde, and sees how she manages Wareham—she pretends to scorn him by burning 50 pounds, but has previously sent Mrs. Paschal out for some fake money. Though she has expected her to be "an unprincipled but still ambitious adventuress" she found she was "cleverer than I had anticipated" and "a worthy antagonist" (263). When a drunken scruffy man turns up and Fanny gives him £50, Mrs. Paschal works out he is the husband and reveals all to Walford—who then shows his limitations by trying to drown himself, but getting stuck in the mud of the River Thames.

Between tragic beauties and somewhat admired adventuresses, Mrs. Paschal does at times recognize some aspects of positivity in women, but mostly it is her own strength of character and purpose which speak up for women through the collection. Kestner suggests there is something like feminism in her opening scene with the police: "The returning of the male gaze is startlingly stressed in this first episode: 'I met the gaze of Colonel Warner and returned it unflinchingly'"—but the continuing text sees this this simply a sign of her personal courage rather than modern gaze theory: "he liked people to stare back again at him, because it betokened confidence in themselves, and evidence that they would not shrink in the hour of peril."[11] What the Colonel does say testifies to Mrs. Paschal's qualities in a more general way: when he is first commissioning her he says, "I am aware that you possess an unusual amount of common sense" (19) and later, in the context of the bad abbess, he says, "You must be courageous beyond the average run of women"—and she coolly replies, "Habit is second nature." (146). Klein has a less positive position than Kestner on the stories as interrogating gender positions, saying, "Only occasionally does it seem that both Mrs Paschal's assignments and her successes are directly corre-lated to her sex."[12]

In keeping with that judgment, Mrs. Paschal operates in largely mas-culine terms, looking into mostly male crimes, though she does, like Miss Gladden, use feminine skills in inveigling confidences from people, mostly women, and in some instances exploits her gender-linked power to enter a household as a servant. Klein, from the position of modern feminism and the development of the fully-fledged tough-girl detective like V.I. Warshawski, was quite severe on the amount of achievement, saying that the stories featuring Miss Gladden and Mrs. Paschal are in terms of inno-vation "qualified by treating them more as neuter than female; they are honorary men."[13] Yet although the authors are male, and the representation of female values and capacities is distinctly limited, it is an advance on what Catherine Crowe had offered over 20 years before. The fact that this material is in the publishing mainstream is a structural step forward for the representation of women, and might even have seemed quite challeng-ing in its period, as in spite of the relative success of the sales there was no contemporary follow-up, and the establishment of women detectives as lit-tle more than routine was a full generation away.

Slow Development

There was almost no immediate follow-up to the female detectives of the 1860s. The forward-looking American women crime writers of the 1860s did nothing with female detection beyond the insights of the detective Mr. Burton's clairvoyant daughter in *The Dead Letter*, though Watson has felt Victor shows some concern for the capabilities of women (see Chapter 1, p. 32). Even more disappointing was the failure in this period of the very productive and energetically varied Australia-based Mary Fortune to produce a gender-authentic parallel to Gladden and Paschal. Irish-born, growing up in Canada, then moving with her father to Australia in the 1850s gold-rush period, from 1865 to 1908 Fortune wrote over 500 full, varied and interesting short stories, many of which were consciously in the detective format. She took over from male writers and dominated this mode in the widely-read and well-established *Australian Journal*. She used the pseudonym "W.W.," a criminographical variant of the enigmatic pseudonym she used for her other writing, "Waif Wander." Her series detective, Mark Sinclair started as a "mounted trooper" in the Victorian small rural towns in 1866 and was relocated to Melbourne by the 1880s. She presumably she did not see either of the 1864 London female detectives or would surely have developed the idea. When she did move in that direction, as has been shown in a study of women detecting in her work by Nicola Bowes,[14] they were slow to appear, intermittent and often contained in gender terms.

Bowes does see Fortune as using at times a "female surrogate" (223) detective, not unlike Collins' very early Anne Rodway, or the women who look into puzzles in some of the sensational novels, as discussed in Chapter 5. The first of these quasi-detectives is Nurse Bennet in "Condemned by a Bracelet" (1876), where, in a re-use of the Road murder story, a 16-year-old girl is found to have killed her infant brother and put the body in her mother's coffin: the investigating nurse notices a stone from her bracelet among the baby's bedclothes. "Brandon's Boy, Bill" (1878) shows Bella, a 14-year-old girl, helping a rather unpleasant and unsuccessful private detective—she is disguised as Bill. In both of these stories the female investigation fades out before the end of the story, as did those Collins created for Anne Rodway and Marian Halcombe. Another form of containment appears in Fortune's "Mrs Larner's Revenge" (1890). Abandoned by her own husband, Mrs. Nemo, as she calls herself (she or Fortune apparently recalling *Bleak House*) is hired by a man, not specifically as a private detective, though she does identify his former wife as the thief. Then in old-style sensationalism the thief and the detective's husband, now a pair, are killed in a fire and the intelligent employee marries the deserted widower. "The Spade Guinea" (1893) shows how a young woman named Melie, acting as a housemaid, helps a police detective resolve the case, and he seeks to enlist her in the profession. This has evidently by the nineties become an acceptable approach, but is still rare in Fortune's work. Some element of that mode is in "The Major's Case" (1895) where Eliza Barret (not related to the 1876 nurse) works with her brother as a pair of detectives in a Melbourne case—she is the more successful. The most striking sign of Fortune's slow uptake of female detection is that only in 1898 in "The Diamond Cross" does Mark Sinclair, after more than 30 years of police inquiries, gain the detective help of his wife Nellie, whom he calls "one of the cleverest" in his profession (quoted by Bowes, 256). As Lucy Sussex has shown,[15] from the start, Fortune's work is notable for its use of women in the discussing and representing of crime and its containment, but she moved very slowly and incompletely towards using a female detective, a mode that would seem in principle very well-suited to her approach.

As is discussed in Chapter 5, there were some movements towards female detection in the work of the mainstream novelists. Collins, with Magdalen Vanstone in *No Name* (1863), and Valeria Brinton in *The Law and the Lady* (1875) certainly envisaged a woman inquirer, if not one who managed a complete inquiry, and Mary Braddon could involve women in investigations like Eleanor Vane in *Eleanor's Victory* (1863) and Margaret Wilmot in *Henry Dunbar* (1864), as did Ellen Wood with Barbara Hare in *East Lynne* (1861). But after the male-generated, market-varying beginnings of the 1860s, the real emergence of a female detective would essentially wait until apparently stimulated by later interest in the "New Woman."

The Fin De Siècle *Woman Detective*

The 1864 female detective appears to be a variant on the short-story collections of the early 1860s, and the sudden rise of detective novels in the mid 1880s seems to have operated as a similar stimulus. Gaboriau and to an extent du Boisgobey were selling well in the early-mid 1880s from Vizetelly in London, and then in later 1887 at the same time there appeared both Fergus Hume's sudden best-seller *The Mystery of a Hansom Cab* (see Chapter 6), and the much less-noticed, then at least, *A Study in Scarlet* by Arthur Conan Doyle. In apparent response, a young man born as Leonard Miller, after working in the Kimberley gold mining region of South Africa, who returned to London in 1885 and worked as an actor, then started writing fiction as Leonard Merrick. He first deployed a woman detective, presumably as a variant, though Mike Ashley suggests he might have read *The Lady Detective* published in America in 1880, probably written by the prolific Harlan Page Halsey, author of the "Old Sleuth" novels (see p. 30).[16]

Mr Bazalgette's Agent appeared with the respectable London firm of Routledge in July 1888. It is only novella length, barely 40,000 words, and Merrick never wrote another mystery—indeed he apparently tried to suppress this one, to the extent of buying up copies to destroy them. As is discussed by Baker and Shumaker,[17] he presumably thought it was a vulgar start to a career that would before long gain for him from J.M. Barrie the title "the novelist's novelist." The central figure, Miriam Lea, is 28, younger than both of the 1864 female detectives, and has been an actress and a governess, sacked from the latter job because of the potentially bad influence of the stage on her charges. Running out of savings, she sees an advertisement by Alfred Bazalgette, whose business is "suspected persons watched for divorce, and private matters investigated with secrecy and despatch."[18] She applies, but is kept waiting by the two less than imposing men who run the business. When finally out of money she goes back, and they say they were about to contact her for work—it seems Merrick is spinning out his story.

Her task is to find Jasper Vining, a gambler and bank clerk who has absconded with at least £4,000 in bonds, as in a mid-century short story. Before that was discovered he had said he was leaving for Australia, so they assume he will not be there: with a slightly tough maid who is also a detective agent, Miriam searches through Europe, starting in Hamburg. The narrative is more a matter of sensitive responses to travel than detection as such; from Hamburg they go to Lisbon, then head office directs them to Monte Carlo. During more sightseeing, she there spots a likely candidate and, pretending to be a weak female, obtains his handkerchief, which bears the initials J.V. He goes under the name Jack Vane, but they are sure they have found their man.

Certainty grows when he disappears to South Africa and they find him in the Kimberley area of Merrick's own experience. After more tourist material, she makes herself known, he is friendly, and she realizes she is falling in love with him. He is doing badly, needs more money and seems to have cashed some bonds. She writes Bazalgette a report about him as Vining, but just after it has been posted, the pair admit their love for each other. He asks her to marry him, so she plans to save him from cruel justice—but then a cable arrives saying the real Vining has just been arrested in New York. James Vane she realizes with joy "is not Jasper Vining; he is a gentleman" (137). There follows a quick happy ending, and a prosperous one: James is suddenly doing well with his new diamond claim.

By no means all of the 1864 female detective stories ended with a conviction, but none was as suddenly reversed as this. This is in effect a pastiche of a detective story, with travel scenes, and some fluent and engaging writing. Barrie was not wrong about Merricks' literary appeal, and he continued with lightweight romance-focused fiction such as *The Man Who Was Good* (1892) and short-story collections like *A Chair on the Boulevard* (1919). His distinctly minor novella has been celebrated by Kestner as the first major female detective story, initially stating, "Merrick's strategy in *Mr Bazalgette's Agent* is a brilliant one" then going on to speak about "Merrick's remarkable querying of the detective profession, its suggestion of twistedness, lack of respectability, lying and spying."[19] But the dubious features of the Bazalgette agency have been in the genre since Vidocq, and there are crooked lawyers, insurance agents and thieving gamblers right through the short stories of the mid-century, whatever the gender of the detectives. Kestner also feels the treatment of Miriam offers some "proto-feminist insights about gender construction during the Victorian period,"[20] which suggests he, unlike Merrick, is not familiar with *The Woman in White* and its mix of weakness and strength in the female, there split between Laura Fairlie and Marian Halcombe.

Almost unknown at the time, and largely forgotten since, *Mr Bazalgette's Agent* is little more than a curiosity. The real work of creating the *fin de siècle* woman detective will be in other hands, both female and male, and like so much else will be stimulated by the further boom in crime fiction caused by the supreme success of Sherlock Holmes in *The Strand* in 1891. A response to Sherlock Holmes from a different gender and attitudinal position was by Catherine Louisa Pirkis, 1841–1910. She was connected to the English professional establishment—her father Lewis Stephens Lyne ran the Inland Revenue, and so after him did her brother; her husband was a Royal Navy Paymaster, a major administrative role. They had two children in the 1870s, and in an apotheosis of Victorian family life lived with her husband's brother and her sister, another married couple. She published *Disappeared from Her Home* in 1877, a woman-focused mystery, and produced three-volume novels steadily until in what became her last book she turned to a woman detective with six stories that appeared in *The Ludgate Magazine* in 1893 and were collected as *The Experiences of Loveday Brooke, Lady Detective* in 1894, with the addition of a seventh.

Loveday is "a little over thirty,"[21] and though Pirkis calls her a "lady detective" this seems more a courtesy title than a class marker, though rather more accurate than Klein's negative description of her as "an older spinster."[22] It is noted that "five or six years previously, by a jerk of Fortune's wheel, Loveday had been thrown upon the world penniless and all but friendless" (8). She "had chosen for herself a career," and when for some

Figure 9. Loveday Brooke, lady detective, advising her employer. Illustration by Bernard Higham to Catherine L. Pirkis, "The Black Bag Left on a Doorstep," in *The Experiences of Loveday Brooke, Lady Detective* **(London: Hutchinson, 1894), p. 9.**

time she had "drudged away patiently in the lower walks of her profession," after "an intricate Criminal case" she was offered work with a "well-known detective agency" (6) on Lynch Court off Fleet Street, run by Ebenezer Dyer, though it is she who introduces the first case to him (Figure 9).

In the first story, "The Black Bag Left on a Door-Step," the bag of the title contained a clerical collar, a book of sermons, some gloves, a brush and comb, and other clerical items. This is discovered after Loveday has been engaged to trace Lady Cathrow's apparently stolen jewels. Her employer Dyer is annoyed that she is interested in the strange bag, but she will, in a characteristic intuitive procedure, relate the two events through the fact that the Cathrow safe had written on it "To be let, unfurnished." There is a missing girl as well, and she links these things through her knowledge of texts in the popular anthology *The Reciter's Treasury*. With the help of the handwriting on the safe door, she identifies the criminal and jokester as "Harry Emmett—footman, reciter, general lover and scamp" (23). Routinely, Loveday mixes like this some close observation with surprising and often popular knowledge, to make connections that completely elude both her employer and the police, with whom she is often working.

As in this story, the processes can be both detailed and somewhat strained, but Loveday is also shown to be calm, efficient and very quick in her decisions—she often routinely leaves the site of a crime well before she is expected to and pursues arcane inquiries elsewhere. She also shows herself very good at dealing with awkward people, like the surly Italian maid in the last story "Missing" or the over-talkative woman neighbor in "The Ghost of Fortune Lane." With courtesy and apparent understanding, she teases out of them crucial pieces of information. Her employer Dyer says at the start that she is "one of the shrewdest and most clear-headed" (7) of his lady detectives and also that she is "the most sensible and practical woman I have ever met" (8). Loveday is often low-level in her approach, posing as some form of servant or humble worker, or even just watching a house for long periods. Dyer says at the beginning of "The Redhill Sisterhood" that "the idea seems to be gaining ground in manly *[sic]* quarters that in cases of mere suspicion, women detectives are more satisfactory than men, for they are less likely to attract attention" (47). Loveday exploits her relative anonymity, social as well as gendered, in routine inquiries but also in some dangerous contexts.

She is often acute in observation—in the highly effective story "Dream Dagger" she knows from a glance that a bedroom is being used by a maid, not the lady who is supposed to have just returned from China—because arrangements have been made for the next day's dressing. The mistress has in fact suborned her maid to represent her so she can go off with her disapproved-of beloved, and the missing jewels are with her. In "The Redhill Sisterhood," though Loveday herself is under scrutiny by an associate of the criminals, she manages to identify the house where they will next strike, and so absolves completely the secular charity workers—the "sisterhood" of the title—whom the villains are linking to their crimes. In this process studying a bicycle and spotting electrician's wire in a man's pocket are crucial, but she also notices that the sisters treat the disabled children in their care with real tenderness, and doubts the guilt the police have assumed they are hiding.

The stories are fairly long—all around 8,000 words—and Pirkis cannot resist repeating the opening story's trick of condensing into one narrative two apparently separate weird events. In "Dream Daggers" the drawings of daggers sent through the post come together with the missing necklace, when she notes they are in fact all heraldic illuminations and this gives her the name of the man who is behind the absence of the lady represented by her maid. In "The Ghost of Fortune Lane" a comic resonance is made between a reported ghost appearance to a Wesleyan boot-maker's family and a check stolen from a substantial couple. The overdressed and aggressive wife has not taken it—it is, of all things, a gang of millenarians, whose leader's preaching has also stimulated the ghost-ridden dream. Pirkis sometimes, as here, skirts the edge of unlikely comedy, and she can use coincidence and improbability with a light hand at times, but in general Loveday is a steady, calm, knowledgeable figure, seeming rather like a female parallel to Martin Hewitt, the workmanlike detective from the same post–Holmes period.

She certainly has a strong presence as a woman: as Kestner notes, "Loveday and a male frequently disagree," and he sums up that she is "repudiating male cultural gendered expectations about women by being assertive, courageous, defiant and self-reliant."[23] In this context Kestner seems more accurate than the curiously negative Klein who finds that although in essence "Loveday's style of detection is similar to that used by Sherlock Holmes," Pirkis "sabotages the effect of this positive portrayal by subordinating each of Loveday's successes against criminals to male associates."[24] In fact the process shows Loveday working positively and tactfully with the established police forces with less self-assertingly grandiose claims than are made by and for Holmes. A similar misinterpretation is behind Klein's harsh reading of the frequent open ending without police punishment: she states that "Loveday concludes her own investigations only in the three non-criminal cases which result in marriage plans; in the others she is shown incapable of handling the criminals."[25] In fact, in the four criminal cases the ending is consistent with the class-based distaste for police shown by the mainstream writers who deal in mystery and crime and consistently resist a public resolution handled by the police and run through the shamefully public courts, a pattern discussed in Chapter 5. In general Loveday Brooke is the most radically proto-feminist of the early women detectives and, as Elizabeth Miller argues in some detail, she "disrupts norms of gender and criminality that many critics have thought endemic to her time and her genre."[26]

Not long after Loveday Brooke appeared, a little-known woman detective, Florence Cusack, was created by the enormously productive L.T. Meade, the pseudonym for Elizabeth Thomasina Meade Smith (1844–1914)—

Smith was her husband's name. Born and brought up in Ireland, she moved to London in 1874 and wrote busily for 40 years. The author of over 250 books, many of them targeting adolescent girls in the Alcott tradition, she turned to crime with a collaborator and an investigator both named as Dr. Clifford Halifax—the collaborator was in fact Dr. Edgar Beaumont. They produced in 1892 *The Medicine Lady*, a novel mixing scientism and women, but in negative mode: a nurse takes over her dead husband's mission in curing consumption, but eventually fails and goes mad. Christopher Pittard comments, "The subtext that women are not suited to medical practice is clear."[27] In the following year they started a series about Dr. Halifax in *The Strand*—the impact of Conan Doyle worked very widely. She moved on to collaborate with "Robert Eustace," actually Dr. Eustace Robert Barton who would later work with Dorothy L. Sayers on *The Documents in the Case* (1930). Like Beaumont, he seems to have produced the complicated key ideas for stories that Meade then wrote—their first series was *The Master of Mysteries* in *Cassell's Family Magazine* in 1897, described by Douglas G. Greene in his introduction to the Cusack stories as "stories about seemingly impossible crimes."[28]

Evidently prompted by the female detectives of the 1890s, the pair produced six stories featuring Miss Cusack between April 1899 and March 1901 in *The Harmsworth Magazine*. The stories were not collected until the 1998 specialist/enthusiast edition, and this suggests they were less than successful at the time. As Jack Adrian notes in his "Afterword" to the collection,[29] they did not appear in a coherent series in the magazine and he argues that there is, even for a very busy writer like Meade, a surprising number of inconsistencies and loose ends, though Kestner argues against this sweeping critique, noting that some were apparently created by the illustrators and others, notably those involving dates, are not necessarily inconsistent.[30] There is clearly meant to be eventually an explanation of Miss Cusack's saying in the first story, "I am under a promise I must fulfil" (4) and an explanation of the crucial significance in her life of the "two enormous brazen dogs" who are in her study and because of whom, she says, her life is "set apart for the performance of duties at once herculean and ghastly" (4).

The stories are short—well under 5,000 words—and they tend, as is not uncommon with Meade, not to be detective narratives as such, but simply to focus on and eventually reveal a single complicated mechanism by which a crime is committed or concealed, presumably provided by her doctor-collaborators. In Holmesian mode, the stories are narrated by Miss Cusack's friend Dr. Lonsdale. The first, "Mr Bovey's Unexpected Will," starts by proclaiming that a man has left everything to the one of three men whose weight is closest to the weight of the gold. They establish the inheritor, but the gold is immediately stolen, and by noticing an advert for sand and charcoal dust Miss Cusack works out that one of the three has done the robbery and a pawnbroker friend has cast the gold as one of his three emblematic balls. She does not explain how she works this out, and the entertaining opening only leads to a rather banal, even strained, conclusion, though she remains gender-loyal, insisting that "Lettie must be saved" (8)—the fiancée of the successful but then robbed and badly hurt man, as well as being Miss Cusack's cousin.

More effective is "The Outside Ledge" where Miss Cusack looks into the apparent betrayal of a speculator. When he receives advice from South Africa on shares to exploit, he keeps finding the same man acting to take advantage of the knowledge before him. Miss Cusack investigates and finally shows that the speculator's partner makes a copy of the telegram and fixes it on a cat's collar—who then runs along a ledge following a trail of valerian, apparently irresistible to cats, to arrive at a nearby office, occupied by the villain's other partner. Quite entertaining, this is still without much detective detail, and its quirky crime is paralleled in the second story "The Arrest of Captain Vandaleur" when Miss Cusack works out that before they become public, racing results are being passed up a gas-pipe in the form of varied scent. In other stories Miss Cusack does much less than even these unexplained revelations. In "Mrs Reid's Terror," the doctor-narrator handles almost everything, and then Miss Cusack finally outwits a beastly money-lender who is preying on Mrs. Reid's habit of gambling: she gives him a written agreement to repay the debts in an ink which will fade within a month, when he will find the first installment has not arrived. Though a male criminal is again confronted, Mrs. Reid's anxieties, as well as her weaknesses, are central—this negative gender focus was emphasized in the original version, where Mrs. Reid appeared in all four illustrations.

Miss Cusack can be even less engaged. In the finely titled "A Terrible Railway Ride: A Story of the Man with the False Nose" the doctor-narrator is active throughout on behalf of a friend of Miss Cusack—and all she offers is a little brief detection. The doctor engages in vigorous final action involving the use of solid carbon dioxide to drug a man about to be robbed, but disappointingly the titular false nose plays no part in the narrative.

Meade seems not really interested in Miss Cusack. She is represented as a wealthy single woman, with a large house in Kensington and an unexplained mission to help people, as mentioned in the first story, but the series tapers off. The sixth and last story, "The Great Pink Pearl," a lost jewel adventure, only features Dr. Lonsdale—who eventually finds the pearl deep inside a healed wound of a man who has been a pearler off the Queensland coast. Even this story does not explain very well how the puzzle is solved—the man mutters a clue when under chloroform—but Meade seems to have been as interested in the doctor as the lady detective: she had already, with "Halifax" produced *Stories from the Diary of a Doctor* in *The Strand* in 1893–94. She seems to have had only limited and perhaps imitative

THIRD EDITION NOW SELLING.   6s.

The Baroness Orczy's

GREAT NEW WORK

Lady Molly of Scotland Yard.

PRESS PRAISE EPITOMISED.

" *Sherlock Holmes in Petticoats* "—*Daily Graphic.* " *Thrilling and absorbing throughout* "—*Black and White.* " *Quite out of the common* "—*Evening News.* " *Clever and ingenious* "—*Bookseller.* " *Cleverly worked out* "—*Queen.* " *Ingenious* "—*World.* " *Fascinating* "—*Christian World.* " *Sherlock in Petticoats* "—*Globe.* " *Told with conspicuous cleverness* "—*Liverpool Post.*

Figure 10. Publicity for the Lady Molly stories. Advertisement, October 29, 1910, *The Times Literary Supplement*, p. 347.

interest in Miss Cusack, making her a flat and in terms of her own narrative an unresolved figure, and as a result she is quite unlike the other inquiring women of the 1890s.

The *fin de siècle* woman detective runs into the next century and the figure's capacity for self-assertive confidence reaches its height in Lady Molly, created by Baroness Emma Orczy, author of the immensely successful *The Scarlet Pimpernel* (1905). After success with her *The Old Man in the Corner* stories featuring a detective who does not stir from his restaurant chair, beginning in 1901 in the *Royal Magazine*, Orczy produced 12 stories about *Lady Molly of Scotland Yard*, which were published in *Cassell's Magazine* from 1909 and then, with excellent publicity (Figure 10), in book form by Cassell in 1910.

The daughter of an earl, and maintaining a distinct sense of style, Lady Molly Robertson-Kirk takes a junior position as a police detective in order to establish the innocence of her husband, who has been wrongly jailed for the murder of his grandfather. In the last two stories, she establishes his half-brother committed the crime and framed her husband. The criminal is, bizarrely, the son of a French woman who then ran off with Molly's own father—presumably spice Orczy felt not inappropriate to a crime story. By then Molly has risen through her skill to be head of "The Female Department" at Scotland Yard and has handled a range of cases successfully—

though she seems to operate in an independent way, either taking on cases that interest her or being called in when the police are at a loss. The stories are told by Mary Granard, at first a junior detective and then resigning to become Molly's secretary in her increasingly personalized activities—they live together in a flat in Maida Vale.

Many of the stories deal with criminal women, and Molly sees through them partly by her often-stressed intuition, and partly with simple female observation—she deduces the murderess in "The Woman in the Big Hat" was small, not the tall beauty she is framing for the crime, because waitresses said that the hat obscured her face so much. She decides the sister of "The Man in the Inverness Cape," being so tall and bony, is in fact the man in disguise. Molly tends to work out the criminal's scheme by a mixture of distant and sometime improbable insights, and occasional small clues—such as those found when her assistant at her suggestion scans personal advertisements in many newspapers. Molly is more interestingly successful through a range of excellent disguises, from being a Central European princess to a grubby charwoman, even "the landlady of a disreputable gaming house."[31] In this last mode she gains information which enables her finally to confront the criminal and force a confession—which is as usual almost never followed by conviction. Male criminals tend to kill themselves, others escape the country or after confessing and offering restitution, are allowed to continue their respectable and normally upper-class lives. Molly can show courage and decisive action, as well as intuition: in the opening story she and her assistant walk some 12 miles to and from the case, though in a later story they have the use of a motor-car.

In spite of the publicity it received, the series was were not nearly as successful as "The Old Man in the Corner," and the cases tend to be of limited interest, rather woodenly written, lacking extensive mystery plotting, and making Lady Molly a mix of clear-headed observation and over-femininity, capable of, her assistant says "kissing me in her pretty, engaging way" (46). She has a "tiny hand" (54) and "beautiful kind eyes" (53) which are also perceived as "luminous dark orbs" (115): Molly is summed up as "one of those women whom few men can resist" (328). She has a stronger side, and can show "the glitter of triumph in her eyes" (103), and will eventually release her husband, though that whole story, from its origins, is strangely not itself revealed until the eleventh story—a structural oddity not unlike the way Molly often does not appear until the last third of the story, after a very long exposition of events. Even when she appears in the frame of a story Molly still seems an unconvincing mixture of feeling and distance. She fell in love with the tall handsome Boer war hero Captain Hubert de

Mazareen, and knowing he was about to be arrested married him, against his offers to release her, by special license—but when he escapes from jail she feels, because of her police connections, she has to return him to await exculpation.

The narrator-assistant feels Lady Molly is "the most wonderful psychologist of her time" (27), which seems an exaggeration of her limited observational capacity. Kestner is extremely positive, identifying "the detective's shrewd and calculating ability to impersonate across class lines" and he also feels the cases "are striking for their focus on female transgressive behaviours."[32] The emphasis on female crime is notable, but hardly operates in any feminist direction, and the cross-class disguising is merely a function of Molly's all-powerful mastery of her world, itself only a means towards her often less than convincing power to read the secrets of the criminals. Not very successful in their time, Orczy's stories seem to have hardly developed from the interesting initiative of Pirkis, Meade and even, as discussed below, Hume, to shape a credible version of a modern female detective.

Male Authorial Responses

There were in the 1890s, as in the 1860s, also women detectives produced by male writers, none achieving anything like real independent status—or even the quirky self-assertion of the 1860s male-authored women detectives, but deserving notice as part of a survey of female detection in general. *Dorcas Dene, Detective: Her Adventures* appeared in 1897, offering five cases over 11 chapters, with a second series in 1898. The author George R. Sims had a long record of journalism and public writing, much of it quite radical and sympathetic to the poor. Dorcas is less than a radical feminist as she is always thinking of the welfare and wishes of her husband Paul, an artist who has gone blind. She also suffers containment from an aggressive mother and a large bulldog named Toddlekins—Klein feels the family context "clearly mocks and diminishes the detective's ability."[33]

Dorcas took up acting when her father, also an artist, died and the family were left with many bills, but a neighbor who was a former police superintendent led her into detecting. Her Watson is Saxon, a playwright she knows from her acting days, and the stories show her very good at disguise— she becomes in a single story a parlor maid, an American tourist and an old German woman. She often employs close observation and lucid analysis—there is a low-level Sherlock Holmes tone to much of the narrative. The first adventure, "The Council of Four," does give the family the kind of role that annoys Klein, but the stories themselves offer Dorcas more self-assertion, and although the link to the blind but respected husband remains unbroken, Sims does appear to be enacting at times through the stories some elements of his radical instincts in terms of gender independence. Klein is overall negative, seeing the figure as "submerged within the confines of patriarchal marriage" but Kestner's recurrent positivity seems for once valid—he finds a "total self-awareness of, even self-irritation at, her role as Victorian wife,"[34] while Craig and Cadogan find the stories "have a fairly vigorous, forward-looking tone."[35]

Almost simultaneously appeared a figure notable more for curiosity value than feminist detection, created by Grant Allen, a Canadian who specialized first in factual and science writing and turned to fiction in the mid-eighties. This included science fiction like the well-regarded *The British Barbarians* (1895), but in *The Woman Who Did* (1895) he engaged with the "New Woman"—the heroine, a graduate of Girton College Cambridge, loves a bohemian artist, has his child, and finally commits suicide. The novel was widely discussed at the time and is now seen as essentially masculinist.[36] Under the pseudonym "Olive Pratt Rayner," Allen wrote the less excitable *The Typewriter Girl* (1897), a brisk account of a clever, active young woman (also from Girton) who eventually passes the man she loves to her wispily feminine friend: in her edition, Clarissa Suranyi notes that Allen was interested in the New Woman, but as a Darwinian he felt she was "a deplorable accident of the passing moment."[37] He produced a successful early crime thriller in *An African Millionaire* (1897) and then responded to the rise of female detectives first with *Miss Cayley's Adventures* (1899—serialized in *The Strand* 1898–99), in which a bold, genteel girl, again from Girton, defends herself and her aristocratic employer spiritedly against a set of dubious men across Europe, some criminal, and ends married to the best of them. Then Allen produced *Hilda Wade: A Woman with Tenacity of Purpose* (1900, in *The Strand*, 1899–1900), which has the intriguing feature of having its last two chapters, "The Episode of the Officer Who Understood Perfectly" and "The Episode of the Dead Man Who Spoke," written, apparently after discussion with the dying Allen, by his friend and Hindhead neighbor Arthur Conan Doyle.

This can hardly be said to involve the great man in feminist detection. After the final story details how Miss Wade forces her dying medical boss to reveal how he ruined her father's reputation, it shows her, in spite of his crimes against her family, expressing her continuing deep respect for Professor's Sebastian's powers. This rejection of female independence links back to the beginning where Hilda Wade aspires to work for the Professor because of his grand status. Chapter I states that her intellect, her excellent memory, her "subtle knowledge of temperament,"[38] and especially her "intuition" are of high value both with his patients and his research into a new anesthetic—she projects human and animal responses to the use of Indian hemp successfully to predict results of his invention—but she is in several ways disempowered from being anything like a "New Woman." The opening of Chapter I says she "stands intermediate mentally between the two sexes," but is only seen as "a valuable adjunct to a medical practitioner," and she is also conventionally feminine, having "wistful, earnest eyes" and being "gentle and lovable." Yet, to remind readers of the danger of clever women, Chapter III notes that she can exhibit "a frank open smile with just a touch of feminine triumph in it." Kestner finds in the stories an "intelligent, professional, independent and brave protagonist,"[39] but while strength and ability is demonstrated in Nurse Wade, there is also a good deal of containment of her by conventional gendered ideas, and had Klein looked at these stories she would surely have seen them and their central figure as being, like those of Sims, as essentially subjected to patriarchy.

The idea of subversive feminism also seems foreign to the work of Mathias McDonnell Bodkin, an Irish doctor's son who became a barrister as well as a novelist. In 1899 he produced a volume of stories about Paul Beck, "the rule of thumb detective," a more legally-oriented and less charismatic version of Sherlock Holmes, and he followed this up with Dora Myrl, *The Lady Detective* (1900). Though the first page states "there was certainly nothing of the New Woman" about Dora,[40] as the daughter of a Cambridge don who did brilliantly in maths and was set to study medicine there, she seems a fine prospect for New Womanhood. When her father dies, legal practice does not appeal, she dislikes the idea of teaching or being a companion, and so after her first success has cards printed reading "Dora Myrl, Lady Detective." Good at sport, she is slim and agile, and can be brave when it is necessary. As a detective she picks up very well on slight but crucial clues, and has some quasi-feminist sense—she tells a bullying and she thinks criminal doctor, "Women are clever and men are confident; their confidence betrays them" (73). The second volume, *The Capture of Paul Beck* (1909), describes her as a "tracker of criminals, unraveller of mysteries" and a "famous lady detective, whose subtle wit had foiled the most cunning criminals, whose cool courage had faced the most appalling dangers."[41]

But Bodkin creates distinct limits to her independence—she is always a lady, in the title and in her behavior, and she has a gentleman very much in mind: the "capture" of Paul Beck is through marriage not detection, and this is built up to by her sense of submission to his authority, both male and detective. She has resisted his approaches and, as Klein comments, "Astonishingly, Bodkin solves Paul's problem by making him the successful detective" and so the basically humiliated Dora "solaces herself with marriage"[42]: she will only return to the field of detection through the medium of their son in *Young Beck: A Chip off the Old Block* (1912).

If Sims, Bodkin and Allen all work to reduce the threat of the New Woman, something both gender-contained and in terms of race and class more inventive is achieved in the 12 stories in Fergus Hume's *Hagar of the Pawn-Shop* (1898), a positive departure from the fairly dull novels he produced for many years after his runaway success *The Mystery of a Hansom Cab* (see Chapter 6). Hagar is not only a strong-minded woman detective, she is also a Romany, as Hume prefers to call her rather than gypsy, who applies insightful and courageous investigation to the mysteries involved with items from around the world presented at the pawnshop she manages in Lambeth, a very poor area of London. At first it is run by Jacob Dix, whose wife, dead for some time, was Hagar Stanley. They had a son Jimmy, who has disappeared but suddenly another Hagar Stanley appears, 20 years old, "Eastern-looking," with "magnificent black hair."[43] She has come to look after Dix because he is alone, and she wants to learn his trade: she is also escaping from a red-haired half-gypsy she calls Goliath.

The frame story develops: Dix's friend the lawyer Vark proposes to Hagar, but she rejects him, saying he is a scoundrel. With a letter forged in Jimmy's hand Vark persuades Dix his son is trying to murder him for his money, and offers him either a new will leaving all to Hagar or one in favor of himself. Dix chooses Hagar, and tries to burn the old will, but she takes it to help Jimmy gain his inheritance—even when Vark reveals Jimmy is in fact her enemy Goliath. Dix soon dies, and the following chapters tell stories focused on pawned objects and Hagar's capacity to resolve the mysteries they generate. A medieval Dante manuscript is pawned by Eustace Lorn, who admires her: he first thinks she is Jewish, then shows familiarity with Romanies. Hagar finds the book contains an invisible ink code revealing where his uncle's money is hidden: she cracks the code, but the money chest is found empty. Eustace goes off for Hagar's sake to find Goliath, but will return for her.

The following stories tell in order varied and notably international stories. An amber necklace from the West Indies is involved in a murder, a jade idol is eventually taken back to China, much as happened in *The Moonstone*. Hagar deciphers another code on an ancient key, then a silver teapot containing letters generates a sentimental mystery which Hagar solves, but promises a terminally ill mother to keep it all secret. Later stories gain in melodrama. A mandarin doll contains a diamond worth £20,000, and in resolving the problem Hagar carries a pistol for defense. Then a pair of boots is linked to a murder case in which Hagar thinks the suspect is not guilty, turns her attention to the dead man's brother, but then finds for the police detective the pistol that was used, in fact by a young woman. The last two stories involve a Renaissance casket of silver and an ancient Persian ring—Hagar is very active in the former, but the second is resolved without her involvement, and then the personal frame is reactivated.

Eustace is still looking for Goliath, but the latter turns up at the shop, having been in jail. Vark says Goliath, who is also Jimmy Dix, has escaped from jail and Vark wants half the £30,000 Jimmy inherits—Hagar calls him Judas. Goliath/Jimmy shoots dead another escaped convict who is after Vark with a knife and though the lawyer dies of his wounds, Jimmy is pardoned as a result of public acclaim. Eustace and Hagar, united again, will marry. Chapter 12 reports Eustace has bought a caravan and they will be itinerant booksellers: finally they "went away hopefully into the green country towards the gipsy life."

The Way Ahead

Hume's effective, well-varied, and quite feminist stories seem to have made little mark in their period, but Hagar is a good deal more independent and capable than the distinctly male-oriented products of the other male writers of the new female detective, and in a number of ways more progressive in gender, ethnic and social terms than either Loveday Brooke or Florence Cusack. But neither Hume nor Hagar were to continue in this mode. Though male writers had responded in partly respectful but ultimately, if variously, containing ways to the *fin de siècle* woman detective, the future seemed to lie in female hands. As has been discussed in Chapter 1, in America Anna Katharine Green took up the theme of female detection first with Amelia Butterworth in 1897 and then with the younger and more self-assertive Violet Strange from 1915. By then both Mary Roberts Rinehart and Carolyn Wells still accepted a supervising male detective but he tended to appear late in their novels and to do little more than had been achieved by an energetic and self-selected female inquirer. But the woman writers had now come firmly into the genre—in her book on the form, Wells mentions four Americans of the period including Rinehart, as well as two British and one Austrian.[44]

The changes in gender attitudes foreshadowed by these American and

English turn-of-the-century women writers would continue and develop. One of their readers was Agatha Christie who would first de-masculinize detection through Poirot, making it distinctly non-macho, often operating through female-style domestic observation, and then she shaped the archetypal Miss Marple, who had her own form of toughness. But female detection would wait for 50 years to become in a real way feminist and challenge the developed aggression, whether intellectual or simply physical and attitudinal, of the 20th-century male detectives—whose own increasingly crass gendering in itself deserves a study.

CHAPTER 5

Major Authors, No Major Detectives: The Response of Mainstream Novelists to Emergent Crime Fiction

Towards the Novel of Detection

As Chapter 3 showed, the crime story emerged slowly, with urban criminal anxieties becoming identified through the emergence of specialists in detection who had clear disciplinary skills, but not through the police, in existence from 1829 in London, or even the police detectives, real from 1842 and known in the literary form of Paris's Vidocq by 1828. Both kinds of police were felt to be irredeemably lower-class, and so not appropriate inquirers into the anxieties and crimes of the main reading social group, the literate middling and middle classes, as well as dramas among the upper class, whose values and status they aspired to.

This narrow range of criminal inquirers was even more evident in the novel—the short story did by 1849 develop a form of police detective, albeit one of gentry origin, in Thomas Waters by "William Russell" (see Chapter 3, pp. 85–89), but such a development took much longer in the mainstream novel, as this chapter will describe. While early novels of some power did engage with mystery and its detection, as Godwin's *Caleb Williams* (1794) and Brown's *Edgar Huntly* (1799) did with some radicalism and Bulwer's *Pelham* (1828) did with matching conservatism, the earliest novels that engage to any degree with crime seem quite old-fashioned against the stories of Warren and "The Philadelphia Lawyer"—indeed Warren himself provided an example in his novel *Ten Thousand a Year*, serialized 1839–41 in *Blackwood's* after his *Passages* stories. In this mixture of social satire and idiotic comedy, Tittlebat Tittlemouse, a draper's clerk, is established by lawyers Quirk, Gammon and Snap as heir to a fortune, so he marries an

Earl's daughter and becomes an MP. But he is shown to be illegitimate, goes to debtor's prison and ends up in a lunatic asylum. Remarkably, the novel sold very well, but it quite ignores the narrative and thematic possibilities of crime and inquiry which Warren had developed through his earlier "Physician" stories. Bulwer himself turned to the Newgate Novel, which sophisticated the simple, modest Newgate Calendar stories of the past to melodramatize proletarian heroes for a reading audience that was largely middle-class—the Newgate super-criminals do not in any way share the politics of the working-class resistance and the Chartists of the period in which they appeared. The Newgate novel form faded: the characters did not fit the mid–19th-century crime fiction context, where lower-class criminals were controlled by the police, and the main focus was on the fallibilities and self-management of bourgeois and gentry figures.

As a novelist interested early in crime, Dickens is more modern, but within substantial limits. Though the London police by then existed, Dickens in *Oliver Twist* (1838) presents some ineffective Bow Street Runners who attempt to engage with the criminals Oliver encounters. In a pattern already seen in *Pelham* and to be repeated throughout the mainstream novels which turned to crime, the story has two basic and dominating features—the key crime is a challenge to the status and wealth of a currently displaced member of the gentry, and that challenge is explored and defeated by members of that class itself. Oliver's inheritance is regained from his half-brother Monks: it is the kindly Mr. Brownlow, not the police or any detective, who organizes inquiries. Monks is forgiven and sent to America, but while there returns to crime and dies in jail: disappearance and/or death are as usual the outcomes for criminals among the gentry. The legal authorities are, however, active against the lower-class villains: the Artful Dodger is, apparently, transported, and Fagin is, with much melodrama, executed. This class separation will remain through the mainstream 19th-century novel's account of crime and its outcomes: Anthea Trodd sums up: "The threat posed by the police force to the privacy and autonomy of the middle-class home was countered in most of the novels discussed by the insistence that domestic affairs could be managed and redeemed within the home."[1]

Though the professional private detective was a known entity, he did not appeal to authors as a positive character. The negative features of the figure, as well as his usefulness to the plot, were memorably created by Dickens in Mr. Nadgett in *Martin Chuzzlewit* (1842–43), "the man at a pound a week who made the inquiries" for the Anglo-Bengalee Disinterested Loan and Life Assurance Company. He is distinctly unheroic, "a short, dried-up, withered old man … mildewed, threadbare, shabby" (Figure 11) but he also has weight: "he belonged to a class; a race peculiar to the City; who are secrets as profound to one another, as they are to the rest of mankind."[2] Nadgett leads against Jonas Chuzzlewit, who tries to kill his father for his money, then schemes against Nadgett's employer, Montague Tigg, himself an insurance fraudster who passes among the credulous wealthy as the

Figure 11. Mr. Nadgett, Dickens' private detective. Illustration by "Phiz," Hablot K. Browne, to Charles Dickens, *Martin Chuzzlewit* (London: Chapman and Hall, 1844), p. 448.

grander-sounding Tigg Montague. Jonas finally murders Tigg to protect his own secrets, but Nadgett exposes him and, like many mainstream mystery villains who come from the socially elevated classes, he poisons himself.

Bulwer (not Bulwer Lytton until 1846) discusses class separation on crime control in his preface to his crime-related *Night and Morning* (1845). He calls lower-class malfeasance Crime, and its socially higher parallel Vice, and sums up: "I say not the Law can, or the Law should, reach the Vice as it does the Crime; but I say that Opinion may be more than a servile shadow of Law."[3] As part of this notionally controlling force of "Opinion," the novel develops a "lost inheritance" story—the parents had married secretly, for family reasons, and the children cannot establish the marriage existed, after the death of both parents. Restitution works primarily through coincidence, courage and good fortune, though there is one sequence when through a coiner acquaintance named Gawtrey, the hero seems to be promised the help of a Paris detective named Favart, clearly a version of Vidocq, but Favart is soon shot by Gawtrey, and the police presence is not renewed. In the end the central disinherited child Philip will marry Gawtrey's daughter, as if the pair are the pure survivors of the classes that can generate both Crime and Vice.

The mainstream novelists' handling of crime within the family and the respectable house is in effect a statement of moral Opinion, as Bulwer puts it, and their approach both explores and resolves threats perceived at this social level. The gentry criminal is allowed to go overseas, commit suicide or be in some other way removed from the functions of higher-class society. An early novel that explores middle-class familial disruption but does not yet quite prefigure either the mainstream mystery or the future crime novel is Catherine Crowe's *Susan Hopley* (1841). This starts with, and finally explains, a murder, and the servant Susan undertakes recurrent investigation, including some clues to the murderer. These elements of the story have interested commentators, both of its crime fiction and its early female-gendered activity, but much of the long and little-known novel is generically foreign to mystery writing, and it has no coherent structure of analysis by a dominant inquirer, so it can hardly be called, as Jean Fernandez does, "Crowe's detective novel."[4]

Early in the story a wealthy wine merchant (curiously, the author's father's profession) is found murdered, and his will has disappeared. His only daughter Fanny admires a man with a share in the wine business, Walter Gaveston—the surname seems to refer to King Edward II's deeply unreliable male friend. Wentworth had told him he was in his will giving two of his own three quarters of the business to Harry Leeson, the son of his dead niece, and one to his loyal employee Simpson: Fanny owned the other quarter. Harry is a close friend of Susan and her older brother Andrew: Harry's mother cared for them when their parents died; after her death Wentworth adopts Harry and takes them in as servants. Andrew is able to protect Harry when he twice almost suffers a fatal accident, first on a horse Gaveston lends him and then on a boat trip with Gaveston, who claims (to Fanny Wentworth's surprise) he cannot swim, and so leaves Harry to drown.

On the night of Wentworth's death Susan has a powerful dream in which her brother is in his grave-clothes, and Wentworth appears with his throat cut: she also hears movement in the house, though the family are away, to return the next day. Wentworth's body is found next morning at a nearby inn, and his will, kept in the house, is missing. Susan's Gothic warning about the crime leads her on to some investigation: she sees footprints outside the murder house, but cannot identify them; she also finds a silver button with WG/JC on it, which she keeps. Gaveston has given Harry a half-crown coin which she recognizes from an inscription it bears as one that Wentworth owned. Her brother Andrew is missing: the inquest finds Wentworth was murdered by him, and it is assumed he has fled with the attractive dairymaid Mabel Jones.

This is a mystery-style opening to a novel, with Susan acting as inquirer: Sussex sees it as "precursive of generic crime,"[5] noting that its original subtitle was *Circumstantial Evidence*, a popular phrase in early crime fiction, suggesting the need for intelligent analysis of what has so far emerged. But from the second edition on, the novel was associated more with class, taking on the sub-title *The Adventures of a Maid-Servant*, and this sidelining of detection is clear in the plot. Susan's limited inquiries into the murder are followed by a cascade of rambling episodes. The story hurries off to Cadillac in France, where Gaveston is sending a local wine merchant a beautiful girl to marry, Amabel Jones; she gets no further than being in Paris with a Colonel Jones (who has a very hooked nose) where they meet, and she admires, the Duc de Rochechouart.

Then Susan finds a job with a Mrs. Wetherall in London, and soon fails to receive £10 sent her by Fanny Wentworth. Simpson, Wentworth's trusted employee, investigates and finds Wetherall took the money because of his financial troubles—Simpson, noble throughout, lends him £200. But he is less kind to Gaveston: suspecting his unreliability, he demands control of the firm. Gaveston is forced to agree, but follows Simpson, planning to throw him in the Thames. At the same time Wetherall is on the way to drown himself—but, with coincidence multiplying, he and Simpson see a woman jump in the river and save her. She is Julia Clark—she will turn out to be the JC on the button, but the novel now lurches off for some 30000 words with her back-story, a melodrama beginning in south-western France with her mother Julie le Moine, who was struck literally dumb by her experiences, especially with two evil men both named Rodolphe. When Julia arrived in London she met a William Godfrey (whose initials, also on the button, suggest Gaveston), who abandoned her and their child to his friend called Dyson, actually George Remorden. We will not hear again about some of these figures until late in volume 3.

Gaveston has married Fanny and maltreats her, and Harry, who runs away to sea. Susan finds work in London with a Mrs. Aytoun and is soon making inquiries to defend her against a charge of stealing silk from a shop—an assistant there is called Nosey and Susan recalls him as having called at the Wentworth house just before the murder. At court a man named Seymour is kind to her mistress, but then he recurrently harasses her. When her husband returns from overseas work he kills Seymour in a duel, but Seymour's brother-in-law, Colonel Alleyn, decides Aytoun behaved correctly and no action is taken—the gentry resolve their own problems.

With some more inquiries from Susan, notably her astute observing of the stolen silk near a house they are staying at in Brighton—coincidence continues to dominate—the theft charge is resolved, but the Aytouns go overseas, and Susan works for the Crippses of Clapham: he is a vulgar retired grocer, with three daughters and plenty of money. The original murder is occasionally mentioned: Mabel's sister gets money sent her every year, and Mabel writes asking about Andrew; Susan has not forgotten her brother or her own power to inquire—she says if she knew where Mabel was "I'll go to her and find out the truth, if I beg my bread along the road" (279).

A new narrative detour begins when the Crippses are visited by Count Roccaleoni (Cripps calls him Rockaloony), who speaks perfect English, even though he claims to come from Transylvania—his friend is Colonel Jones. They briskly marry the two elder sisters and set off, with the third sister and Susan, allegedly to Transylvania. At a rough French inn near Lisle, in the Dordogne, the two men disappear with all the jewels and are reported to have shot the Duc de Rochechouart and his servant. The landlady at the inn used to be mute and the shooting was observed by, of all people, the two Rodolphes. This welter of coincidence and distant connection will soon come together in a trial for the murder of the Duc. In England, Olliphant, the Wentworth family lawyer, has had the lost will found in a blood-stained jacket, and Gaveston is trying to stop a new road being built through the house where the murder occurred. He hears Julia is active (notably in the will discovery) and tries to kill her, but is disturbed by a watchman, and so takes her to France where soon he throws her in the Seine—but coincidence still rules and Olliphant and Simpson, visiting to make inquiries, save her.

Back at the Dordogne inn, Susan hears strange noises at night, and the Rodolphes break out of the cellar where the vengeful landlady, no longer mute, had locked them. The Crippses arrive, as does Harry Leeson: after a fine career in the navy, he aspires to a legal partnership. Remorden/Jones/ Dyson and Dillon/Roccaleoni are charged with the Duc's murder. In a new idea, they claim he looked like Andrew Hopley and they shot him as Wentworth's murderer, but Gaveston, who supports them, is challenged by the prosecution because of his attack on Julia and also through Susan's carefully preserved button and half-crown. The two murderers of Wentworth and the Duc are executed; and in a separate case the Rodolphes are sent to the galleys. Gaveston returns to London and shoots himself, leaving money to Julia; there is no word about Fanny so the Wentworth family disruption is not fully resolved. They find Andrew's murdered body in the now demolished house where Wentworth died, and Mabel enters a convent. Harry will marry the daughter of the solicitor he works for, and Susan will stay with them, becoming his companion after his wife dies: she has herself died just before he gathered together this story.

Dickens' close friend John Forster was impressed by the novel, saying in a review "facts and recollections of apparently the most trivial kind come gradually out into more and more prominence."[6] This mix of revealing events, especially coincidental revelations, and occasional inquires by servants or lawyers will constitute a recurring pattern in the mainstream mystery novel, but *Susan Hopley* can hardly be claimed as a woman's pioneering creation of the crime novel—the plotting is too obvious and clumsy, the narrative sequences both manipulated and random-seeming, the gentry play no part in their own recovery. Susan's detective work is on a very small scale and only when the forces of character, coincidence, and melodrama have played out their role do her button and coin prove of any, and then minor, significance.

An evident interest in crime affecting respectable people, and the role of servant support and inquiry, does not here develop into the structure of a criminal mystery, though that is less true of Crowe's second novel, *Men and Women, or Manorial Rights* (1843). Here the social context is higher: Sir John Eastlake is murdered and his bereaved mother, with a little police assistance, is able to show that the heir is not, as widely suspected, in fact guilty: it was a servant avenging the squire's ruin of his sister. Some ballistic details are involved, but again Crowe suggests rather than develops elements of the future mystery novel, and went no further with it.

If Crowe seems not to envisage, or at least value, the mystery-focused shape of the mainstream crime narrative, another early text is closer to the form, but is consciously located at the social level of lower-class life. *Mary Barton* (1848) was Elizabeth Gaskell's first novel, using much of her experience in the industrial context of mid-century Manchester. There is almost no room for servants in this working world, nor indeed for professional gentlemen and their incisive investigations, but there is still a good deal of familial inquiry and some hostility to the police, which suggest the overarching presence of attitudes from above the lower class.

John Barton works in a textile mill, living among Manchester's "half-finished streets."[7] His wife is pregnant, his daughter Mary is 13; her aunt Esther has left home suddenly. Barton is quite slight, but shrewd and vigorous; he is an active trade unionist and soon becomes a Chartist. This activity is both political, pursuing what "the workman thinks and feels" (21), which is "an eternal subject for agitation in the manufacturing district" (21), but it is also personal—he was out of work when his son died and he was bitter at seeing the owner's wife spending freely. He feels the police are his enemy: when he asks one about Esther, it is the first time he has done such a thing "because of his livery" (9), the term suggesting he sees police as servants of the dominant class.

Barton's wife dies in childbirth, with the baby, and they think Esther has run off to be a lady. Time passes; Mary, now 16, is pretty, and neither Barton nor she want her to go into service: he arranges a dressmaking apprenticeship. Jem Wilson, son of Barton's friend George, a skilled worker, often away from home on special jobs, admires Mary but she becomes interested in Henry Carson, a mill-owner's son, who is evidently attracted to her.

Gaskell stresses the quality of the workers' feelings and capacities—Job Legh is a retired folk scientist and his grand-daughter Margaret has a very fine voice. The workers' commitment to resistance is growing as jobs are harder to find, and Barton heads off to London to take the Great Charter to Parliament—it is evidently 1839. The humiliating failure of this project embitters him deeply, and things grow darker: Esther reappears, having fallen into prostitution when her gentleman abandoned her, and Mary rejects Jem because she thinks Carson will propose. As wages are threatened, in a major scene the union members take one of "the fierce terrible oaths" (179) of early unions, and draw lots to kill Henry Carson. The narrative does not reveal who is chosen, but Margaret suddenly finds her father "haggard and wildly anxious-looking" (184), and he suddenly seems "so strange, so cold, so hard" (186).

Carson is shot dead, and his father offers a £1,000 reward. A gun is found which belongs to Jem Wilson, as a disguised policeman rudely discovers from his mother. There is also a clue, one which will recur in early mysteries: the pistol wadding has been torn from a poem Mary wrote out for her father, so she searches his room and finds bullets and a gun case. Jem Wilson has been arrested, but she will try to give him an alibi—he was accompanying his brother Will back to his ship at the time. Mary's evidence is successful, and Jem is freed: she says in court that she loves him, is insulted by the prosecution, then collapses in illness and delirium. Barton, though not accused, is unemployed because men will not work with him, apparently out of suspicion. Then, in the presence of the wise worker Job Legh, Barton confesses to Carson's father. The mill-owner cannot forgive him, but after thinking about things he feels moved, and calls next day to say he will "acknowledge the spirit of Christ" (367) in any conflict with the workers—and Barton dies in his arms.

Mary marries Jem and they leave for Canada; Esther has died forgiven. Margaret, who went blind but kept singing, has had a successful operation on her eyes and marries Jem's brother Will. The young capitalist, who did eventually propose to Mary, is somewhat forgotten after his political murder: it is the guilt of the semi-justified killer that is in social terms internally assuaged, just as industrial tension is sidelined under the promise of Christian charity. As a result *Mary Barton* is essentially a class-displaced version of the gentry crime novel, and the police play no role of any significance— Mary has proved effective as an inquirer, even recalling Will Wilson from his ship to give evidence.

As Kate Watson notes, Gaskell returns to the theme of crime in quite a number of her short stories, including some in Dickens' magazine *Household Words*,[8] but in the novel she went little further with mystery and detection—though in *North and South* (1854) Margaret Hale, in a reverse replay of Mary's problems, tries to protect her mutineer brother from the police by lying to them, but she only succeeds when her wealthy manufacturer admirer, in spite of having less social status than her, has the power to make the Inspector drop the matter. Gaskell's crucial contribution was to introduce murder and investigation to the mainstream serious novel, condensing the lower-class context of the crime short story c. 1850 with the socially elevated familial investigative approach that her colleagues would follow.

G.W.M. Reynolds, an enormously popular writer in the 1840s and

1850s, made, for all his marked radicalism, little variation to the mainstream middle-class treatment of crime and detection. When he returned from some years in France in 1837, he started writing fiction and stories for magazines, and though he transplanted the French criminal rogue Robert Macaire to England in 1840, he only dealt seriously with crime when he relocated in much altered form Eugène Sue's enormously successful *Les Mystères de Paris* (1842–43) and produced in penny-a-week episode format his four-volume *The Mysteries of London* (1845–48). This includes a wide social range of crime, from unregenerate lower-class criminals like the fearful Resurrection Man, some corrupt gentry, forgers and fraudsters who entrap the hero Richard Markham into jail, and also new-style professional crooks like Eugene Markham, Richard's brother, who is at once MP, company director, fraudster, corrupter of officials and, apparently for the first time in fiction, an agent of corrupt bill-broking. The police do appear, and are not admired—Reynolds' radicalism leads him to show magistrates unreservedly supporting the police, whom he describes as "polite to the gentry and rude to ordinary people."[9]

Detectives are very rare, but one good one, Morris Bensted, both befriends Richard and also in volume 2 saves from conviction a young woman who starts off as the public hangman's niece, and is then framed for murder: she turns out to be Richard's long-lost half-sister, but the existence of the good police detective helping a mistreated ordinary woman, without knowing her gentry connections, itself suggests Reynolds' radical views. Bad characters like the exotic and multi-named Mrs. Fitzhardinge, illegally returned from transportation, have trouble with the police, who also occur in the recurrent memoirs of criminals like Tim the Snammer (the Robber), whose friend George is first framed for crime then executed for a revenge murder. The major criminal-police engagement is when the Resurrection Man both blows up some of them and is jailed by others, but it is a criminal he has betrayed who imprisons him in his own cellar, to die of starvation.

In Reynolds even longer eight-volume series *The Mysteries of the Court of London* (1849–56) police and detectives rarely appear—the criminals are high level, from the brutish Prince Regent, much mocked in the first four volumes (though the satire ends when he becomes king), through *femmes fatales* like Lady Fernanda Aylmer in volumes 1 and 2 and the ultra-criminal Lady Saxondale of volumes 5 and 6, and their male counterparts like the murderous fake Duke of Marchmont in volumes 7 and 8. The police are largely off-stage and there can be effective inquiring by women—in volumes 1 and 2 the very young Caroline Walton, pregnant at 16, inquires into the misdemeanors of the man who ruined her, including her becoming a male Indian male servant at his house for some time. In volumes 5 and 6 there is effective inquiry and some brave defense of her friends by Lady Bess, "The Female Highwayman." In the same volumes Lady Saxondale is both helped and bothered by the professional criminal Chiffin and the police regularly pursue him, with occasional success, but volume 6 offers a classic case of gentry control in the Marquis of Eagledean. A figure with dual class status, born a lord but having lived as a successful merchant banker overseas after an embarrassing love-affair (which produced Lady Bess herself), he says that although Lady Saxondale is murderer of three, procurer of a fake heir after her baby son was lost, attempted murderess of that son when he re-appeared and rejected her sexual advances (to be fair, she was unaware of his identity), there is no need for the police to be involved—and she merely dies after confessing, stabbed by the fake son she has just given a fatal wound. Her lover and assistant in crime, the Marquis's own heir, is, like many gentry villains, sent quietly overseas.

This inherent absence of policing recurs through many of the long novels Reynolds produced in the 1850s, almost all based on the life of a surprisingly young woman—it seems Reynolds knew the nature of the major part of his audience. *Mary Price* (1852) tells of a servant girl, eventually loved by a gentleman who will inherit a great estate. She is good at making inquiries about things that are going wrong in her mistresses' households and lives, the police have no role of any significance other than containing the pair of couple of local thugs who recurrently harass Mary, but some lawyers do become involved in Mary's eventual modest inheritance and the processes which restore her future husband to real wealth and status as Lord Wilberton.

The intriguing central character of *Rosa Lambert* (1854) is a clergyman's daughter who makes her way in the world as mistress to a series of fairly well-selected men. She encounters crimes such as harassment of herself and, sometimes by her men, financial misappropriation, but there is again little police activity beyond their mostly failed attempts to contain the multi-identity comic villain Toby Grayson, who is especially interested in Rosa and her usually well-stocked purse. She is capable of working out what people are up to, but the crimes presented are mostly emotional, or occasionally professional fraud by Rosa's less admirable possessors—who tend to resort to suicide as a result of detection. Somewhat different is *Ellen Percy* (1857): again very young, only reaching 21 as the novel ends with her marital access to the nobility, Ellen is like several of the 1890s women detectives an actress by trade, which may suit her for investigations,

Figure 12. Constable Bensted introduces Richard Markham to the St. Giles criminal precinct. Illustration by George Stiff to G.W.M. Reynolds, *The Mysteries of London* (London: Vickers, 1846), Vol. 2, p. 1.

though her devoted gipsy maid Beda also makes bold and successful inquiries: she and her gipsy boy-friend William even save Ellen from being drowned, locked in a capsized boat. The only male novel-hero in this group, *Joseph Wilmot* (1855), though he is as active as Ellen and rises from servant to his own previously stolen title, does not detect significantly, though he does undertake discreet inquiries for his employers at times. He is once jailed for treason in Paris, but, as he is pretending to be a gentleman, he is treated very well and is able to talk his way out, eventually to regain his purloined title.

Detection Approaches the Mainstream

If Crowe and Gaskell had sent signals that the mainstream novel might embrace detection without police involvement, and Reynolds also essentially excluded police inquirers, a more positive response to police detection appeared in a series of essays by Dickens in the early 1850s, broadly in favor—within social limits—of the detective police. The first of these was published in July 1850 as "The Modern Science of Thief-Taking." It introduces "a superior order of police,"[10] the narrator learns about criminal types and their special names, a story is told which turns, once more, on a shirt-button clue, and then Sergeant Witchem, evidently the real Jack Whicher, defeats "the swell mob," the elite London criminals. More senior police appear in the two-part "A Detective Police Party" in July and August 1850. Here Dickens reports, as he had indicated in *Oliver Twist* and would mention in passing in *Great Expectations* (1861), that the Bow Street Runners were unreliable and self-promoting, but men like Witchem, Stalker (Walker) and Wield (Field) are "well-chosen and trained" (73).

The relatively low social level of even these elite police is registered: they have no gentry element about them—one is "a plain earnest-looking man" (63), while the more potent Witchem is still "a plain honest-looking fellow" (67); in general the detectives are "workman-like" (73), and in "A Detective Police Party" Dornton (Thornton) is "like a sergeant in the army" (74). These "respectable-looking men" (74) deal in these stories with the criminal lower class, not bourgeois, gentry or professional malfeasance—though one of the three short "Detective Anecdotes" (September 1850) does involve a thieving medical student, who in gentry fashion poisons himself in Newgate. With these police, Dickens adventures into the central criminal conclave of St Giles in "On Duty with Inspector Field" (1851)—as had Reynolds' Richard Markham with Morris Bensted in 1845 (Figure 12)—and then he joins the river police inspecting professional water-thieves in "Down with the Tide" (1853). A full account of Dickens' treatment of the police is given by Haia Shpayer-Makov in her book on police detectives in general, with some stress on the later part of the century, though she does not see Dickens' social limitations, finding his treatment merely "extraordinarily flattering."[11]

The origin of Dickens' strong admiration for police seems in part to be his genuine interest in new social structures and people of forceful character, but his attitude also seems to mesh with the horror he expressed in two letters to *The Times* over the execution of Frederick and Maria Manning in November.[12] He deplored the crime, of course, but he was worse upset by the vile celebratory behavior of the huge audience. He evidently shared the widespread admiration then felt for the police, led by Whicher, through the speed and efficiency of their resolution of the Mannings' case, which involved telegraphs and other ultra-modern operations[13]—and it seems Dickens' innate fear of the people at large, as seen in the execution crowds, might have led to his high valuing of the strong, impassive, dutiful police who in these journalistic essays seem to have both the capacity and the intention to keep under control the worst the ordinary citizens can do.

Dickens admired these men and their capacities not only in writing— in 1851 when he arranged and appeared in a special royal performance of Bulwer Lytton's *Not So Bad As We Seem* he personally hired Inspector Field to ensure that Lytton's estranged and uncontrollable wife Rosina did not interrupt the proceedings.[14] But he did not make positive use of these figures in his fiction. In the short story "Hunted Down" (1859), Sampson, an insurance manager, meets a man who arranges insurance for a friend and has with him an alleged niece. Named Slinkton, he will be shown to have murdered another alleged niece for her insurance, and plans to do the same to his friend, and presumably the new niece. This is revealed by a brave fake-drunken friend of Slinkton, actually the dead girl's lover, who with Sampson exposes the crime, and the criminal, in gentry mode, dies in a fit. He is a version of Thomas Wainewright, the famous "Poisoner," who was convicted in 1837 and died after transportation in 1847,[15] but in structure and tone this is much like one of the *Barrister* or *Attorney* stories of the early 1850s, with no police input.

Before that story, Dickens's high valuing of the modern detective did have one major impact on his fiction. In "A Detective Police Party" Inspector Field is described as having "a habit of emphasising his conversation by the aid of a corpulent fore-finger, which is constantly in juxta-position with his eyes or nose" (73). This is obviously linked to a description in the opening of Chapter 53 of *Bleak House* (1853):

> When Mr Bucket has a matter of this pressing interest under his consideration, the fat forefinger seems to rise to the dignity of a familiar demon. He puts it to his ears, and it whispers information; he puts it to his lips, and it enjoins him to secrecy; he rubs it under his nose, and it sharpens his scent; he shakes it before a guilty man, and it charms him to destruction.[16]

Bucket is a metaphorically intensified version of the image of Field. This has excited crime commentators, with Julian Symons saying Bucket "serves as a model for many later professional detectives" and Ronald R. Thomas, over-simplifying the book as "Dickens' first detective novel."[17] The fact that Bucket's wife plays some part in his success has itself engaged feminist commentators, as when Dagni Bredesen calls her "an earlier and more direct precursor" of

Figure 13. Mr. Bucket, Dicken's police detective. Illustration by "Phiz," Hablot K. Browne, to Charles Dickens, *Bleak House* **(London: Bradbury and Evans, 1853), p. 477.**

later female detectives, so preceding Miss Gladden of 1864.[18] But what is most notable about the Buckets is their limitation, their failure to become in the novel itself anything like the controlling, dominating, all-revealing force that is the routine role of the detective in later mystery fiction.

With Bucket the crucial component is class. In dealing with the mystery of the letters that the ominous lawyer Tulkinghorn sees disturbed Lady Dedlock, Bucket moves against the lower-class shooting-gallery-owner and ex-soldier George, and manages with confident ease (Figure 13) George's loyal and comical ex-soldier friend Bagnet and his knowledgeable wife (the name itself is mocking, related to bayonet). Bucket arrests George for the murder of Tulkinghorn as a means of control, not out of suspicion, and in a similar minatory way acts secretly against Jo the crossing sweeper who is causing Tulkinghorn annoyance—Bucket goes to some trouble and distance to remove him from Esther's care at Bleak House itself, and so effectively sends him to his lonely death. Bucket, through the help of his wife in particular, including her identification of the book from which, once again, the pistol wadding came, also has under control the French maid

Hortense who betrays and leaves Lady Dedlock, and then harasses and eventually murders Tulkinghorn—and who is evidently a contained version of Maria Manning, an emblem of a foreign untrustworthy female servant, hostile to her social superiors.

In all this lower-class engagement, Bucket, the son of a butler who became an inn-keeper, so is from a family used to forms of service, is confident and controlling, even cunning and falsely charming, as with the Bagnet family. But with the aristocrats he is a much reduced force: it is not him but the sly law-clerk Guppy who finds the link between Esther and her mother Lady Dedlock. Rather than impose the law, Bucket accepts £100 from Sir Leicester to locate and bring back secretly his fled, apparently guilty, wife. Then Bucket helps reveal the relations of the Dedlock servant Mrs. Rouncewell to her son, the ex-soldier George whom he formerly harassed—and who also in servile mode chooses like his mother to work for Sir Leicester, not continue his challengingly independent life by following his brother into industry. The sudden change of the class domain in which Bucket operates varies his role and contribution remarkably. When he had managed to get the letters from George for Tulkinghorn, the text speaks of "the dread power of the man" (620), but soon when Esther meets him and they seek Lady Dedlock together, she feels he is "really very kind and gentle" (650). As Trodd puts it, after "beginning as a figure of near-magical power, he is progressively tamed, and ends the novel as a kind of domestic servant, offering gratuitous household advice to the heroine."[19]

After Bucket and the distasteful Smallweed, a quasi-criminal whom he has had under firm control, discover the will which establishes Jarndyce and Richard Carstone free of the miseries of Chancery and resolves the threat to this honorable gentry family, he simply fades from the story. Dickens' enthusiasm about senior policing and his ability to realize characters of strength and special meaning have led him to set up something that promises to develop much like a detective story—and has been read as such by inattentive commentators—but his interests in traditional social relations and the power of the benign bourgeois individual have left Mr. Bucket stranded as no more than a helpful agent of gentry requirements, good at keeping the lower orders in their place.

Dickens will not be tempted back towards crime fiction for some time—Mr. Inspector in *Our Mutual Friend* (1865) is merely a pillar around and against which the identity-varying characters relate and identify themselves, but when in his last, unfinished, novel, *The Mystery of Edwin Drood* (1870) he does look again at detection, it is both itself incomplete, though intriguing, and also a product of the work done by his colleagues Collins and Braddon as they generated narratives often centering on mystery, but never resorting fully to the simplicities of the single detective hero or heroine—though in the process they created much that later mystery writers would adapt.

Sensation of Mystery and Detection

The sensation novel is essentially a domestication of the Gothic—instead of amazing and terrible events occurring in mountainous Italy or medieval Spain, they are exposed as the result of disruptive forces in highly respectable English domestic life. That means there is always some form of crime occurring or threatened, and also some element of mystery about what occurs, who is involved, and why this is happening. Wilkie Collins' second, highly sensational, novel *Basil* (1852) is in this earlier Gothic mode, but his third, *Hide and Seek* (1854), introduces a structure of inquiry by a central figure, and makes clear moves towards the mystery novel. Part 1 is "The Hiding" and the longer Part 2 "The Seeking"; there are chapter titles that would seem familiar in later crime fiction like 2.6 "The Finding of the Clue," 2.9 "More Discoveries," and climactically, 2.13, "The Search for Arthur Carr" and 2.15, "The Discovery of Arthur Carr." The plot focuses on a beautiful deaf-mute girl, adopted by an artist (who by being genial, disorganized and less than successful, is very unlike Collins' father) after her mother died, abandoned by her lover. The girl is Mary, called Madonna by her adoptive family (as was the wife of Alaric Watts, who had helped Collins with his biography of his father). The detection is carried out by Matthew Grice, who turns out to be the girl's uncle, and recognizes his sister in her from the start. But as he has been overseas adventuring in the Americas, he does not know his link to Madonna—and indeed calls himself Mat Marksman. He is a striking figure, very strong and active, speaking in an uneducated way, scarred in the face, and hairless, having been scalped—Collins seems to be looking back towards Cooper's Leatherstocking as a model for his inquiring hero. The processes Mat undertakes—travelling about, interviewing people, copying a key to examine a locked trunk—are familiar enough from the short crime and detection stories which were thriving around 1850 (see Chapter 3), but Collins by no means makes the amateur detective a disciplinary figure—his simplicity may in part relate to the working-class qualities of Dickens' *Household Words* police. Mat is a socially involved character, notably in his friendship with Zack Thorpe, son of the finally revealed seducer, now turned severe moralist (and as the latter more like Collins' own father). Zack is therefore Madonna's half-brother, and so there is no resultant romance as might have been expected—

in fact Mat and Zack go overseas at the end, while Mr. Thorpe, alias Arthur Carr, like most respectable villains, dies contrite and Zack soon returns to his now extended family. The novel is by no means fully a mystery—much of it is leisurely and colorful recounting of the characters' feelings and activities, presumably one of the reasons Dickens admired the novel a good deal. It did not do very well—coming out as the Crimean War started was not helpful, but it may also have seemed generically challenging. In 1861 Collins issued a revised version—no doubt exploiting the success of *The Woman in White* in the previous year—which reduced the character-rambling a little and finally brought Mat back to Britain and happiness with his niece.

After this Collins moved towards the existing structures of the short story mysteries, using as his dominant mode of crime and inquiry inheritance fraud and familial betrayals, but revealing them by character-based detection. That provided the structure on which Collins was to construct his first major novel, and the one which is held, with Braddon's *Lady Audley's Secret* (1862), to have co-started the true sensation movement: Trodd comments, "The 1860s saw the emergence of the new popular genre of sensation novels which made the interaction of crime and family life their paradigmatic structure."[20] *The Woman in White* (1860) was immediately very popular, both as a story and as a fashion and celebrity triumph. As is common in the mainstream mysteries, a key theme is double identity, usually linked to the question of improper seizure of an inheritance. Laura Fairlie looks very much like Anne Catherick—they turn out to be half-sisters—and Laura's villainous husband and his worse cohort Count Fosco plan to put Laura in Anne's asylum, allow, or perhaps help, Anne, already in very poor health, to die, and so cash in on Laura's inheritance. This scheme is frustrated by the inquiries first of Laura's older half-sister, the strong-willed and lightly-mustached Marian Halcombe, and then in the second half of the novel by the energetic activities of Walter Hartright, the drawing master who loves Laura but, when she is forced to marry the evil Sir Percival Glyde, headed to South America and dangerous activities—to return as a more sophisticated version of Mat Marksman.

There is very little detective activity by professionals. Hartright—symbolic meaning is often close to Collins' names—has the help of a calm and shrewd lawyer, Mr. Kyrle, and at one moment Marian employs unspecified people to watch, detective-like, the house of Count Fosco. It is puzzling why Deborah Wynne felt Fosco is based on Vidocq[21]—though *All the Year Round*, where the story appeared, was reprinting Vidocq adventures at the time, the characters seem far apart. Beyond the two central figures of Walter and Marian, detection is almost completely absent, and it is striking that

Marian withdraws from this activity. She does become very ill, having been soaked by rain on a ledge while she listens to the villains plotting, but there also seems a strong gender element in her constraint: she takes on the housework as the three hide from the villains after rescuing Laura from the asylum, and Walter goes bravely to seek the proof that will destroy their enemies.

In fact the villains, as usual if they are not lower-class, auto-destruct. Sir Percival blunders to his death by setting fire to a church as he tries to suppress evidence his parents were not married—a very common theme in these inheritance-anxiety narratives; Count Fosco is murdered in Paris as a renegade from an Italian secret society. All these elements shape a mainstream mystery, with property at the base, and realizing the maltreatment, and the resistance, of women, and also the power of the respectable classes to defend themselves, with some professional help—and overall there remains the strand of romance that is as strong as and will eventually triumph over the mystery of the crime. The novel also exhibits the tendency for coincidence to be an almost supernatural force in resolving problems—when Walter meets Marian and the rescued Laura at the grave of the alleged Laura, it is as if they all deserve this amazing accident.

Collins' succeeding novels explore with flair and ingenuity the themes of identity, inheritance and intrigue, with legal help and sometimes dubious detective assistance. In *No Name* (1863) two sisters are left without inheritance in a plot starting curiously like Bulwer's *Night and Morning* (1845): the older is resigned to her state, but Magdalen Vanstone seeks to help them both with her energy and shrewdness, and especially with the assistance of the memorable Captain Wragge, a distant relative who had previously blackmailed her long-unmarried parents and now uses his dubious and at times quasi-detective powers to help her, with her actress's skills of impersonation, to marry the son of the man who took their inheritance.

Magdalen is successful, and after her husband's death even learns to be a housemaid to infiltrate his inheritor's house to search for his will. But just as Marian Halcombe withdrew from detection to domestic duties, Magdalen eventually just gives up, finding it all too distasteful—she feels that in the process "I have lost all care for myself" (333). Romance saves her, both by her sister's marrying into love and money and, when she herself is both very poor and very ill, coincidentally meeting again in London a man she briefly met before—he is, like some other noble rescuers in the period, an ex-maritime officer, and they will live happily together, without thinking of the inheritance.

The same spirit of hyper-melodrama focusing on identity and inheritance enriched *Armadale* (1866). One of the two Allan Armadales is the son of a semi-criminal disinherited heir, while the second had a father who took the name as the chosen heir—and then murdered the bad Allan in a sinking ship. A dream of this event haunts the murderer's son, who changes his name to Ozias Midwinter, after a gipsy mentor. The two Allans meet the spectacular red-haired villainess Lydia Gwilt, who plans to marry Ozias-Allan under his real name, have property-owning Allan murdered, lose the remaining Allan, and inherit all as Mrs. Allan Armadale She nearly brings this all off, but finally the wrong Allan is being gassed in a Hampstead clinic, and having learned to love Ozias-Allan, she saves him and, finally giving up all her malignity, lets herself be gassed.

On the way there has been some detection of limited effectiveness: the Rev. Decimus Brock, acting for rich Allan's mother, is tricked into thinking a servant is Lydia and so clears the menacing beauty of suspicion. There are several dubious figures, including a professional private detective, who act for unsavory people, without much impact. The gentry are supported by father-and-son lawyers, the Pedgifts: with their help both Allans survive, and Ozias-Allan takes up life far from inheritance melodrama as a busy European journalist. The novelty of *Armadale* is, as Mariaconcetta Costantini comments, "confirmed by its distance from Dickens' literary influence," having been serialized outside his control and mostly conceived when Collins was overseas: its vigorous mix of innovative ideas and quite unVictorian concepts has stimulated a collection she edited of searching essays from the Italian scholarly community.[22]

The richness, even eccentricity, of sensation that Collins realizes in these potent novels is restrained in his more mystery- and detective-oriented *The Moonstone* (1868), which has been hailed by T.S. Eliot and Julian Symons as the first detective novel.[23] It starts with a puzzle—the loss of the Moonstone itself—and ends by revealing the surprising identity of the thief, but unlike the classic mystery novel it is not based on murder, there is no single dominating and successful detective, and much of the story is a romance. It is also more than a mystery novel, suggesting that stealing the Moonstone was a very disruptive act, and includes a highly liberal account, for the time, of how Indians, here the three patient noble Brahmins, might respond to English imperial depredations. By contrast, Dickens had in late 1857 in *The Perils of Certain English Prisoners*, co-authored with Collins, written a section with what seems like angry vengeance about what was being called "The Indian Mutiny," see Chapter 7, p. 189.

The first policeman to explore the case of the missing Moonstone is Superintendent Seegrave, a stupid bully, common enough in fiction of the period and long to survive alongside sensitive amateur detectives. But here the apparently more successful detective is Sergeant Cuff: his investigation is reminiscent of Whicher's actions in the famous Road murder of 1860, especially with regard to the paint-stained nightgown. Cuff is, like Dickens' men of 1850, a forceful lower-class person with a blunt name; he deals confidently with servants, as the lower-class police were expected to, identifying Rosanna Spearman as a convicted London thief and treating amiably the argumentative gardener and especially Betteredge, the long-winded butler. But like Mr. Bucket, when he turns to the gentry his power weakens. He appears effective—he soon sees the crucial paint-smear—but he quite misreads the puzzling hostility of Rachel Verinder, daughter of the house, deciding she has, with Rosanna's help, stolen the stone to pay off her expenses: he reads her as that classic mainstream mystery figure, an errant lady. When Lady Verinder insists this is wrong, he is dismissed, with a handsome check—police detectives were still available for private cases. In spite of his skills, and ability to relate to staff, Cuff has never fitted in with the family. He even threatens to extend his own intrusion, suggesting that the dead servant Rosanna be replaced by a "woman accustomed to private inquiries of this kind" (177), but his own presence is the real problem. Lady Verinder says, "There is something about that police officer from London that I recoil from" (116), and later she twice refers to him as a "stranger" in the house (183, 187).

Rachel Verinder has actually remained silent and hostile to the inquiry because she saw Franklin Blake, whom she loves, and for whom she has rejected another cousin, Godfrey Ablewhite, banker's son and philanthropist, actually take the Moonstone from her room that night. But she keeps this secret, and Franklin operates as the dashing young European-educated gentleman, full of charm and wit. When harassed by a pompous MP at dinner who asks him what we will have left if we lose our democratic liberties, he grandly replies, "Love, music and salad" (81). He feels central, having brought the Moonstone from the bank for Rachel's birthday, and he takes charge of the inquiries in Cuff's absence—but is himself steadily drawn into them.

Rosanna's own love for Franklin Blake—a very positive name in English and American tradition—leads both to her tragic suicide and also the preservation of the key evidence, his own paint-stained nightgown. The second third of the novel ends with Franklin realizing "I had discovered myself as the thief" (314). The story is slowly untangled through the only real detective of the story, but hardly a heroic figure. Ezra Jennings is part-white, a medical man, facing an unhappy life and public hostility—and an illness that leads to the heavy use of opium, so he shares with Collins himself what he calls "the spiritualized intoxication of opium" (392). Jennings has taken over the practice of Mr. Candy, who was at the fateful birthday dinner after which the Moonstone was lost, but is now very ill—like Marian Halcombe he was soaked by rain—and Jennings has been piecing together his rambling reminiscences of the evening. It turns out that, cross with Franklin for mocking doctors, Candy gave him laudanum to make him sleep. Jennings, interested in subconscious phenomena, has the event re-enacted: they see Franklin sleep-walk to Rachel's room, take the replacement for the Moonstone, then fall asleep and drop it.

Detection has solved one issue—Franklin is not a thief; but opened another—how did the stone get to London? When the Indians attack Luker, the London-based money-lender, they indicate they know it has been mortgaged. Franklin contacts Cuff, who has now retired, and as the anniversary of the diamond's loss is coming up, when they expect the loan to be renewed or the stone redeemed, they will watch Luker. Two people arrive at Blake's fine London house—he is now rich, his father having died: one is "Gooseberry," a small energetic boy named for his protuberant eyes; the other is Cuff, who has heard about the re-enactment from Franklin, and no doubt kept up with events in London. He gives Blake an envelope with a name in it.

They see Luker in the bank, and detain people he bumps into and possibly gives the stone, but without success. Gooseberry is sharper: he chases a tall black sailor, who is found in a riverside inn, murdered, with the stone gone. Cuff pulls off his wig and his beard—it is Ablewhite. Cuff manages to establish, and report to Blake, largely from Luker, what happened. Ablewhite heard Blake moving about late at night after the birthday dinner, went out, and Blake, clearly not awake, gave him the stone and asked him to look after it. Crippled with debts from his theft of trust funds, and also his secret life with exotic ladies, Ablewhite borrowed on it for a year, and was now off to Amsterdam to have it cut—but the Brahmins have won, after all their dedicated commitment, and the stone is restored to its temple in India.

In the envelope Cuff had written "Godfrey Ablewhite." That is as far as police detection actually gets in this story: with the re-enactment and the London events before him, Cuff agrees with Mr. Bruff, the Verinder's lawyer, and the London clubmen who all believed the rumor that Ablewhite, also attacked by the Indians, had the stone. The rest of Cuff's report to Blake is explanatory tidying-up. The revelation of the criminal's identity is in fact, not a detective outcome at all, but a mixture of in-family activity, amateur work of a general sort by Blake, and a quasi-scientific sort by Jennings, and of course also by the other crucial element in all these melodramas, coincidence—as when Ablewhite met the sleep-walking Franklin—though Gooseberry's speed of eye and thought should not be forgotten.

Though he was well aware he had developed a strong sense of "detective-fever"—the phrase is used four times (162, 308, 312, 432)—which is felt by all his inquirers, Collins never did more than this with the detective model, though he would re-use elements of it, notably in *The Law and the Lady* (1875) where a brave wife, with a lawyer's help, lifts the stigma of being a possible murderer from a husband whose guilt over his previous wife's death was in Scotland found "Not Proven"—though no retrial is sought, and all remains in respectable middle-class secrecy.

Dickens disliked the technique of *The Moonstone*, saying "the construction is wearisome beyond endurance"[24]—he probably meant the way it relegated the authoritative author to being a mere recorder of other people's revealing statements. This was an approach Collins apparently drew from a murder case he attended in 1856, when he was very struck how the separate testimonies wove together into a complete narrative, and from *The Woman in White* on he usually constructed his novels from personal statements of varying length. In modern critical terms developed by Roland Barthes, to Dickens, the master of the "writerly" voice, this technique would have seemed annoyingly "readerly," even unauthorial.

But Dickens did prove willing to adopt the familial mystery and at least amateur detection: that was the structural basis of *The Mystery of Edwin Drood* which he left half-written at his death in 1870. This would have been a well-focused quite short novel about the disappearance of Edwin, a young engineer who was engaged to the beautiful—and in future very wealthy—Rosa Bud. His uncle John Jasper, not much older than him, is a musical specialist at Cloisterham Cathedral (the setting is clearly Dickens' own Rochester), and he appears suspicious on several counts. He is first found in an opium den in London; we later hear the owner has heard him threatening someone called "Ned,"[25] and only Jasper called Edwin that; he is definitely very attracted, even in a slightly unbalanced way, to Rosa, and when he harasses her after Edwin's death his face appears "wicked and menacing" (239); he is very interested in the crypt of the cathedral. Most strikingly, when after Edwin's disappearance Jasper is told that Edwin and Rosa had decided to separate, he is "open-mouthed," a "ghastly figure" (194), gives "a terrible shriek" (195) and collapses—just as if he has committed murder for no reason.

These suspicions are all presented in the narrative, and it appears detection is going to be conducted by the figure of Dick Datchery, who suddenly appears in Cloisterham, has a suspiciously thick white head of hair, black eyebrows, and seems not to like wearing his hat—he apparently has a large wig. He collects data, using the rough and eccentric small boy "Deputy" for minor detective tasks, and at the end is watching the London opium-den owner as she watches Jasper in the cathedral. The original cover illustration (Figure 14) seems to feature his thick-haired figure, including in some crucial encounter with Jasper,[26] and his identity has been much discussed, as have Dickens' plans for the ending of the novel.[27] As he has "robustness and breadth of shoulder" (223) he can hardly, as has been occasionally suggested, be Helena Landless, the clever friend of Rosa, nor yet, a more popular idea, Edwin himself, having survived the murder attempt—he is "youthful" (29) and in the illustrations fairly slight. Some have thought Datchery might be the clerk to the lawyer Grewgious, named Bazzard, who is said to be away from the office when Datchery appears, but nothing else suggests him.

It seems obvious that Datchery is in fact the quite young ex–naval officer named Tartar, who is found in London living near both Grewgious and Neville Landless, Helena's brother, whom Jasper is clearly setting up as the murderer. Datchery chooses rooms in Cloisterham very like Lieutenant Tartar's small ones in London, which reminded him of cramped life on a corvette. He admired Rosa when they met in London, and she responded; Datchery is described as clasping his hands behind him as he walks "as is the wont of such buffers" (300): the gesture and term have maritime resonance—and then a long simile about Datchery begins with the words "As mariners on a dangerous voyage" (302). Perhaps clearest of all, as Tartar has just been discussed at the end of Chapter 17 the story cuts to Cloisterham and we immediately meet Datchery. This seems a bravura Dickensian signal of the connection that will be the basis, no doubt with exciting action and also romance with Rosa, for bringing the sharply-focused mystery narrative to an end. Then the gold ring Edwin had for Rosa will reappear, and there will be, as Forster's account, from Dickens himself, suggests,[28] a grand prison-based climax exploring in unparalleled psychological meaning and symbolic complexity that familiar feature of the mainstream mystery, the murder's confession and death, probably by suicide, without any real engagement by the police—a modern socially elevated version of Fagin's end.

While Collins was surely an influence on Dickens' final engagement with a mystery structure, another important model was no doubt the work of Mary Braddon, herself rather like a sensational heroine in that John Maxwell's wife was in an asylum and from 1860 to 1874 she lived with him unmarried, producing five children and caring for his previous five. He was a publisher, and, apart from some periods of illness, she was a richly productive author, often of mystery-involved fiction. Her first novel, *Three Times Dead* (1860), republished with some re-writing as *The Trail of the Serpent* (1861), starts with a murder, develops a fantastic Europe-wide and

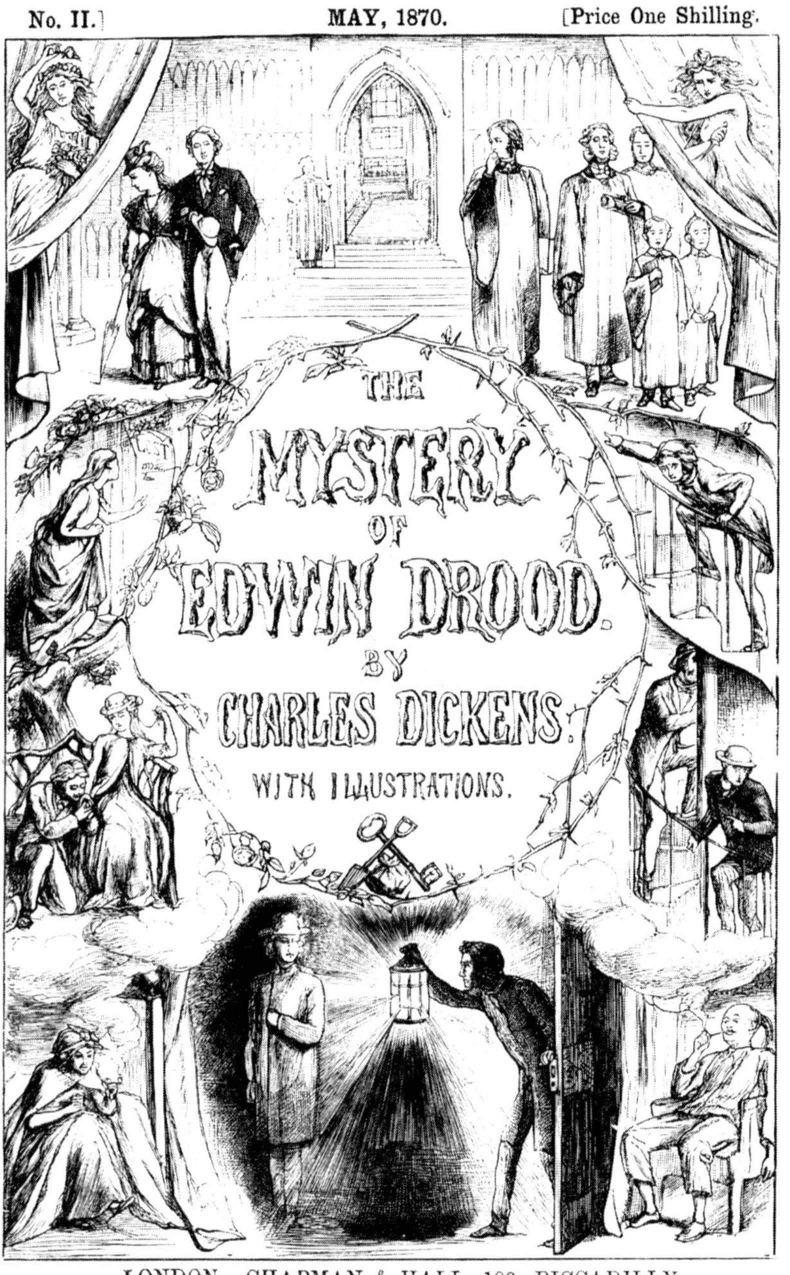

Figure 14. Cover illustration of *The Mystery of Edwin Drood*. Cover illustration by Luke Fildes to Charles Dickens, *The Mystery of Edwin Drood* (London: Chapman and Hall, 1870).

multiple-identity plot with a multiple criminal and a determined detective figure, who is mute—but not, as some bad people find, including the murderer, therefore deaf.

Braddon wrote a good deal for the popular end of the market, producing what were called at the time "newspaper novels," stressing melodrama rather than mystery and detection,[29] but she involved detection in a direct form in her higher-end fiction. In *Lady Audley's Secret* (1862) the heroine, villainess, and now baronet's wife has been married before and pushed her returned-from-Australia husband down a well, she thinks to his death: this is her "secret," and she resumes "her impersonation of domestic perfection."[30] As Jenny Bourne Taylor comments, she is "a subversive parallel of Laurie Fairlie,"[31] but that status also means the gentry family is available to act against her for its self-protection. The languid and inactive barrister Robert Audley, nephew to her doting elderly husband, starts by looking for his apparently murdered friend her former husband George Talboys, and then with considerable concentration, and a great deal of travel, gathers the evidence that will lead to Lady Audley. After her failed attempt to murder him, by setting fire to his inn, she confesses her bigamy (though not her husband-murder) and so by typical gentry in-class arrangements is sent to an insane asylum in France until she soon dies. Though Lady Audley's mother was mad, Braddon implies she herself may well be just genuinely bad, not mad at all—as she reaches the asylum the text calls her "Sir Michael Audley's wicked wife" (379). Her attained class status keeps her from the law, and the importance of that for respectable people is etched when Robert thinks of "the agony of shame" (370) a court case would have caused. The family hides its disgrace and the novel turns to romance: Robert can marry George Talboys' calm beautiful sister Clara; Sir Michael's daughter Alicia marries a handsome squire; and Robert even starts up a lively legal career.

Trodd argues that female authors are more likely to create intrusive police, while male writers worry more about untrustworthy servants.[32] Janice Allan sees Braddon as the writer "who engages most closely with the construction of the servant as domestic spy,"[33] but she is also less negative towards police detectives than her women colleagues, giving them space in some of her mainstream novels. In the highly sensational *Aurora Floyd* (1862–63), Aurora, suspected of shooting dead her first husband, a groom, appeals to her gentlemanly former admirer Talbot Bulstrode, and he and a police detective bluntly named Grimstone eventually isolate as the criminal a malign servant: in the best, and here overdetermined, tradition, a crucial clue is a brass button which actually functions as pistol wadding. The detective withdraws towards the end, but eventually the police process operates, presumably because the villain is not himself a gentleman, and he is hanged. In *Henry Dunbar* (1864) a serious and hard-working London police detective leads a character-based inquiry in what Beller calls a "participatory detective process"[34] but cannot solve the mystery. Joseph Wilmot, a fraudulent bank-clerk, has killed and impersonated the man who made him a fraudster, the banker Dunbar. At first his daughter Margaret, helped by her fiancé and a lawyer, looks for Dunbar's murderer, but finding it to be her errant father, she manages to conceal everything. Finally her father dies, she can marry, and gentry order is restored.

In these two successors of *Lady Audley's Secret* Braddon moves closer to the mystery and detective narrative structure than her colleagues but it was a later novel that came closest of all these writers' work to being a fully-formed detective mystery, *Wyllard's Weird* (1885). From the opening scene, where a girl falls or is pushed from a train on a viaduct near Bodmin in Cornwall, to the final confession and death by poison of the murderer, though romance is still strong, this is shaped like a classic mystery. The girl is from France and she has been seeking a mysterious man who did very well in share-trading in early 1870s Paris. The local Bodmin lawyer, Edward Heathcote, takes up the detection: at first a London lawyer with some detective achievements helps, but he soon withdraws from the case; then a Vidocq-style retired French police detective named Drubarde is fairly useful, but before long Heathcote "began to lose faith in the old sleuthhound"[35] and carries on alone, mostly in France, where he "was slowly, patiently, laboriously following this thread of circumstantial evidence" (228) which would explain all. He finally uncovers the Bodmin banker Wyllard as the villain, who confesses and kills himself, clearing the young ex-officer from local suspicion so he can marry Heathcote's younger sister Hilda and release the romance strand. In a typical Braddon complication Heathcote himself loved and was engaged to the beautiful and admirable Mrs. Wyllard. She rejected him for Wyllard, but may in time, the novel finally suggests, return to her first love. Though Braddon's title does not attempt to conceal the mystery, *Wyllard's Weird* operates primarily with the focus, detail and recurrent incrimination of what will become the classic form of the murder mystery.

It may have had wider influence. Braddon's husband Maxwell was an energetic publisher and routinely sold proofs to newspapers in the USA and Australia. From early November 1884 to the end of May 1885 *Wyllard's Weird* appeared in the well-known Melbourne newspaper *The Leader*—and Fergus Hume arrived in the city early in May 1885. There are distinct resemblances to *The Mystery of a Hansom Cab* (1886), discussed in Chapter 6, see pp. 170–71: Braddon's energy may well have not just popularized mystery and detection within the middle and higher levels of society; she may well have played a substantial part in shaping the first British best-seller in the form.

Other writers were involved in the complex inter-relation of main-stream novel and crime writing. Ellen Wood, always known at the time as Mrs. Henry Wood, has in her hugely popular *East Lynne* (1861) a plot based on Lady Isabel Carlyle, the young, noble, beautiful and sensitive wife of a wealthy solicitor who grows jealous of her husband's dealings with Barbara Hare. She yields to the charming but evil aristocrat, having become Sir Francis Levison after his father's death. But her husband and Barbara were in fact consulting secretly about a murder thought to have been done by Barbara's brother, and though Barbara always loves Carlyle, and will marry him after Isabel is reported dead, he, and also she, are trying like detectives to solve a complicated case with multiple figures involved, confronting determined lying by the only woman involved—whose father was killed—and, it turns out, two different army officers surnamed Thorn.

After Isabel is abandoned by Levison—now a knight, he is seeking a less tainted woman to marry—she returns incognito as her own children's governess after wounding her face in that common occurrence in the new mystery fiction, a railway accident. The novel continues the emotional melodrama of her experiences and feelings, and she will eventually die contrite, at least having loved her three children with Carlyle (though one son and also the one she has with Levison both die). But to the end Carlyle and his new wife and some other helpers pursue the murder mystery, seeking identifications and evidence, quite without police involvement. The eventual break-through, in both the case and the overall plot, is the discovery that Levison, calling himself Lieutenant Thorn, was toying with the murdered man's daughter—she lied for him and was with him in London for two years. There are two quite full trial scenes to complete the mystery and detection aspect of the novel, and Levison is condemned to death. It is unusual for someone of his class to undergo this, but it seems justified because he is unusually villainous: his reprieve from the gallows to a life prison sentence has no class basis, but is founded on the sudden, disagreement-based nature of the murder.

This novel is very well-developed, a surely-plotted and sharply-written combination of mystery and romance to a level that nobody else achieved: as Sussex comments, "The crime plot is inextricable from Lady Isabel's story."[36] It may well have stimulated Braddon within a year to reverse its fallible heroine into a genuine villain in Lady Audley. Wood remained aware of the possibility of mystery: Watson notes that she produced several short stories focusing on crime and its discovery,[37] and she even has in the 1858

story "The Diamond Bracelet" a police detective "of gentlemanly appearance."[38] Immediately following *East Lynne* both *Mrs Halliburton's Troubles*
(1862) and *The Channings* (1862) make fairly minor use of police detectives.
Jonas Butterby, the comically-named latter of these two inquirers, is upgraded
in *Roland Yorke* (1869), effectively a sequel to *The Channings*, in which a
lawyer is shot at the start, perhaps by himself, then people are steadily elim-
inated as suspects by the detective—who even looked at one stage "more
inexorably hard than a granite stone,"[39] and near the end he "knew the truth
now" (450). But he does not tell it to anyone, and a final confession by the
gentry criminal, who kills himself, will reveal all. In one way this novel offers
a complete mystery and detection model, but Roland Yorke himself, like
Lady Isabel in *East Lynne*, plays no direct part in the mystery: it acts as an
intriguing parallel to Roland's adventures, which end in him being elevated
to a baronetcy and marrying his chosen woman. Wood was the last of the
mid-century sensational novelists who turned at times to what would become
the patterns of crime fiction, but never fully or influentially espoused the
genre in that way. She continued from 1874 to produce her "Johnny Ludlow"
stories, focusing in the rural context of her own origin on a range of puzzles,
some of them criminal mysteries though they tend to be small-scale in-
family studies, like "Lost in the Post" which opens the second series.[40]

There were other writers who came close to being fellow-travellers in
early crime fiction. Charles Reade wrote a range of sensational novels which
could engage with varied crimes, but they usually lack the structure of mystery and detection. After using a minor private detective figure in *Hard Cash*
(1863), in *It's Never Too Late to Mend* (1856) he made central a falsely accused
young man who is transported and battles back personally to respectability,
and *Foul Play* (1868) more politically exposes bad practices in the shipping
industry. *Griffith Gaunt* (1866), which Reade thought "my masterpiece,"[41]
has the hero leave his wife out of mistaken jealousy—over a Catholic
priest—and then bigamously marry an innocent girl. Then his wife is
charged with his own murder: she defends herself capably through some
long court scenes, and all hinges on two men with the same name and even
very similar moles on their faces. The real Thomas Leicester has drowned
when drunk, and Griffith, who took that name for bigamous purposes, eventually returns to his at first rather distant wife. She warms to him again
after he gives blood to save her in childbirth; the other woman marries into
the gentry and has nine more children, the one she has had with
Gaunt/Leicester having died. Clearly a reworking, mostly with gender rever-
sals, of *East Lynne*, and as usual with Reade having a somewhat mechanical
sensationalism, this is as close as he comes to mystery fiction. Anthony Trol-

lope had used a minor and less than impressive detective figure, Samuel
Bozzle, in *He Knew He Was Right* (1869) and then made a detour towards
the crime fiction form in *The Eustace Diamonds* (1871), essentially an ironic
reversal of *The Moonstone*—with Lizzie Eustace actually the money-seeking
jewel-stealing fraud that Cuff thought Rachel Verinder was, and with competent inquiries led by the banally named police detective Bunfit.

It is evident the structure of the mystery novel had by now become
recognized, and novels with no other generic claim were appearing—in
the Grahame Greene and Dorothy Glover crime fiction collection more
than 80 come between 1871 and 1890.[42] This development essentially ended
the curious genre of mainstream mystery novels which never fully accepted
the processes of specialist inquiry in the way that the short story had by
the late 1840s. In this long-lasting generic compromise, which involved
many of the century's major writers, the most remarkable feature, especially
to modern readers, was that negative attitudes about police intervention,
based on devotion to the myth of respectable people's self-management,
especially with discreet professional help, made the real work of detection
tend to be shared among the members of the disrupted family, guided by
events and often sheer coincidence, and only if the villains were themselves
lower-class was any final legal penalty seen as tolerable.

The social element of those attitudes was to continue—Sherlock
Holmes stories almost never deal with lower-class crimes and they remarkably rarely end in trial and even less often with execution. But as Collins
showed in *The Moonstone*, as Dickens surely acknowledged in *The Mystery
of Edwin Drood*, and Braddon achieved structurally in *Wyllard's Weird*, the
process of at least some investigation, part of it possibly in police hands,
had become accepted as central to the structure of the mainstream mystery.
The road was open for the one-volume mystery-focused, revelation-
concluding mysteries of the future, whether or not they retained the
romance sub-structure. But it does remain tempting to wonder what would
have emerged if class anxieties had not stopped writers of Collins' capacity
to plot, Braddon's intensity of focus, and Dickens' flair for symbolical
enrichment, from feeling able to work with a dominant detective figure.
What bravura, what grandiose characterization, what richness of complication and even complexity might have illuminated the stage of early crime
fiction then—Hartright as a Police Inspector, Robert Audley as a proto–
Lord Peter Wimsey, Lady Dedlock herself as a mix of Miss Gladden and
Sara Paretsky. Then Sherlock Holmes would not have been needed to
apotheosize the detective.

CHAPTER 6

Why Did Hume's
The Mystery of a Hansom Cab
Move So Fast?

The Puzzle

Crime fiction has many authors, very many readers, and also a number of myths. One is that the whole thing started with Poe, a view favored by those unaware of earlier authors who developed the form before the brilliant Philadelphian made myth out of mystery and detection. Another is that Raymond Chandler was a great popular private-eye author—in fact his first novel sold in sober hardback and he was always better-received among the English literati of his own origin, a context which gave class and confidence to his reshaping of Hammett's edgy populism. The myths also have it that Sara Paretsky was the first of the feminist mystery authors—in fact several others preceded her by a decade or more, but they have been effectively obscured by the firmness and flourish which in her Chandleresque way she brought to the form, or the anti-form. A negative myth is the topic of this chapter—why has no-one ever offered any explanation for the runaway success of the first novel by an author who went on to write many with nothing of the same success, who set it in far-away Melbourne, Australia, and yet saw his novel *The Mystery of a Hansom Cab* take London by bibliocommercial storm in very late 1887, so much so it gained the title of the first best-seller in crime fiction? Unlike Fergus Hume's more than a hundred other novels, 40 more years of mysteries and sensational stories, the book has almost always been in print, usually in a cheap format and occasionally with a short, gesturing introduction. It has been at times mentioned as a freak and very rarely described in very limited detail. There is now from the Melbourne scholar Lucy Sussex a full account of the context, production and promotion of the book, and it seems time it came in from the critical cold.

The Person

Ferguson Wright Hume (some versions give Fergusson, the spelling of his mother's maiden surname) was born in Powick, Worcestershire, England, on July 8, 1859—six weeks after Arthur Conan Doyle in Edinburgh. Hume's father was a man of lower-class origin who worked in a mental asylum: after emigrating to Dunedin, New Zealand, he became in 1863 an asylum Superintendent and ultimately co-proprietor of one. He was clearly very good at his complex job, but was not, as he is often reported to have been, a doctor. Fergus and others in the family grew up to a cultured middle-class New Zealand life—two sisters were professional-standard singers and the young Fergus wanted to be a dramatist. Sussex records that he "made a theatrical start with farce and low comedy"—*Once Bitten, Twice Shy* and *Dynamite, or the Crown Jewels* were early titles, but he moved on when in 1885 his *A Woman Scorned*, "a cynical comedy of married manners"[1] was professionally performed in Christchurch. Hume studied law at the University of Otago, working as a law clerk to support himself, qualified as a Dunedin solicitor in 1883, and wrote for theatre and in newspapers, where he had an uncle with contacts. But the larger world called, and in early May 1885 he and his sister went to Melbourne, she 30 and an established singer, he 25, planning to make his name.

He made contacts in local theater and did get as far as "localizing" some plays, that is writing topical references, especially jokes, into the text of imported comedies—one was a burlesque *Dr Faustus*—but he found it impossible to be taken on as an author of plays. Melbourne was a city of over quarter of a million people; the major gold rush starting in 1851 had made it a center of real wealth, and its position as the first stop in eastern Australia for the ships from Europe—they came southabout the continent—made it a major focus for import and export. It had a very busy professional theater world, well above the more relaxed and easily penetrated New Zealand context where Hume had made some headway, and was a major shopping city, with grand blocks and arcades, including book shops— "Melbourne stood out as marvellously bookish" comment Martin and Mirmohamadi in their study of its reading habits, especially of Mary Braddon.[2]

Logically enough, Hume thought of publishing fiction. In his preface to the 1895 Jarrolds edition of his famous novel, he says:

I enquired of a leading Melbourne bookseller what style of book he sold most of. He replied that the detective stories of Gaboriau had a large sale; and as, at this time, I had never heard of this author, I bought all his works—eleven or thereabouts—and read them carefully.[3]

Eleven was a fairly full set of what Vizetelly had been publishing by Gaboriau in English in London since 1881; Hume very likely also had a copy of du Boisgobey's *The Mystery of an Omnibus*, which Henry Vizetelly produced in translation in 1885, so generating both the title of Hume's novel and a reference to du Boisgobey at the end of Chapter 1.

He started work: Sussex suggests he had finished the novel by the end of 1885, and it must have taken at least three or four months, especially if, as he also says in the preface, he made a major change to the plot when he had a complete draft, as is discussed below. He was also working in a legal office, and appears to have had a fairly busy social life—Sussex finds evidence of him being a "masher," a young man about town with lively interests.

Publishing the book was as difficult as getting on in the theater. The author of a memoir of George Robertson (the Melbourne publisher and bookseller, not to be confused with the slightly later Sydney man with an identical name and role) believes he rejected Hume's novel "because of the coarse language it contained, as well as scenes of low life in Melbourne."[4] There were more general problems: Hume's 1895 Preface says

every one to whom I offered it refused even to look at the manuscript on the ground that no colonial could write anything worth reading. They gave no reason for this extraordinary opinion, but it was sufficient for them, and they laughed to scorn the idea that any good could come out of Nazareth, i.e. the colonies.[5]

But though Hume had joined the list of famous rejectees—reaching from Melville's *Moby Dick* to Rowling and *Harry Potter*—like them he did not give up, and finally with money borrowed from friends and supporters paid for publication himself from the small firm Kemp and Boyce. It does not look an imposing novel: quite short, especially by 19th-century standards. Four copies have survived of the early Australian editions—a bibliophile's dream (Figure 15).

Hume had assets as well as the novel itself. Frederick Trischler, another UK migrant to New Zealand (whom Hume seems not to have met until both were in Melbourne), combined literary and business interests and Hume said in an interview he "took a fancy to the story and undertook to arrange for its publication."[6] This was done with some panache—the book came out on October 23, 1886, the Saturday before the week when people flooded

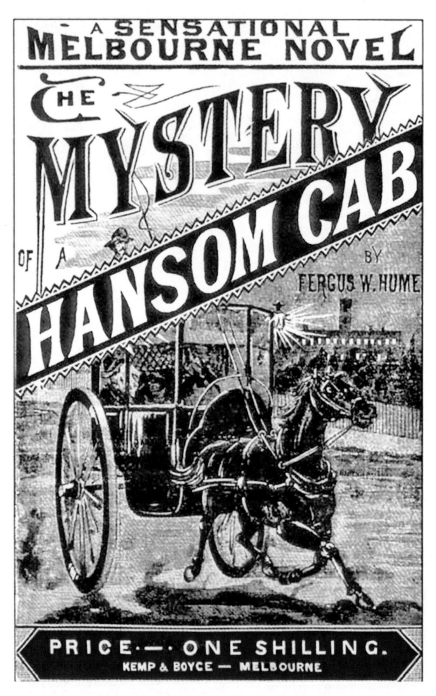

Figure 15. *The Mystery of a Hansom Cab*, the original Melbourne edition. Cover of Fergus Hume, *The Mystery of a Hansom Cab* (Melbourne: Kemp and Boyce, 1886), copy in Rare Books, Baillieu Library, University of Melbourne.

into Melbourne, then as now, for the major horse-race, the Melbourne Cup. There were publicity stunts, with Hume himself delivering copies of the book in—of course—a hansom cab. The novel apparently sold well from the start, and soon had excellent publicity when the major local newspaper *The Argus* printed on a Saturday—always a big day for Australian papers— Hume's detailed panegyric of "The Block," the always busy center of the downtown shopping area that Melburnians so much celebrated.

Sales of the novel in Australasia have long been disputed—the claimed first print run of 5,000 copies has been thought improbably large, and even less likely seems the story that a reprint in the same number was needed in a few weeks. Nevertheless, there were contemporary reports that the book sold very well: Sussex cites one saying that 2,000 sold in New Zealand in the week the book appeared there,[7] and there certainly were new editions printed in Melbourne, as examples have survived. Clear evidence for excellent sales in the original location is that both Trischler and Jessie Taylor, wife of a Melbourne bank manager, were willing to back with substantial funds a London publication, which would be the basis for the novel's bestseller status.

The London edition appeared in November 1887—in another Conan Doylean coincidence, only a few days before Sherlock Holmes first appeared in *Beeton's Christmas Annual*, which carried the novella *A Study in Scarlet*. Conan Doyle later claimed to have finished this by April 1886 so it seems unlikely, unless he was lying and someone posted him a Melbourne copy of Hume's novel, that there is any direct influence—but when the American *Lippincott's Magazine* wanted more Holmes from Conan Doyle in 1889 and when George Newnes of *The Strand Magazine* was so keen on the Holmes stories in 1891, it may well be that Hume's remarkable sales for crime fiction had been noticed.

The London publisher was Trischler's specially formed Hansom Cab Publishing company, but it was hardly a lavish production, again a small paper-jacketed book. The London sales figures are not easy to trace with confidence, but the major success was indisputable. Later copies exist with the cover boldly asserting the novel has achieved sales of 600,000, and it seems clear that 25,000 were printed and sold every month for over a year. Trischler claimed 360,000 by mid–1888 and however inflated such claims might be, the *Illustrated London News* reported "Persons were found everywhere devouring the realistic sensational tale of Melbourne social life."[8] The language of the report itself accepts the novel's self-representation— the Melbourne edition was on the front page labeled "Startling and Realistic," while the London one carried above the title in bold print "A

Sensational Melbourne Novel." Eric Sinclair Bell's report states that by August 1888 340,000 were sold and by the Jarrolds edition of 1895 the number was 373,000. Jarrolds then claimed 500,000 in 1910 and by 1916, 550,000.[9]

Hume was now famous around the word, and set off for London in April 1888, still thinking of theater—his close friend the actor Philip Beck was on the ship with him—but also willing to keep writing mysteries; *Madame Midas*, both novel and play, having some overlap in minor characters with the first novel, would come out in Melbourne in in July 1888, and do well there and in London. That and the theater version of *The Hansom Cab* at least brought in some money: Hume had—amazingly, in retrospect—sold the copyright of his first novel to Jessie Taylor for £50, just as Conan Doyle at the same time gave *A Study in Scarlet* to the publisher for £25.

At least as great a disappointment as the financial loss would be that Hume never came close to matching his early success. His future life and work were to be a long distance from the excitement of that first novel. No doubt the publicity skills Trischler brought, Taylor largely funded, and Hume helped fulfill, were important, but they are not enough to explain the mysterious success. The context and the text itself deserve analysis. And, like the final explanation of the death of Oliver Whyte, that analysis needs to come from a range of positions and in a variety of voices.

The Structure

The story begins with a ten-page chapter offering a newspaper report of a man found dead in a cab headed from the city of Melbourne to St. Kilda, an attractive bay-side suburb. The second chapter, of the same length, describes the inquest, giving the limited report of the cab-driver and also saying that a man like the one who left the cab with what turned out to be the body in it was driven to the fashionable residential suburb of East Melbourne, arriving a little after 2:00 a.m. The third chapter is a half-page announcement offering £100 for more information.

No-one claims the reward. A police detective, Gorby, sees after several days a landlady's advert for a missing Oliver Whyte: as the body had on its face a chloroform-soaked handkerchief with the initials OW, he visits, and after a rambling comic discussion establishes that a tall man, like the one the cab-driver saw pick up the drunken Whyte before his fatal journey, had previously called to threaten him about a girl. While Gorby is searching the dead man's room Whyte's friend Moreland calls, having, he says, just returned from the country. When told of Whyte's death he "stared at the detective in a puzzled sort of way,"[10] then says he was drinking with him on the night of his death. He reports Whyte was pursuing Madge Frettlby, daughter of a very rich man, and that Brian Fitzgerald, another suitor, was hostile to him.

Frettlby's story is told under the chapter title "A Wool King." He arrived in Victoria before it was called that, so before 1850 when it was still part of New South Wales, and there was yet no gold discovered. He had done very well with land-buying and sheep-farming, and the gold boom had only amplified his wealth. Now he is faced with a choice of sons-in-law. For no evident reason he had favored Whyte but gave in to his daughter's interest in Fitzgerald. Interspersed with an account of the Frettlby social life, Gorby pursues Fitzgerald, visits his landlady (another comic, talkative one) and finds he was home a little before 2:00 that Thursday night, but her clock may be slow. After Hume has celebrated Melbourne social life, and Fitzgerald has taken Frettlby and Madge to his lodgings for tea, Gorby arrests him for murder.

The second section of the novel opens with a news report, and a visit to Fitzgerald in jail by Calton, an accomplished lawyer engaged by Frettlby for the defense. Fitzgerald says he was the man the cab-man saw pick up the drunken Whyte and hail the cab for him, but he left when he realized who it was, and then went elsewhere. He claims he did not return to the cab, as the driver reported—and so denies he was Whyte's murderer—but will not say where he went, as revealing that would have a negative impact on Madge. Ignoring this, she and Calton investigate at Fitzgerald's lodgings and Madge finds a half-burned letter inviting him to call—it is reproduced in the text. Calton interests Kilsip, a police detective who dislikes Gorby, in the case and he traces the letter to the semi-criminal Mother Guttersnipe, living in Melbourne's dangerous inner slum area. The letter was written on the day of the murder by "the Queen," who was staying there, and was it is later revealed often visited by Whyte. It was delivered to the Melbourne Club by Mother Guttersnipe's grand-daughter Sal Rawlins, who is now missing.

Chapter 17 is a description of the long trial: the evidence against Fitzgerald is strong, Sal is not there to provide an alibi, and Fitzgerald will not speak for himself. The only evidence in his favor is that he seems to have got home a little too early, and both cabmen say the second tall man in a light coat and soft hat had a diamond ring on his first finger—Fitzgerald has never worn such a thing. But suddenly Sal appears. She joined the

Salvation Army after "the Queen" died, then left it, went off to Brisbane with a Chinese man, abandoned him, and was ill for some time. Now she gives firm evidence for an alibi, and Fitzgerald is cleared.

The novel enters its third sequence with a long newspaper summary in Chapter 20 of the events so far, fairly repetitive in nature, and then a three-month break follows until a hot Christmas at the Frettlby country estate. Sal is now a family servant, and Madge is educating her. They have found that "the Queen" was named Rosanna Moore and that there were papers concerning her which Whyte had on him, no doubt in the jacket-pocket which was found torn. Calton writes a lengthy letter to Fitzgerald summing things up and basically demanding information, as he feels the secret told him at Mother Guttersnipe's is the key to the murder. Fitzgerald knows he must tell: but still delays.

Fitzgerald has been wary of Frettlby, and Madge even mistakes her father for him one evening, in a long light coat and soft hat. When he is told this, Fitzgerald has "a cold feeling at his heart" (335). It seems he thinks Frettlby did it, and this now appears quite possible. However, Kilsip tells Calton he suspects Moreland—who does wear a diamond on his first finger—and suggests Moreland threw guilt on Fitzgerald deliberately by the cab-ride to East Melbourne. Suddenly Mother Guttersnipe sends a message that she is dying: they hurry to see her and she tells them Rosanna was her daughter, a much-admired dancer, who married Frettlby in Melbourne, and they had a child, Sal. Rosanna went off to England and reported both the child and herself dead, but she recently met Whyte there and they returned to blackmail Frettlby for money—and Whyte also demanded to marry his daughter. It looks as if Frettlby is indeed the criminal.

His doctor has told Madge he has a weak heart. He is visited by Moreland one evening, and the next day he sits in his office writing. That evening he is sparkling at dinner—an old Scots nurse says he is "fey," meaning fated and also far-sighted. That night he appears sleepwalking with in his hand the wedding certificate of himself and Rosanna. Sal seizes it; Madge screams and faints; Frettlby wakes up, and drops dead.

This outcome is told in the novel after a discussion of Frettlby's possible guilt between Fitzgerald and Calton—they have heard separately, from Rosanna and Mother Guttersnipe, about Frettlby's prior marriage. Then a telegram comes, recounting Frettlby's death. Calton says, "It is the Judgement of God" (351). It was his confession he was writing, and when his executors, Calton, Fitzgerald and the doctor, meet to read it, they agree they will then burn it to protect the family name from the shame of bigamy: as in the mainstream English mystery novel, the respectable classes do no not hand over their wrong-doers to the police. But before they can burn the confession, Kilsip arrives and says he has found the coat Moreland wore, and hid in a park near Fitzgerald's house: it still contains the fatal chloroform which he has discovered Whyte had bought. They read the confession which occupies all 12 pages of Chapter 33. The Rosanna story is told by Frettlby, and he then states Moreland did the murder, knowing of Whyte's power over Frettlby and wanting to have the money for himself. He told his guilt to Frettlby, knowing he could not expose him. Frettlby had watched Whyte that last night: he had earlier told him he had the certificate, and Frettlby hoped to get it. He had seen him drunk, and Fitzgerald hail a cab for him, but when the second man appeared—whom he did not then know—he gave up and went home. He gave Moreland a check for £5,000, but the executors-cum-investigators find he has been unable to cash the check, and foresee he will go to Frettlby's lawyers about it. They are requested to bring him to Calton's office, and there he confesses. The police take him away: the doctor correctly predicts he will commit suicide. The three men conceal all the details and the murder is put down to conflict between Whyte and Moreland, as two English incomers.

So all is resolved without police action. Sal is now better educated, and working for fallen women. No-one has told her she was Frettlby's older and only legitimate child. The executors were anxious about her and the inheritance but Frettlby's will, as they had hoped, named Madge as his complete beneficiary. The treatment of Sal—in fact the proper inheritor—seems surprising and can annoy modern readers, especially women. Even in the English mainstream mystery Sal would have had some claim on moving into the family—she is after all the actual heir, and Madge is illegitimate, in the situation of Magdalen Vanstone in Collins' *No Name*: hence the stress laid on the need for Frettlby's will to name her. But the novel ignores this problem and Sal's treatment—the only compensation is that she has now been educated and becomes a social worker. Finally in a reversal of the English tradition where the displaced person was allowed to disappear overseas, Madge when she gets better, marries Fitzgerald and they finally sail away, but not to anonymity. It is "towards the old world and the new life" (410)—Fitzgerald has previously had fantasies about re-establishing his family's fortunes and their ruined castle in Ireland, and Madge's inheritance will achieve this.

The novel's story moves quite rapidly, with some slower, repetitive and reader-reminding sequences, notably those in court, or from the newspapers, as well as Calton's letter to Fitzgerald and Frettlby's confession. But against the model of both the three-volume novel and the extended sensational novels of Braddon and Collins, the whole seems quite brisk, and being at most a hundred thousand words it fits comfortably in the early editions into a small single volume, not much over 200 pages, and that including quite a few advertisements at the end. The format itself bespeaks modernity.

Hume's interest in the theater may well lie behind not just the comic landladies but also provide the basis of a structural feature that seems quite new against the existing crime writers—the novel falls readily into three acts, with an epilogue. Collins had divided novels into Scenes or Acts, but not in a stage-oriented triune way like this. When Fitzgerald is arrested at the end of Chapter 10 we are just less than a third of the way through, and the next third, or act, ends with his acquittal in court at the end of Chapter 19—and both scenes are fine *coups de théatre*. Act 3 appears to end with the dramatic evening at the Frettlby mansion when he appears sleepwalking, Madge faints and he dies: this is Chapter 30, making a neat three-act partition overall. But that is not the end of the novel, though it may well once have been, when Frettlby, as both Fitzgerald and Calton have been thinking, was indeed the murderer. In his 1895 preface, Hume says, "In the first draft I made Frettlby the criminal, but on reading over the MS I found that his guilt was so obvious that I wrote out the story for a second time, introducing the character of Moreland as a scape-goat."[11] Frettlby clearly had motive, and when he is mistaken by Madge for Fitzgerald, it looks as if the hints are gathering to his guilt, to be both revealed and punished in the fine theatrical finale of the sleepwalking death. A surviving theatrical reference to Frettlby as murderer is a direct connection to Macbeth made in Frettlby's confession where he seems to see Moreland as Banquo and so Whyte's murder resembles that of Duncan (see 354–55).

Through the early stages of the rewrite, Moreland is shown as acting rather suspiciously when he hears of Whyte's death, and the comment to the cab-driver "Yes I've changed my mind and will see him home" (5) suggests Moreland—who knew where Whyte lived—as being possibly suspicious from the start. Moreland tells Gorby Fitzgerald looks like him (54), clearly a clue for the observant reader. Other early elements appear to have been altered substantially, and as a result if the existing text was meant to be based on Frettlby as the killer, there would appear some puzzles, such as how did Frettlby get hold of Whyte's coat, with the chloroform in it? Then if Frettlby did kill Whyte in the cab why did he then take a cab to near Fitzgerald's lodgings and hide the coat—surely he would not have wanted to cast suspicion on his daughter's beloved? Presumably the East

Melbourne detour was, like Moreland having Whyte's coat, invented with Moreland becoming the murderer, and originally Fitzgerald was suspected by Gorby only on the basis of Whyte's landlady's evidence. The only other unresolved puzzles in the story do not bear on the change of murderer: it is not clearly explained how Fitzgerald had one of Whyte's gloves in his coat pocket—an important early clue that is persuasive for Gorby. Presumably Calton is right to assert in his final speech for Fitzgerald's defense that he picked it up when helping the drunken Whyte. Nor is it clarified why Whyte had bought the chloroform which Moreland found in his coat pocket—did he perhaps mean to finish off Rosanna now he felt close to the money and Madge?

The change of plan over the murderer and the evidently fairly extensive early rewriting are inherently successful, as the revelation of Moreland's guilt is both quite subtly suggested early on and then, when finally presented, provides a good climax to a concealed-criminal pattern, arising from the early hints and then the ignoring of Moreland for a long time—the structure is quite Christie-like in that way. The pattern also fits very well with the surprise revelations found in early successful crime fiction, but while Hume's story attracts attention immediately to the writer whom his typesetters in Melbourne and London spelled as "Gaboreau"—suggesting his fame was limited—there are more complex patterns in the relation of *The Mystery of a Hansom Cab* to the already established successful patterns of mystery writing.

Sources Around the World

Successful though Gaboriau was in the 1880s through the flow of new translations published in London by Henry Vizetelly, he does not seem to have offered a major structural model for *The Mystery of a Hansom Cab*. In his first detective story *L'Affaire Lerouge* (1866) the successful analysis is by a retired amateur with some Dupin-like tendencies, and then M. Lecoq takes over, though in only five novels. As discussed in Chapter 2, he is a busy Parisian police inspector who studies the scene with care, then pursues leads and suspects with dedication in what seems an early form of the police procedural crossed with inspirational detection: Lecoq's devotion to duty never falters. In several novels, notably the very successful *Monsieur Lecoq* (1869), there is a lengthy sequence back in time and there, as commonly elsewhere, the guilty persons are aristocrats, real or false. None of this meshes with Hume's pattern, though *Le Dossier no. 113* (1867) does offer the model of the initial suspect being involved with a delightful and wealthy young lady; when the true criminal is identified they will live happily ever after, a structure Hume does deploy, at least in the first two-thirds of his novel, though he could have found it elsewhere, especially if he read Braddon's *Wyllard's Weird* (1885), as is discussed below.

A stronger candidate than Gaboriau for influence is also mentioned in passing by Hume—the wide-reading man-about-town Rolleston likens the events to those in *The Leavenworth Case* (67). Published in 1878, set in New York, this first and very successful novel by Anna Katharine Green (as discussed in Chapter 1, pp. 35–39), uses a professional and very competent, if rather reserved, detective Ebenezer Gryce, and some investigations by other men—but not by Leavenworth's two lively daughters. For some time the novel presents as a possible murderer of the rich Mr. Leavenworth the admirer of his lovelier and less intellectual daughter, Henry Clavering—he is a figure not unlike Brian Fitzgerald, and is also a well-born but impoverished traveller from overseas, in this case England. A late turnabout, with a confession, exposes the surprise villain, and romance can finally flourish—so there is a reasonable overall similarity to Hume's pattern.

Some detailed resemblances exist between the two novels. Green's is notable for opening with a very long inquest. It takes several days, so some other action does occur, but it occupies the first 11 chapters, a third of the book—which like *The Hansom Cab* is in three sections, with a short part 4 "The Problem Solved." It includes a map, which Hume does not offer, but a torn letter is illustrated in both texts. A number of newspaper reports appear in *The Leavenworth Case*, shorter than most of Hume's, and a long confession in a very late chapter, matching, apart from the final guilt, that written by Frettlby. It looks fairly clear that Hume was familiar with this novel, though he does not use its focus on a single detective or its largely domestic setting—Green's New York has little of the overtly-described flair of Hume's Melbourne. The novel was very successful and highly likely to have been read by the young Hume.

Another possible source for *The Mystery of a Hansom Cab* is Mary Braddon, mentioned when Fitzgerald thinks this "romance in real life" in fact "beats Miss Braddon hollow" (79). Through figures like Eleanor Vane in *Eleanor's Victory* (1863) and Margaret Wilmot in *Henry Dunbar* she provided examples of strong women involved in detection to acquit a lover who is suspected. Madge plays that role quite forcefully for a while—when she plans to investigate for Fitzgerald's sake "her eyes were hard" (147). Braddon had responded to the popular detective of mid-century short stories when she created both a skillful amateur (Robert Audley) in *Lady Audley's Secret* (1862), and a police detective (Sergeant Henry Carter) in *Henry Dunbar* (1865). Though she largely moved away towards emotional and sensational structures, Hume may have found some ideas in *A Strange World* (1875) where the suspected hero refuses to say where he was on the night of the murder, where the heroine is called Madge, and an appealing lawyer is involved in the detection (though he turns out to be the murderer): there is also a girl much like Sal Rawlins who, when her birth secret is revealed, might well inherit everything.

There is a closer link between Hume's novel and Braddon's *Wyllard's Weird,* to be discussed below, but a few points might have been picked up from *The Cloven Foot* (1879) where a prior marriage to a dancer threatens to be a serious problem for a respectable family, and the murderer is a disreputable Englishman. However, these ideas are not uncommon in the literature of the day, and the sense of strong-willed female involvement that Madge represents might easily have come from Hume's own sisters, and a more substantial set of parallels can be found in a novel that Hume surely knew, but makes no reference to, Willkie Collins' *The Moonstone* (1868). Collins does like Green have a letter in the text in *The Law and the Lady* (1875) and has a woman inquirer in the same novel; he also uses characters giving their own narratives like Frettlby, going right back to Joanna Grice in *Hide and Seek* in 1854, but *The Moonstone* has a set of structural patterns that seem to be essentially replicated in Hume's novel—as well as the use of the unusual name Rosanna for two characters who die fairly early and, curiously in the light of their actual emotive, even moral, impact, are never of more than secondary interest in the story.

The Moonstone offers a police detective hired to solve the apparent theft of a very valuable diamond, but he is far from the imposing authority of Lecoq or the restrained mastermind of Green's Ebenezer Gryce. Sergeant Cuff's name itself suggests he is personally limited: he turns out to be wrong in almost all his decisions and he only returns at the very end to rationalize discoveries not made by him (see p. 148). Commentators often link him to the way Dickens was impressed with the police in his magazine *Household Words* and in that spirit created the insightful Inspector Bucket of *Bleak House*—but Bucket's name is itself diminishing; as discussed in Chapter 5, both he and the real police have distinct limitations and Hume's self-confident and erroneous Gorby is in that tradition. After a while Hume introduces a second detective, hired by Calton, Fitzgerald's defense lawyer, who is at first seen as not just "the cleverer of the two" but also "tall, slender, hawk-like" (162)—though the last element was apparently not a hint for

Conan Doyle's Holmes. Kilsip turns out to be right about the murder, in his sudden and it seems instinctive way, and it seems credible to link that, and his personal awkwardness, with Collins' second and real detective, the mixed-race health worker Ezra Jennings, who has deep perceptions and real problems, and, with his drug habit, even some traces of the author.

But Collins offers more. The early-suspected person in *The Moonstone* is both a gentleman and lover, Franklin Blake, who will clear his name and win his bride—though more slowly than Fitzgerald does—and he also plays a part in encouraging the successful inquiries, as if standing in for Hume's Calton. These eventually identify the criminal, who was around at the same time on the same night, saw his opportunity and took it—like Moreland. It was diamond theft that Godfrey Ablewhite perpetrated, not murder, but the circumstances, the final structure and the death of the villain before justice are comparable in terms of novelistic development. There is a clear difference between justified vengeance by the Moonstone-loyal Indians and Moreland's prison suicide, but the shape of the story feels familiar to someone who knows *The Moonstone* well, and the repeated name Rosanna even suggests Hume wanted to leave for select readers a trace of his deep-laid inheritance. *The Moonstone* also uses very little in the way of chance or coincidence, apart from the two suspected men being in the same location on the crucial night: Hume borrows that feature, but carefully, and mercifully, ignores the ludicrous web of coincidence which is found in Collins' *I Say No* of 1885, and also the deeply improbable occurrences of du Boisgobey's *The Mystery of an Omnibus*.

There may have been a more immediate stimulus, at least for the first version with Frettlby as murderer. As was noted above in Chapter 5, Mary Braddon's most crime-fiction like novel, *Wyllard's Weird*, was actually finishing its serialization in the Melbourne *Leader* in the month when Hume and his sister arrived in the city, and copies of the whole text would have been on sale directly.[12] The novel starts with a sudden murder on public transport (a train): the victim is bringing written evidence from the past that will potentially disgrace a very successful and wealthy man, who reacts instinctively and fatally—the opening of the original *Hansom Cab*. A younger man is suspected and this affects his romance—in Braddon not with the murderer's daughter but with the sister of the lawyer who undertakes the inquiry, with police support rather less effective than that of Kilsip: presumably Gaboriau and Green here are acting as partial influences on Hume. Braddon's story also ends with the confession and death by suicide, of the murderer, and the happy marriage of the former suspect and his love, though neither have been as active in the story as Brian and Madge.

While it does seem that *The Moonstone,* combining two semi-detectives, one of the two disposable Rosannas, a gentleman suspect who then works on the case, a sudden villain long unobtrusively present in the story, and a resumed romance for the gentleman suspect who loved a young woman affected by the crime, appears to be the richest detailed source for the published version of *The Mystery of a Hansom Cab,* though elements do derive from Green and perhaps elsewhere in Braddon, it also appears that the structure and premise of *Wyllard's Weird* is what Hume was initially imitating, and somewhat varying, in his first, superseded, version of his murder mystery. With all these sources, offering many varied and effective elements, Hume's novel is in general a skillful combination of up-to-the minute structural elements from the best of recent mysteries around the world.

Sources in Australia

But *The Mystery of a Hansom Cab* is also an Australian novel, and its success in that mode was the start of its triumphant journey. Its relations to the local fictional tradition are both of inherent interest and also a topic of apparently no value at all to commentators, including those who offer themselves as Australian experts.

There had been no shortage of crime fiction in a country set up to accommodate people convicted of crime. Identities could be easily changed on the long journey and confidently maintained at such a long distance from records, but at the same time events and crimes from the past country could re-emerge to the embarrassment of newly-established respectable immigrants. These topics provided material for stories about both the unjustly criminalized and also still-concealed villains, and local readers also soon developed admiration for bold criminals, known as bushrangers, operating in the massive spaces of the new land.[13] Major writers dealt with these themes, such as Marcus Clarke in *For the Term of His Natural Life,* the revised novel version of which appeared in 1874 and a new edition was published in both Britain and Australia in 1885, while the original serial version, the more subtly-titled *His Natural Life* (1870–72), was reprinted in Melbourne's *Australian Journal* from September 1886. Mary Fortune (discussed in Chapter 4, pp. 109–10, in terms of gender themes in her crime fiction), a long-term provider of high-quality police detective short stories, was still busily at work when Hume was pondering what to write; she still tended to focus in rural areas, though in 1880 two of her *Australian Journal* stories were Melbourne-set and by 1886 her detective, Mark Sinclair was based in the city, though still likely to travel to the country on detective business.[14] Hume's use of the developed city and the lack of any connection back to convictism or to bush adventures mark his pattern off from the well-known tradition of Australian rural fiction which was in the 1880s being strengthened by the very successful bushranger novel *Robbery Under Arms* by Thomas A. Browne, writing as "Rolf Boldrewood," serialized in 1882–83 but not published in book form until 1888.

By turning his back on that tradition Hume realizes a new world for crime fiction in Australia—the murder involves young men out from England, but they bring no crimes or secrets with them that originate or belong there. Frettlby's marriage to Rosanna took place in Melbourne, and though Mother Guttersnipe sounds as if she grew up among English-born convicts, her role is entirely to do with her daughter and grand-daughter in Melbourne's criminal slum. There is one sequence deploying property-owner comfort, at Frettlby's rural palace, but his landed wealth is never explored—the family and their friends spend most of their time in an urban context in the fine house on the beach at St Kilda, a cab-ride from the city. The other personnel are Melbourne moderns like Rolleston the writer and aspiring politician, Calton the polished lawyer, and the women who gather round them, entertain them and are, unlike the men, at times quite sharply satirized.

That air of actual modern Melbourne must have been a major part of the novel's appeal to the busy people who thronged the shops, and notably the book-shops. Martin and Mirmohamadi have devoted a chapter to the active, even excitable, ways in which fashionable and often young women engaged with literature by authors like Braddon, and by extension Hume, and Sussex has noted that of the four remaining copies of the Australian edition three were evidently owned by young women.[15] But Hume was not the first to take this path in the city. Apparently unknown to most scholars of Australian literature is the 1873 novel by Donald Cameron, unconcealingly entitled *The Mysteries of Melbourne Life*.[16] Cameron was still about in Hume's Melbourne: he had been a member of state parliament for the very distant seat of West Bourke in 1877–80, Ned Kelly's first self-exculpating letter was directed to him in December 1878, and he wrote fiction steadily until his death in 1888.

Cameron's novel is set in Melbourne in the present, recognizing both that "Collins Street was now in all its glory" (7) and that the inner-city slums are both disgusting and dangerous. The central problem is conflict between three young men, one rich and landed, one a charming opportunist, and one a murderer—so, they are much like Fitzgerald, Whyte and Moreland.

Here they compete for one woman, but not a rich man's daughter, just the beautiful Linda. Though the story starts with a murder on the river-bank, its recurrent crimes are against Linda's marital choice, the charmer of the three, and they are brought about by the murderous friend, stimulated by a high-class prostitute, jealous of Linda. Hume has inserted a Green-style murder mystery into this world, but also re-deploys Cameron's sense of busy city mobility—cabs and trains are prominent in *The Mysteries of Melbourne Life.* The murderer is finally killed by a train, the city scenes are vigorous, and the climax is, like Hume's publication day, in Melbourne Cup Week where the police reveal their incompetence (and, in the case of Detective Meddle, corruption); the noble friend supervises the happy outcome, like a combination of Fitzgerald and Calton, but without their detective activity.

Cameron seems to provide for Hume a ready model of the busy but also mysterious city, but there are other stories in this modern mode, including Fortune in the *Australian Journal.* It is evidently an important part of Hume's success in Melbourne that he is offering a new type of Australian story, bound neither by the convict past nor the colonial present. He took advantage of this idea of modernity by recurrently realizing the vitality of the thriving city he had come to visit—Hume is, like Conan Doyle, Chandler, Paretsky and Rankin,[17] another novelist who uses crime fiction to create a vividly lasting memory of a city he did not grow up in.

He seems to have consciously recreated the exciting modern Melbourne: in his Preface Hume says "the story was written only to attract local attention," and a reminiscence of him published in *The Bulletin* of 1902 reports he told friends, as he was about to write his first novel "I'm going to put on the local colour with a spade."[18] The last chapter of the first part of the novel begins with an emphatic presentation of how "all fashionable Melbourne was doing the Block" (102), the city's shopping heart, at its busiest on a Saturday morning, hot already in late winter August:

> With regard to its "Block" Collins Street corresponds to New York's Broadway, London's Regent Street and Rotten Row, and to the Boulevards of Paris. It is on the Block that people show off their new dresses, bow to their friends, cut their enemies, and chatter small talk [102–03].

A parallel water-side sense of the unique Melbourne experience has already been offered as Gorby follows Fitzgerald and finds him on the St. Kilda esplanade

> watching the white waves breaking on the yellow sands, the long narrow pier running out like a black thread into the sheet of gleaming silver, and away in the distance the long line of the Williamstown lights like a fairy illumination.

> Over all this fantastic scene of land and water was a sky such as Doré loved—
> great heavy masses of rain clouds heaped one on top of the other like the rocks
> the Titans piled up to reach Olympus [77].

The same pair share the landlocked "but equally classical beauty" of a Melbourne park a little later as Gorby follows Fitzgerald through the Treasury
Gardens

> along that noble avenue of elms, which were in their winter dress, and the moon
> shining through their branches wrought fantastic tracery on the smooth asphalt
> beneath. And on either side Gorby could see the dim white forms of the old
> Greek gods and goddesses ...

They leave the gardens memorably "by the end gate, near which stands the
statue of the Dancing Faun, with the great bush of scarlet geranium burning
like an altar before it" (83).

Not everything is urban glamor—Hume also gives a full account of
busy Bourke Street at night where the "restless crowd which jostles and
pushes along the pavements is grimy in the main, but the grimyness is
lightened in many places by the presence of the ladies of the *demi-monde*,
who flaunt about in gorgeous robes of the brightest colours" (175) and not
far away are "the darkness and narrowness of the lanes" and many a "low,
dark, ill-smelling passage" (180) in the criminal slum off Little Bourke
Street—where the classical resemblance is to Dante's "Infernal Regions"
(179) and the modem avatar is stated to be London's ferocious Seven Dials.
Two recent critics have linked Hume's dark scenes of this kind to *fin de
siècle* slum literature in general, and seen this as a major theme of the novel,[19]
but the extent of the scenes is limited and all the residents who play a part
there are dead or become respectable by the end. However, the swearing
of Mother Guttersnipe in the first Melbourne and London editions is quite
strong, and in his 1895 Preface Hume said he had painted "perhaps too
vivid a picture of her language and personality. These I have toned down
in the present edition."[20]

The final set-piece is a hot Christmas in the country at Frettlby's
property Yabba Yallook, where Madge sits on "the wide verandah" and stares
"at the wide plains lying parched and arid under the blazing sun" (250).
But this hot dry environment can be recuperated for culture, and she also
looks at the garden, seeing

> great bushes of oleanders, with their bright pink blossoms, luxurious rose trees,
> with their yellow, red and white flowers. And all along the border a rainbow of
> many-coloured flowers, with such brilliant tints that the eye ached to see them
> in the hot sunshine, and turned restfully to the cool green of the trees which
> encircled the lawn. In the centre was a round pool, surrounded by a ring of white

marble, and containing a still sheet of water, which flashed like a mirror in the binding light [250].

By representing the city and its wider context in such emotive and memorable detail, Hume was no doubt calling on self-identification in his audience, much as a century later writers like Helen Garner and Peter Corris would engage modern Australians by setting novels in their self-consciously independent cities of Melbourne and Sydney—that was in response to Britain's new Europe-oriented isolationism. Hume's instinct was to capture an earlier and exotic world, without the negative past connections or the rural fantasies that Australian literature had been dominated by in the past—and still would be for decades to come.

But there is also distance, in a real sense. For all its detail and investment in modern Melbourne, this is also not ultimately an Australian story. Brian and Madge in the final words sail away "towards the old world and the new life" (410). The novel, like its future fame, and very soon its author, moves on, away to old Europe. That is where its best-seller status was fully established, and it is appropriate to consider what aspects of the novel led to its remarkable achievements in the London of 1887–88.

Success in London

A major feature of the London success of *The Mystery of a Hansom Cab* was its marketing. Having seen the novel catch on in Melbourne, Trischler had some confidence, and with Jessie Taylor's support a good deal of money. It has long been known that the novel was well publicized, but Sussex's research provides specific details. Innovatively, a "prospectus" about the book was sent by Trischler to newspapers, "as if floating a mining concern."[21] In this he called the book "a Literary Tribute to the Mother Country"—somewhat enigmatically, it would seem, as people from the mother country only cause trouble in the story—and claimed sales of 25,000 in three days in Melbourne. Journalists picked up the prospectus as in itself a news item, and Trischler also advertised very widely, stating, "The one topic of conversation in London literary circles is the phenomenal success that has attended the publication in England of the Australian novel, 'The Mystery of a Hansom Cab.'"[22] These moves were successful—from November 1887 the novel was printed and sold at a rate of 25,000 copies a month for over a year.

But there was necessarily some quality of content that meshed with the publicity. One element, in London as much as Melbourne, must have been the direct and accessible style of the novel. While *The Leavenworth Case* has similarities in its use of legal scenes and detection in a major city to uncover an unsuspected murderer, Green's style of writing is quite formal and distant. In the same way, though Braddon and Collins had produced novels about sensation and crime, their tone is inherently elevated and knowing, seeming to be a literary gift to the reader. Hume's work reads much more plainly and directly, he moves the story on a good deal more quickly than the others. The comparison is remarkably like setting the first Sherlock Holmes short stories, with their sharp pace and wit, against the often boring, sententious and self-aggrandizing stories and articles that also appeared in *The Strand Magazine* in 1891.

If the tone of the novel seems new and briskly urban, its format also had innovative force. The Braddon and Collins model was at least twice as long, and the one-volume cheap novel was quite new. There had been single-volume stories in the past like Charles Warren Adams's relatively short *The Notting Hill Mystery* of 1865 (only about 80,000 words, published under the pseudonym "Charles Felix"), but it had appeared in installments in 1862–63 and is through its use of the epistolary mode quite antique in form, though also an innovative achievement with its murder by mesmeric transference. Peter Drexler has argued that the single-volume form which was increasingly popular in the 1880s itself led to "a resurgence of detective themes,"[23] as the three-volume novel did not focus so much, or so early, on investigating a mystery, but had extensive character- and sensation-based issues to handle.

There was also an element of innovation in the way Hume handles his Australian setting and theme. England-based novels had long used sequences in one of what were consistently called "the colonies." As Coral Lansbury has shown,[24] novelists like Lytton, Kingsley and Trollope routinely sent a character to Australia to experience living in the huge and often threatening, as well as ultimately lucrative, country. They usually brought the characters back with plenty of money—Charles Reade did it moralistically in the very popular *It is Never Too Late to Mend* (1856), Dickens ironically in *Great Expectations* (1861). In the very popular crime-without-detection narratives such as those produced by Reynolds (see pp. 135–47), not read by literary critics but consumed by thousands of readers, it is not uncommon for an English criminal to escape from transportation (however improbable that actually was) and return to England for vengeance, or just continued criminality.

Hume's novel uses none of the traditional Australian themes of convictism and bush life, and the interest in its setting for Londoners might well be linked to the late 19th-century widening awareness in the actualities of the overseas and imperial world. While it has often been fashionable among scholars, especially Americans with their sense of having eluded empire early, to see imperial themes in early 19th-century literature, the emergence of actual recognition of England's imperial status is quite late—as is argued in Chapter 7, Conan Doyle's use of characters returning somewhat damaged by empire, like Watson himself and a number of the criminals, is notably original. After Conan Doyle, Stevenson was to amplify this new awareness before its major development by Conrad and Kipling. Hume's account of the complex city life of Melbourne has innovative force, exposing both the threats and the attractions of the modern nature of the empire to readers back at home.

It has always been tempting, especially with the curious propinquity in time, both of birth and publication, of Hume and Conan Doyle, to see *The Mystery of a Hansom Cab* as an achievement swamped by the Sherlock Holmes phenomenon, and Hume's failure to produce another major seller seems part of that formation as well. But the collocation also points to a special feature of Hume's work—it does not offer the consoling simplification of the great detective, that narrative sedative which has been so compelling a force on anxious readers over time. *The Mystery of a Hansom Cab* can be read as the culmination of the broad-based 19th-century tradition of mysteries that are resolved through a variety of means, not just a genius detective, and so resemble much more closely the actuality of events in society rather than the simplistic romanticism of the all-knowing inquirer. In this model, which is shared by Collins and Braddon, and by Dickens in *Bleak House*, and was no doubt to be the basic revelatory method of *The Mystery of Edwin Drood*, the truth emerges through the interaction and efforts of the characters and also events as they develop.

This can be seen as the tradition of Balzac—and is also the basis for the all-conquering Mysteries, those of Paris by Sue and of London by Reynolds, and others around the world from St Petersburg to New York and even the Vatican.[25] But it was also recognized in London as a central element in its persuasive quality of Hume's novel. One of Trischler's many activities was to seek a review from Clement Scott, a literary journalist who had in 1884–85 published some of Hume's poems in the magazine he edited, *Theatre*. He wrote a long review for *Echoes of the Week*, edited by George Augustus Sala, who had famously visited Australia in 1885, and christened "Marvellous Melbourne." The review appeared on December 3, 1887, a fine book-buying time of year: in his 1895 Preface Hume called it "a very kind and generous criticism."[26]

Scott stresses many of the novel's innovations. He starts by noting it is quite short and might be seen as a "shilling shocker."[27] He agrees that "sensational it may be called" but insists that here the term "means sustained interest, artistic treatment and dramatic glory": he also insists "it is a pure book, it is a good book." (157) This mix of excitement and values is up-to-date: the characters "all wear modern dress. They all speak colloquial English" (158). The novel is also realistic, especially downwards: he comments on the social range and realism—"the hags and harridans, the dissolute and the drunken of lower Melbourne life speak with their accustomed coarseness, and act with the conventional brutality" (158).

The review does not however talk about the quality of detection or the personality of the detectives: the Sherlock Holmes pattern is not yet born, Dupin's position has not yet been apotheosized. Instead, the climax of Scott's praise is for the complexity of the puzzles and their resolution. He concludes, "It is a tale of accusation, of doubt, distrust, and the complications of evidence, and those who take the book up, be they lawyers or laymen, are not likely to put it down until it has been finished" (158).

This account indicates, as does a well-informed modern reading, that *The Mystery of a Hansom Cab is* the culmination of the tradition of the mystery novel—before it is displaced by and into the heroic detective story. That overall coherence and strength, allied to its good publicity and the innovative nature of its setting and treatment, appear to be the basis for its sudden acceptance as a major success. *The Leavenworth Case*, bringing formal discipline to the structure that Gaboriau had developed, was an achievement of the same kind as Hume's in terms of quality and public acceptance, but the French and the American authors had both already foreshadowed the triumph of the all-knowing detective over the ambiguities of plot-based discovery. Hume coupled modernity of attitudes and a setting both exotic and familiar, with the socially mimetic drama of the mystery story resolved by broad-based causes.

The dynamic encounter of mystery and sensation, before the closure of the fully-controlled detective story of Sherlock Holmes and the early 20th century, is a crucial, deeply effective basis of the power of Hume's novel. Though more recently writers like "Francis Iles," Julian Symons and Margaret Millar have worked hard to resurrect the mystery form from the imperialism of the detectives, Hume's novel retains its status as the best, and last, of a long tradition of balancing a recognition of the threats of crime and an aspiration towards the possibilities of discovering their causes, human, social, and psychological.

No Next Cab

The massive success of the novel had immediate impact. In mid–1887 Francis Adams, an English *litterateur* in Melbourne, produced, apparently in three days,[28] *Madeline Brown's Murderer:* he was made by Kemp and Boyce, Hume's now quite wealthy publisher, to use the subtitle of *The Mystery of a Hansom Cab*, "A Realistic and Sensational Novel"—in the proofs he desensationalized it to "Madeline Brown: Australian Social Life," but his change was ignored.[29] A closer imitation-cum-repetition was Henry Hoyte's *The Tramway Tragedy*, also from Kemp and Boyce in mid–1887, but though trams had just been introduced to Melbourne this was set in inner Sydney; it is a well-constructed body-substitution mystery, with a less than effective detective named Geoffrey Hamlin, recalling the title of Henry Kingsley's well-known rural Australian crime-focused novel *The Recollections of Geoffry Hamlyn* (1859). It also shares Hume's theatrical structure, being deliberately offered in "Five Acts" and is dedicated to "The Theatrical Profession."

Even stronger evidence of the power of *The Mystery of a Hansom Cab* was the London parody *The Mystery of a Wheelbarrow* by an author named "W. Humer Ferguson," a full-length, determined, even obsessive, parody of Hume's novel, with the sub-title *Gaboriau Gaborooed: An idealistic story of a great and rising colony*. The comic cover (Figure 16) calls it "An Australian Blood-Curdling Romance" but the publisher's name, Walter Scott, is, surprisingly, not another joke—at the end they advertise pages of their respectable fiction and classic poetry. The action largely follows the original novel, with the body of Oliver Black in a wheelbarrow, not a cab; it will be revealed he was murdered by Lessland. Suspected is Fitzdoodle O'Brien, who loves Peggy, daughter of Fred Frecklenose, but is exculpated through the dealings of lawyer Caldron and the detectives Clawby and Cowslip. For the joke to have seemed worth sustaining so long, and so ponderously, the impact of the inspiration must have been remarkable.

The period offered little better than shadows of Hume's work, and that, sadly, would also be his own authorial fate. Two more novels are set in Melbourne—*Madame Midas* (1888), a melodrama about a very rich woman who owns a gold mine is based on the real Alice Cornwell who went on to buy London's *Sunday Times* long before that modern Australian Midas, Rupert Murdoch. This is effective, re-uses Kilsip, has a new strong central young woman, and sold reasonably well in both Melbourne and London. The semi-sequel *Miss Mephistopheles* (1890) is both slighter—it even drew on Adams's *Madeline Brown's Murderer* for material—and sold disappointingly.

Figure 16. *The Mystery of a Wheelbarrow* cover. Cover of W. Ferguson Humer, *The Mystery of Wheelbarrow* (London: Walter Scott Publishing, 1888), copy in Rare Books, Baillieu Library, University of Melbourne.

In England from 1888, Hume kept writing. He had no real success in theatre but there were some pieces of successful work. The *Hagar of the Pawnshop* collection (1898) (discussed as female detective stories in Chapter 4, pp. 124–25), where the young gypsy girl inquires with recurrent success into mysteries that pass her way, deserves re-reading as a contemporary social commentary, and Hume created a credible series detective in Octavius Fanks of Scotland Yard: he assumes the role of Octavius Rixton, West End gentleman, to gather information, but the four Fanks novels, starting with *Monsieur Jules* (1892) are fairly slow-moving and uninterestingly written. Hume's novels seem to lack the spirited setting and action that he offered in his first effort, and at times they can seem almost casual in the structure and writing—the very short *A Midnight Mystery* (1894) suggests that Hume could be less than dedicated in his work.

Never able to move into the new mode of the character-rich and confidence-bestowing detective figure, and losing the power, perhaps through being a stranger in the structurally elusive social world of England, to construct a socially dynamic mystery and its resolution, Hume lived a simple, even humble life, dying alone and poor in 1932. He became a theosophist, one seeking esoteric knowledge into the mysteries of humanity, nature and divinity, an interest which seems entirely understandable for a man who had experienced such strange extremes as a writer of crime fiction—at first exceptional, if under-rewarded, success, and then a recurrence of unremarkable monotony in both the novels and his life.

CHAPTER 7

Watson's Wound and the Speckled Band: Imperial Threats and English Crimes in Conan Doyle's Fiction

Crime and Imperialism

The world of Sherlock Holmes is suffused with an awareness of Britain's sea-based international contacts. Sometimes the imperial connections seem casual or innocent, like the Chinese tattoo borne by Jabez Wilson in "The Red-Headed League" or the Indian seaman landlord who is wrongly suspected of murder in "The Man with the Twisted Lip." But it is more usual for there to be something threatening in the influence of the world across the oceans—not only in the British political empire itself, but in the country's wider business connections, including China and Central and South America. Sometimes the products of empire are merely causes for crime, not motives, nor criminals. In "A Case of Identity" Mary Sutherland's money comes from an uncle in Auckland, and that is what her stepfather is primarily after when he humiliates—and in a way violates—her by masquerading as a fiancé. In the same mode, the much-desired "Blue Carbuncle" derives from the Amoy River in South China, but a loss of international wealth can also trigger crime: the trouble for "The Stockbroker's Clerk" starts with the failure of a Venezuelan loan.

These references come in early Holmes short stories, all but "The Stockbroker's Clerk" being in the first series, *The Adventures of Sherlock Holmes* (1892), and that is in the second, *The Memoirs of Sherlock Holmes* (1894).[1] While the later stories tend to move away from imperial and empire-related themes, as will be discussed below, in his early material Conan Doyle seems highly aware of ways in which the imperial connections can be negative for people back in the country of origin. The international impact can operate either upon a victim, such as Watson and his wound, or through a villain, as in a series of travelers who return to Britain and bring with them the danger of the imperial project. Through their impact London can be characterized in *The Sign of the Four* (1890)[2] as a kind of jungle, an "eerie city" "with monster tentacles" that can be home to a "wild, dark business"[3] in which the negative features of imperial behavior are imported.

This alarming return of empire to terrorize its point of origin, this suggestion of the dark side of the imperial project, is a striking feature of Conan Doyle's work. In his study of literature and empire Joseph McLaughlin talks of London as "the most dynamic frontier of the empire,"[4] but does not trace the idea before Conan Doyle: this appears to be an area in which Conan Doyle is notably progressive, at least in his earlier work. But that is not a uniform or simple pattern in his fiction and deserves to be looked at both in terms of its own inherent complexity in the Sherlock Holmes stories, and also in the wider context of previous and contemporary ideas of crime and internationalism.

Before Conan Doyle, there had been some associations of empire and crime. The imperial returnee in general fiction might have many characteristics, not only malign ones. Jos Sedley in Thackeray's *Vanity Fair* (1848) is merely rich, foolish and vulgar, but a few returned-officer criminals lurk in the undergrowth of mid-century periodical crime fiction, and ticket-of-leave men were held to be leaders in the garroting panics of 1850s London. Villains whose service in the imperial military seems part of their threat are found in "Circumstantial Evidence," one of the "Experiences of a Barrister" stories published in 1850, and in "The Two Widows," from the second series of the "Waters" police detective stories (1859) by "William Russell," there appears Captain Burt, "a grim Indian sun-bronzed veteran," who is involved in abduction and interference in the exploitation of an over-trusting widow, but he is confidently frustrated by the detective.[5]

These seem rare instances among many stories, but interweaving empire and crime is the recurrence of transportation to Australia as a punishment feared a good deal more than imprisonment, even if on the hulks. Dickens included a story about this, "The Convict's Return," in *The Pickwick Papers* (1836–37), but there is no Australian detail, just an undramatic, humble and Christian return to England when the sentence finishes. Convict returnees play a minor role in both *Oliver Twist* (1837–38) and *Nicholas Nickleby* (1838–39) but, as Grace Moore notes, they only operate as minor and grim memories.[6]

Transportation stories soon become a good deal more melodramatic.

In the multi-volume narratives by G.W.M. Reynolds, *The Mysteries of London* (1845–48) and *The Mysteries of the Court of London* (1849–56), characters are quite often sentenced to the colony but by influence or good fortune have their sentences commuted and soon return to the action. There are also some improbable occasions when, as with Crankey Jem, in Volume 2 of *The Mysteries of London* (1846), he manages to escape from transportation and return to Britain. Jem's case is a fairly detailed and mostly accurately-described one—Reynolds had no doubt read accounts of the convict world like the well-known *The Memoirs of James Hardy Vaux* (1819, republished in 1827). He has Jem work in a Port Macquarie logging camp (though he later seems to confuse it with the very different Macquarie Island), and then escape into the bush with two other transportees from Volume 1 of *The Mysteries,* the crooked lawyer MacChizzle and the property fraud Stephens. These three at least refrain from eating human flesh during their long and difficult time on the run, but are recaptured. Jem is then sent to Norfolk Island, but eventually escapes with others on a boat; when it sinks off New Zealand he is the only survivor, and having represented himself as merely a seaman is brought back on the rescuers' ship to London—where he resumes an important part in the action as the enemy, and eventually the nemesis, of the main criminal, the money-demanding, body-snatching and murdering Resurrection Man.

Remarkable as Jem's story is, there are equally improbable fictional accounts of escape from transportation, not restricted to men. In the second narrative sequence of *The Mysteries of London*, Volumes 3–4 (1847–48: each pair of volumes is a coherent "series" as Reynolds named them) Mrs. Slingsby is a dubious character, just short of a brothel-keeper, with several lovers and husbands. She eventually evades a charge of murdering a rich elderly lover—whom she was in fact helping to deflower an innocent girl, the beloved of her nephew—and she is transported merely for forgery in Volume 3. Many years later, towards the end of volume 4, she returns from Sydney, apparently escaped, or possibly time-served, with the daughter who was born in Newgate, the appropriately named Perdita—meaning in Latin "lost girl." She is a great beauty but shares her mother's personality flaws, and the pair of them, under many names, raid wealthy male society with great vigor and some success, until the mother is killed by accident when trying, with a thuggish accomplice, to rob her daughter's house; shortly afterwards the daughter is murdered by one of the two men to whom she is currently married.

Richly melodramatic as these adventures are, well-designed to enthrall the audience who consumed in great numbers the eight-page weekly episodes, each costing one penny, and having one illustration, Reynolds's transportation dramas have at least some sense of reality, unlike the extravaganza offered by the popular mid-century French writer Paul Féval. In *Les Mystères de Londres* (1843)—which, as discussed in Chapter 2, pp. 50–51, borrowed and displaced Eugène Sue's idea of urban narrative in *Les Mystères de Paris* a year before Reynolds did rather more substantially. It features a frenetic plot led by an Irish patriot, Fergus O'Brien, to blow up the Houses of Parliament and the Bank of England and reclaim Britain for the combined forces of Ireland and France—he was given the blessing of Napoléon himself at St. Helena 15 years ago. As if to validate this bold narrative, Fergus has escaped from transportation to a rather vaguely conceived New South Wales—Féval not only misspells Sydney as Sidney, but also locates a huge tropical forest just outside the non-tropical town. Fergus and his convict friends seize an 18-gun navy sloop and he ranges the world as a pirate captain for four years, amassing a huge fortune and making diplomatic connections, notably with Russia, Brazil and Portugal, who all enthusiastically support his planned take-over of Britain. Fergus's deeply unlikely escape from transportation was evidently based on a real parallel, the convict seizure from the coast south of Sydney of the brig "Cyprus" in 1829, but that remarkable attempt at freedom ultimately failed, and the escapees were captured in Canton.

Imperial Crime: Australia

The idea of the return from empire, usually Australia, was itself a feature, if a less melodramatic and crime-related one, in general English fiction. As Coral Lansbury outlines in *Arcady in Australia*,[7] a recurrent theme in mid-century novels was the exotic and exciting nature of the Australian bush, but so was the possibility of English emigrants returning with substantial wealth. The major source of the idea was Samuel Sidney, to whom Lansbury devotes an entire chapter, as writing recurrently about Australia as an ideal country with "a working-class Arcady in the bush."[8] Though he never visited Australia, he deliberately gave the impression of authenticity and authority, starting with his first title *A Voice from the Far Interior of Australia* (1847). He influenced Dickens especially through his extremely popular *Australian Hand-book* (1848), which was repeatedly referenced in *Household Words*: he contributed six essays to the magazine in its first year, 1850.

Novels on this basis appeared, such as Lytton's *The Caxtons* (1849), where the hero and two friends, all in difficult circumstances in England, go out and make money: the hero and one friend return enriched and save their families from the disgrace of relative poverty. The book was very popular, and Dickens appears to have drawn upon it for the Micawber in Australia sequences in *David Copperfield* (1850).[9] A pattern similar to Lytton's is followed by Charles Reade in his very successful *It Is Never Too Late to Mend* (1856), and an even blander account was given by Henry Kingsley, brother to the very successful novelist Charles, but himself a failed gold-seeker in the 1850s. The effect of his actually visiting Australia was, as Lansbury comments, that he filled *The Recollections of Geoffrey Hamlyn* (1859) "with every known cliché of Australian life" and in it "every known popular anecdote about Australian life is gathered up."[10]

This was a strongly pro-empire context, combining the excitements of an amazing new land with the prospect of real financial gain, but there is also a recurrent sense, especially for Lytton, that the emergent Australian society is without the strains and dramas of modern industrial and urban Britain. The social myth of the bush is felt attractive: its largely egalitarian attitudes and its strong connections with nature, both sensational and benevolent, seem the structures of a better and as far as contemporary Britain was concerned a past world. Lansbury sees the attitude as "an elegy to a way of life that had passed away before the age of industry and machines,"[11] and in this respect the Australian myth is like a distance-based version of the time-constructed medievalism that was attractive to many in England who were seeking relief from the strains of modernity: David Matthews draws attention to a "Romantic Middle Ages," a time of "romance and chivalric deeds, but also of simple communitarian living and humanely organized labour, a pastoral time when the cash nexus was unknown, a time of intense romantic love," and he later notes that "in their different ways, Ruskin, Carlyle, Morris and Disraeli yearn for some kind of return to the Middle Ages."[12]

There was much to admire and approve for writers of fiction in the Australian version of empire, though most of the responses were hardly complex. An interesting contradiction of that situation, and an ironic engagement with the whole myth of the wealthy criminal colony, is one of the many challenging elements of Dickens' *Great Expectations* (1861) in that the convict Magwitch is, in one of the novel's many fallacious expectations, seen as likely to be both threatening and an embarrassment on his return like Reynold's Cranky Jem or Mrs. Slingsby. But in fact he turns out to be the other kind of returnee—wealthy and benevolent, in spite of his not fitting that model in terms of, again, the expectations of his class, and though he dies content to hear from Pip that his child Estella has thrived, he is also in the prison hospital under threat of a death sentence.

Imperial Crime: India

The treatment of India in fiction was quite different from that of Australia. As Mukherjee shows,[13] English interest in Indian criminality was parallel to the home-based development of the Newgate novel, as expressed in William Hockley's series of novels starting with *Pandarung Hari* (1826) offering like others in the same mode what Mukherjee calls "a detailed representation of criminality and corruption that allegedly pervaded all layers of Indian society."[14] As in the Newgate novel, the narrative expressed with both excitement and alarms the potential power of the people who, it is felt, should be kept powerless. As Brantlinger outlines,[15] the phenomenon of Thuggee was frequently taken as an archetype of colonial criminality, going far back in time, and indicating by its disruptive and damaging effect an actual need for British rule. The theme emerged in factual, or allegedly factual, writing, including an 1853 essay in the authoritative imperial journal the *British and Foreign Review* by Philip Meadows Taylor, who had already produced the novel *Confessions of a Thug* (1839), which was decidedly popular—Queen Victoria is said to have sent for the proofs, she was so keen to read it. Meadows Taylor, who had been a police superintendent in India in the 1820s, Brantlinger comments, "showed the worst side of Hinduism to British readers."[16] In his second novel, *Tippoo Sultaun* (1840), Meadows Taylor continues to represent the need for British control over native disorder, in this case a great sultan who is seen as effectively criminal, but the novel, apparently responding to contemporary accounts of real imperial activities, does also show the British army as violent and notes that official versions and imperial reality can be at odds. The same motif, suggesting that for all their confidence in doing good, the colonialists inevitably have recourse to their own crimes and breaches of order, is found in *Long Engagements* (1846), a novel whose title suggests the situation is not at all simple—its author J.W. Kaye was an Indian army officer who returned to London, worked as a writer and then held a position in the India Office.

After 1857, when occurred what the English called, and still do, "The Indian Mutiny"—for most Indians it remains a justified rebellion—there was a flood of factual England-based writing deploring the events as treason, first, as Brantlinger reports, "sensational eyewitness accounts" and then "histories" which could be like Sir George Trevelyan's *Cawnpore* (1865), both savage and inaccurate.[17] As Mukherjee notes, a more subtle conservatism is found in George Lawrence's *Maurice Dering* (1864), which essentially both "questioned that version of 'criminal India,' and struggled to restore the idea of enlightened colonialist rule and its future in India."[18] The theme was popular: Henry Kingsley returned to imperial fiction, in India this time with *Stretton* (1869), a relatively unsuccessful and banal novel. Meadows Taylor's *Seeta* (1872) works much harder towards a liberal reading of the situation: Brandon, a serious and successful administrator, loves the Princess Seeta and marries her in a Hindu ceremony. Both are ostracized by their own contexts, and all will end in tragedy. The novel does indicate that the sepoys were goaded towards mutiny, though the imperial theme is inherently supported by Brandon, hoping Seeta will eventually become a Christian, which she does move towards in her death scene. The novel is, though, not so much a rejection of empire as, Brantlinger comments, "a moral idealism that calls upon British imperialism to practice what it preaches."[19]

Crime fiction would also offer a moderated, even somewhat critical response to knee-jerk hostility to India and Indians, in Wilkie Collins' *The Moonstone* (1868). This was quite a radical step. Dickens was closely interested in events—his son Walter was in the British army in India in 1857 and although, as Moore comments, *Household Words* had made through the 1850s "repeated exposures of the brutalities committed in the name of the company,"[20] Dickens reacted negatively to the events. Moore shows that the essays on India printed in *Household Words* in later 1857 were quite moderate, but for Christmas that year Dickens, with Collins writing one chapter (which is frequently omitted from later editions), produced a novella *The Perils of Certain English Prisoners*. This is set on an island off Belize in the Caribbean, but, as Dickens indicated in a letter to Mrs. Burdett Coutts,[21] is basically very hostile to the events in India: it is a conscious displacement from the East to the West Indies, treating the natives as treacherous criminals, especially vile in their treatment of women, as had been widely and sensationally reported of Indian soldiers in 1857. As Siddiqi puts it, this is the "first Mutiny story to be written in England."[22]

Garrett Ziegler has shown that in his chapter Collins "undermines the imperial ideologies and anxieties"[23] of Dickens' material with ironic elements, making a pirate captain prefer men to women and a comic English diplomat lose his mind. Collins certainly seems to have been less extreme about the 1857 events than Dickens and most others. He wrote an essay for an 1858 issue of *Household Words* which condemned anti–English violence but also praised as worth following the values of the Hindu and Islamic religions, and he seems to pursue this idea of distinct quality among colonized people in *The Moonstone*, also bringing to bear the idea that the colonists themselves might at times be involved in criminality. Collins' novel seems to predict Conan Doyle's concept of the unacceptable possibilities of imperialist aggression, reaching into criminality.

In *The Moonstone* the initial crime is theft and murder by a greedy white officer, Herncastle; after the great yellow diamond is stolen, it is brought to England and again stolen, this time by a hypocritical *haut bourgeois* called Ablewhite—evidently an ironic surname. None of the immediate suspects are guilty—not the reticent heroine, nor the lower-class servant, nor, especially, the three Brahmins who seek to restore the stone to its rightful religious home. Both the frame story and the dedicated behavior of the Indians offer serious challenges to mid-century English imperialism.

This complex interrogative novel finds greed and guilt at the heart of the English national enterprise, both international and domestic. Collins contrasts the casual criminality of the theft of the jewel by, it turns out, an apparently highly respectable Englishman against the supreme, skillful—and ultimately remorseless—commitment of the Indians. He goes further than this in questioning convention, by representing the only person who can understand events, and who sets up the revealing scene which explains the theft, as the half-white Ezra Jennings. He combines an understanding of science with an intuitive reading of other people, and his role supports that of the Brahmins as figures who are not English, but fully valued by the novel.

It is true, as Ashish Roy has argued—Mukherjee both reports and somewhat moderates his position[24]—that Collins does not reject empire as such, but appears to imagine, especially through the continued reporting and authority of Murthwaite at the end of the novel, that Britain will maintain its colonial rule, if hopefully in a less unacceptable fashion, but Collins' critique is still one of some weight and unusual independence at the time. It also has future effect: the mix of political skepticism and a sense of human complexity, even imposed misery, that are revealed as involved in the imperial project will recur in Conan Doyle's work.

Closer to Conan Doyle in time and place, and a fellow-graduate of the University of Edinburgh, though they apparently never met, was Robert Louis Stevenson. He offered much, notably the new idea of the degenerate beast at the heart of respectable urban man (*The Strange Case of Dr Jekyll and Mr Hyde*, 1886). But he also created the exotic all-knowing master of narrative ceremonies in modern London, Prince Florizel, featuring in the multi-novella series *New Arabian Nights* (1882). These books can be seen as providing in essential terms the basic pattern for both the villains and the hero for the Holmes saga. Stevenson also offered the core idea of Conan Doyle's first two Holmes novellas: American animosities causing chaos in London in *The Dynamiter* (1885) led to *A Study in Scarlet* (1887), and when Stevenson refocused the *Moonstone* concept as an Indian jewel-theft with its eventful aftermath in London in the *New Arabian Nights* story "The Rajah's Diamond," he provided the key to *The Sign of the Four*.

Imperial Crime and Conan Doyle

The well-known 19th-century anxiety about human degeneration lies behind Conan Doyle's sense of imperially generated errors, even monstrosities. While Utilitarians and Darwinists both imagined a steady improvement of species, human among them, other thinkers, especially in the context of urban crisis, speculated that humanity might go in the opposite direction—reverse evolution, or as Tennyson put it, when man "Reels back into the beast."[25] This is already a powerful motif in the series of *Mysteries*—of Paris, London, New York and Philadelphia—that thrived in the 1840s. A criminal character who ignores the conventions or the need for morality and good works is also a basis of the sensational novel: such aberrations of conventional morality and respectability include Sir Percival Glyde, hypocritical force of malice in Collins' *The Woman in White* (1860), Mary Braddon's Lady Audley, mistress of her own criminal secret, Sir Felix Levison, who in Ellen Wood's *East Lynne* (1860–61) plays the role of what Deborah Wynne calls "the dandy murderer,"[26] and Godfrey Ablewhite, the ultra-respectable gentleman who is eventually revealed as the thief of the Moonstone itself. The slide into the abyss of selfish crime is central to criminal motivation in mystery stories and novels. Many of Conan Doyle's stories, especially the early ones, follow the same path, showing bourgeois morality to be unstable, and the self-interest that is central to bourgeois activity to be easily enhanced into cunning aggression.

It could be argued, in skeptical mode, that Conan Doyle uses imperial monstrosities as a way of morally simplifying a challenge to English bourgeois morality, as a form of euphemizing displacement of actual local English criminality, much as he begins to use Moriarty as an all-purpose villain by the end of his second series of Holmes stories. But the amount and variety of overseas trouble and imperial monstrosities is so substantial, at least in Conan Doyle's earlier work, that a real cloud of doubt must be cast by them over the imperial adventure. The stories often reveal what Mukherjee calls "the murderous contradictions of imperial ideology" as people trained to use violence for imperial control turn their dangerous skills against their own people—or, to put it from a different evaluative position, still with Mukherjee, the texts realize an "awareness of the 'manufactured' nature of civilized norms."[27]

Conan Doyle had well before his Sherlock Holmes days been aware of the role of empire. In 1881 he published "The Gully of Bluemansdyke," a story set in Australia long before he visited it. Serialized in the empire-oriented *Boys' Own Paper*, this is basically an American-style vigilante adventure, where a brave young mounted police trooper proves himself, helped by a very large mature American, Chicago Bill. Bill is a veteran of the gold rushes in America and Australia, who is not only brave and supportive, and in an early scene he can read from a horse what has happened to its master. His skill in interpreting data may well look forward to Holmesian analysis, but here he primarily represents American male physicality in full benevolence. Though the story is firmly set in Australia, the heroes and villains all have overseas connections, and the colonial localizations can be vague—the place-names seem mostly to belong to either England (the town of Trafalgar) or New Zealand (the Tápu mountains), though the Wirriwa river's name has a credible indigeneity, which is more than can be said for the bushmaster snake (an American species) or the fact that at one point "a wombat rushed past to gain its burrow"[28]—this is a large slow earth-bound quadruped, that does indeed have a burrow but does not "rush" like any kangaroo or wallaby.

Another early story, "J. Habbakuk Jephson's Statement" (1883), is a less naïve and heroic representation of imperial activity, dealing with native resistance to Belgian African imperialism, and even involving an American violent pro-black "return to Africa" movement as an explanation of the mystery of the drifting, empty ship the Mary Celeste—here, as usual, misspelt as Marie Celeste. Conan Doyle would remain long concerned with this area and in later years wrote to the papers about Belgian malpractice in the Congo—it was on this subject that he agreed with Roger Casement, and that and his partial sympathy for the Irish cause, short of armed action, led him to speak up for Casement when he faced, and then suffered, execution in 1916.

Conan Doyle was also interested in India before producing in 1890 *The Sign of the Four*, and in that area felt both colonizers and colonized could behave in criminal ways. A story of some complexity is "The Mystery

of Uncle Jeremy's Household," published in early 1887, when he had com-
pleted *A Study in Scarlet* and was waiting for it to appear in *Beeton's Christ-mas Annual* late that year. As if in parallel to a Holmes story, a young
medical student named Lawrence visits the home of the uncle of his friend
John H. Thurston—Lawrence does most of the detecting, and his being
also the calm narrator is all that separates this substantially from the
Holmes-Watson structure. At the house there are complexities around a
governess, Miss Warrender. Her mother was English, her father an Indian
prince—her paternal blood-line, it finally appears, goes right back to
Genghis Khan. In a story combining a calm tone with highly melodramatic
material, she is revealed as herself one of the Thuggee, and has killed in
the past. But she is now involved in a local conflict based on sexual jealousy
by the uncle's secretary, who also wants his master's money. Threatened by
this domestic crime drama, Miss Warrender is rescued by a mysterious vis-iting Indian, also a Thug, who kills her enemy—as if her tainted past is
her salvation. She escapes from the threatening environment, and from both
the story and any evaluations of her position.

Siddiqi sees this story as having great importance in marking Conan
Doyle's complex response to empire: she comments that "the contours of
character and plot not only express but also contain anxieties about the
efficacy of imperial rule" and notes the story is "open-ended" without
"orderly or conclusive closure."[29] She sees Conan Doyle as here developing
hints from *The Moonstone*, and even suggests that the name Warrender is
a deliberate reference to the name of Rachel Verinder, the possessor of the
Moonstone, which she suggests sounds suspiciously like a Sikh name, and
so she hypothesizes that Collins had imagined the theft of the stone as
also the rape of Indian native innocence.[30]

While that might conceivably be a deep-laid element in Conan Doyle's
imagination, and that of Collins before him, the immediate and striking
power of the story is to realize a complex of guilt around an apparently
British woman, and also a sense of vulnerability in someone who is directly,
and not innocently, a product of empire. It is an imaginatively rich repre-sentation of Conan Doyle's awareness of "the anxiety of empire"—to use
the title of Siddiqi's book—which in his other stories will take more direct,
and so more readily contained, forms.

Conan Doyle wrote *The Mystery of Cloomber* (1889) in 1888 after he
had completed *A Study in Scarlet*. This novella of some 50,000 words deals
directly with imperial guilt—possibly to an extent which would later prove
bothersome, as this was omitted from the otherwise full and author-approved collection of his work known as the Crowborough edition of 1930.

The central character, Major-General Heatherstone, was a colonel in an Indian Army regiment in the First Afghan War. In 1841 he was responsible for a substantial number of native deaths, but the crucial event was when a Buddhist holy man of very high standing, Ghoolab Shah, addressed him, in good English, seeking a less aggressive approach—and Heatherstone killed him with his sword. He was visited that night by the apparently otherwise invisible leader of three avenging Buddhist priests, who said Ghoolab Shah would in time be avenged. Heatherstone had no remorse— he referred to his actions as "vermin killing,"[31] but the pressure he felt from occult powers, which included a recurrent hearing of a bell, led him before long to withdraw to a remote castle in Scotland, where he refused social acquaintance, kept lights burning at night, and was continuously on the watch—he suspects the narrator at first, as he has a somewhat dark complexion. On the fortieth anniversary of the killing he is visited there by what Barsham, one of the few critics to have discussed this story seriously, describes as "three avenging Buddhist chelas,"[32] and through their powers the general and a corporal who was with him at the murder are transported to their death in "the Bog of Cree" which is "a perfect maelstrom of mud" (250).

This drastic story of guilt and supernatural vengeance reads like a hyperbolic version of *The Moonstone*, but just as that offered English values as well as crimes, this story is told by a young law student from St Andrews University whose father is a great authority on Oriental and Sanskrit and is working on a translation of Buddhist holy texts. The scholar has some understanding of the events as they occur, and at the end of the story is appointed to a senior position in the library of the University of Edinburgh. He and his son take the view that science needs to give consideration to the possibility of occult forces, though Barsham goes further, suggesting Conan Doyle is implying that the English crimes of the general are both understood and sidelined through the sympathy and interest of the lawyer and his father, and that theirs is an essentially Scottish position, wiser than the brutal English imperialism of the general.[33]

The Sherlock Holmes saga is never as dark or as searching as this account, but the first we hear of empire is negative. As *A Study in Scarlet* begins, Watson has been wounded in the shoulder, and has been ill. His imperial service has left him shattered, poor, with no discernible future. Holmes helps resolve his problem as he will do those of so many others, but Watson's past is the only precisely imperial connection of *A Study in Scarlet*. Its international negative force is from America, which for Conan Doyle, with some evaluative distinction between North and South, is a major part of the overseas world that enriches his fiction and can overshadow his London. Conan Doyle was always fascinated by America: Mayne Reid and Bret Harte, yarn-spinners of masculine American adventure, were his early models, and he always believed in the link between Britain and America, hopefully even that they would make a political reunion. In 1891 he dedicated *The White Company* to "the Hope of the Future, the Reunion of the English Speaking Peoples"; he described the bond between America and England as "that deep-lying race feeling in the development of both countries."[34] Holmes himself advocates an Anglo-American "worldwide country" in "The Noble Bachelor."[35]

Like Stevenson's *The Dynamiter*—even embarrassingly like it—*A Study in Scarlet* explains contemporary disruption in London by a substantial digression into American history. It is so much an American book that an early stage version in the U.S. managed without Sherlock Holmes.[36] We learn of the brutal violence which has made, here in London, a cunning vengeful murderer out of Jefferson Hope—such a positive-sounding American name. But this, like the later *The Valley of Fear* (1915), is not in fact a critique of America as such, just of a doubtful and damaging element in America—in *A Study in Scarlet* the Mormons, in *The Valley of Fear* it will be workers' unions past and, by implication, present. The Mormons are represented as if they are themselves savages, in need of being imperially civilized, with their polygamy, their secrecy, their cruelty. The story basically absolves Jefferson Hope of crime, and he is permitted by the narrative to die in peace, having brought rough and ready justice to those who have destroyed his own happiness, traduced the name of America, and so damaged that "deep-lying race feeling" that Conan Doyle felt existed between America and Britain.

A British-focused version of the same pattern, inspired both by Stevenson's *The Rajah's Diamond* stories and *The Moonstone* was Conan Doyle's response to the commission offered—by the American *Lippincott's Magazine*—for what would become *The Sign of the Four*. Here Conan Doyle switches firmly to the context of imperial violence and theft. As in "The Rajah's Diamond," and *The Moonstone*, native riches are stolen, but the tone and ambience are less grand than in the source. It is treasure, not a stone of great religious meaning, that is stolen and the white officers dishonestly, disgracefully, hijack it from the original thieves, where Collins' diamond-stealer Herncastle was at least a real fighting gentleman. And rather than noble Brahmins seeking to recover their cultural treasure in England, in *The Sign of the Four* Conan Doyle has a disabled soldier, along with a savage pygmy, seek to steal again the stolen property. The imperial context is itself recurrently degraded, and that negativity is emphasized by the secretive, obsessive nature of Major Sholto, the thief who brought the treasure to England, and also by the feeble eccentricity of his son, who dies quite early in the story. There is a challenging, itself negative, hybridity about this relocation: the Sholtos are heavily orientalized, and yet they and the treasure have come to rest in bourgeois suburban outer London. Their address, Pondicherry Lodge, Upper Norwood, bespeaks this strange world, ambivalent in both cultural and moral terms.

The action follows suite. Holmes's rational deduction is, as so often, a set of show-pieces rather than a structural part of the narrative.[37] The real tracking is physical and quasi-imperial, as men with dogs hunt a savage through the streets. Then, even more imperial and military, comes a hectic armed chase on the river through the center of hyper-urban London, as if we are among wild nature, and the adventure ends with an exchange of gunfire and death in the water. The images quoted above of the city's "tentacles," its "eerie" quality and this as a "wild, dark business" all suggest that a world of savage natural violence has come to London—and has been attracted there by the ferocious reflex of empire. Where Watson was just wounded and alienated by his imperial adventure, now it is suggested that the far-flung world of savage conflict can rebound back to the center that stimulated it. The chase down the Thames is especially potent. Conrad in the opening of *Heart of Darkness* will deploy the same image of the river as the other heart, itself potentially dark, from which English maritime adventure began, but Conrad's image is more displaced and symbolic than Conan Doyle's direct realization of actual imperial violence on the river in the darkened heart of London. Brantlinger calls this kind of theme "Imperial Gothic," and sees an element of "cultural regression and social atavism," usually called "going native," typified by "white savages" like Conrad's Kurtz and the figures found in Stevenson's late, post–Holmes stories *The Beach at Falesa* (1892) and *The Ebb-Tide* (1895).[38] Conan Doyle, it seems, has not been given adequate credit for his innovative percipience.

Conan Doyle's Imperial Critique

The theme of regression, located across the world of imperial capitalism, is recurrent among the short stories of the first period—those collected in *The Adventures of Sherlock Holmes* and *The Memoirs of Sherlock Holmes*, before in 1893 Conan Doyle decided to free himself from his detective albatross and, in the last of the *Memoirs* stories, killed Holmes off in conflict with Professor Moriarty. There are other negative themes to be found in the stories: moral corruption among the English bourgeoisie is recurrent and there are a few thrusts at the degenerate aristocracy, including in the first story, "A Scandal in Bohemia," where the Prince of Wales is plainly in the dock; there are also a few strands of the "Eurocriminal" theme that will engage Holmes increasingly in the later stories. But the empire and international business and their potentially destructive impact at home also provide a significant theme in the first 24 short stories.[39]

A classic example is the fourth story in the first series, "The Boscombe Valley Mystery." Imperial connections seem to have become normal in the English countryside: the wealthy landowner John Turner "made his money in Australia" (77) and his neighbor Charles McCarthy is also an "ex–Australian" (77); Turner's son even wants to marry a barmaid who has a husband in the Bermuda dockyard. But this imperial domesticity can also bring deadly danger into the locale: McCarthy's body is found, and a verbal play links crime enigmatically to the colonies. As he dies, he says "a rat" (82), but only Holmes locates this apparently ethical critique in imperial geography: McCarthy and Turner fell out over events on the Victorian goldfield at Ballarat. The distinctive Australian bush cry of "Cooee" (82) is also used and this story suggests that the kind of men who are tough enough for success in the empire may well have done things and have personalities that are disturbing to the domestic English peacefulness.

A different international threat is central to "The Five Orange Pips," imbued with the British sense of a naval empire—Conan Doyle had already made major voyages himself as a ship's doctor to Greenland and West Africa—and finds ferocity stemming from the American south, formerly a prosperous part of the empire, closely linked to England and supported in the Civil War by a range of conservative British forces. The mild-mannered client has an uncle who was "a singular man, fierce and quick-tempered, very foul-mouthed when he was angry" (106). He became a fierce anti-black and the story involves Ku Klux Klan activities around the world including, it seems, in the continuing British empire—the Klan letter comes from Pondicherry in India, suggesting a subliminal link to the Sholto family of *The Sign of the Four*. The melodramatic story opens with terrible London weather as if the storm that will swallow the *Lone Star* is, like the dark side of empire, coming home. The story is a much more potent emotional experience than "The Boscombe Valley Mystery," and this process of intensifying emotion and drama is continued in "The Speckled Band," the most trenchant of Conan Doyle's stories about the dark side of empire.

Dr. Roylott has, like Watson, returned from India, but he bears no visible wound. As so often, a pale pretty girl, Miss Stoner, is the focus for threat. Roylott, her step-father, suffers "violence of temper approaching to mania" and this has been "intensified by his long residence in the tropics" (177). This curious *non sequitur*—how could heat alone invoke mania?—and the Doctor's interest in tropical animals suggests the form of inhuman degeneracy that he will soon reveal. The story toys with other possible threats—there are gypsies near the house, and a suggestion of a ghost story in the whistling at night. But in a well-managed piece of violent final action, Roylott represents the masculine, even incestuous, id rampant, forcing a snake through a hole in his step-daughter's bedroom wall. It is clear that he is a figure of taboo-ignoring desocialized male sexual violence—and financial violence, as he keeps the snake in a safe and is seeking his step-daughters' money more directly than their bodies. There are resemblances to the plot of "A Case of Identity," where an apparently harmless London step-father turns out to recycle himself as his typist step-daughter's fiancé, in order to retain within the family her money, itself from New Zealand. But that curious and ultimately impractical scheme has little contact with Dr. Roylott's murderous and sexually suggestive assaults on his step-daughters. Empire, it seems, has driven a fierce man totally wild.

These, as Holmes says, are "very deep waters" (182), and the story appears to suggest that the fine old Stoner house symbolizes English antiquity, at risk from these new forces liberated by empire, in a world where "a clever and ruthless man had an Eastern training" (200). Unlike the murderous Tonga of *The Sign of the Four*, a pygmy Andaman Islander who represented Eastern danger, if in a loyally pro–Englishman way, Roylott with his massive strength and uncontrollability, is a monster of degeneracy, and finally the swamp adder that was his phallic agent is wrapped around his head in a sign of the self-destroying element that Conan Doyle seems to detect, or want to detect, in the negative aspect of the imperial experience. Where Watson's wound was sudden and debilitating, the result of courage in a harsh context, Dr. Roylott's mania and wickedness are like a combination of the subhuman ferocity in "The Five Orange Pips" and the sense of inhuman behavior in "The Boscombe Valley Mystery."

It is also notable that the controlling power of Holmes's rationality, both cerebral order in general and his own powers of analysis, are put under real pressure by these imperial challenges: he is shown to connive at an essentially illegal but at least equitable injustice in "The Boscombe Valley Mystery"; he is actually defeated in the following story, "The Five Orange Pips," when the criminals sail away—apparently to death out at sea, but well out of Holmes's policing control; he has to resort to desperate and

Figure 17. Conan Doyle's Dr. Roylott dead, with the "swamp adder." Illustration by Sidney Paget to "The Speckled Band," Arthur Conan Doyle, *Sherlock Holmes, The Short Stories* (London: Murray, 1928), p. 149.

dangerous violence in "The Speckled Band," and the outcome is in fact brought about by Dr. Roylott's over-confident casualness with the allegedly deadly snake (Conan Doyle apparently invented the "swamp adder") that eventually wraps itself around his head and kills him (Figure 17).

Imperial threat returned to England is not Conan Doyle's only area of alarm, nor is empire, or former empire, always hostile. It is notable that North Americans in particular are often highly valued—as in "The Noble Bachelor" and "The Copper Beeches," and to them will be added the admirable black American John Hebron, the former husband in "The Yellow Face," early in the second series. Damaging criminal degeneracy can derive literally at home, as in "The Beryl Coronet" or, in the *Memoirs*, "Silver Blaze." Though this domestic treason may lack the high melodrama of the imperial stories, it can increasingly have a European dimension— or displacement—as with the German scientist criminal Dr. Stark in "The Engineer's Thumb" in the first series or, in the second series, "The Greek Interpreter," where foreign menace is not fully identified or deplored as such:

European enemies are not yet as clear as they will be in the approach to the First World War. In the same elusive way in the early "The Naval Treaty" the threat of serious espionage is strikingly dissolved into the familiar theme of domestic treachery for money.

The image of international danger is still present in the second series of *Memoirs*: "The Gloria Scott" is a curious mélange of "The Boscombe Valley Mystery" and "The Five Orange Pips," focusing on the wicked past of "rich colonials," this time at sea. The return of distant criminality is visited on a now respectable landed gentleman, through the hostile intervention of a returned convict. This raises what Siddiqi describes as the two levels of imperial criminals, the lower class and the officers, or workers and gentry. She sees this as a form of class vengeance: "The imperial vagabond is the nemesis of the successful repatriated colonial, destroying the latter's life in England."[40] Jonathan Small and the Sholtos in *The Sign of the Four* are instances of this division, and it recurs in "The Gloria Scott" where the crewman Hudson returns to disrupt the calm life of the wealthy returnee Trevor.

While "The Gloria Scott" has an air of repetition about it, another story has the highly-strung emotive grotesquerie of "The Speckled Band." In "The Crooked Man" the dark aftermath of military empire appears: a fine young soldier has been turned into bent beggar with a monkey, who again meets Nancy, his early beloved (Figure 18). But this story is imperially critical in a more complex way: the real degeneracy is in fact moral, and resides in the honored colonel who sent his rival in love on an impossible mission in order to destroy his attraction—and so created his present deformity. Where Dr. Roylott's focal image was that of a villain united with his degenerate selfishness, here the innocent is deeply marked by cruelty: "The man sat all twisted and huddled in his chair in a way which gave an indescribable impression of deformity, but the face which he turned towards us, though worn and swarthy, must at some time have been remarkable for its beauty" (453). Here sits a victim of imperial rage, the male version of Roylott's dead step-daughter.

Although the main thrust of Conan Doyle's concern in his first two series of Homes stories is how easily the respectable English bourgeoisie, both *grande* and *petite*, can turn to selfish crime, he reserves a substantial place for the imperial variant of that domestic vulnerability to disrupt order, and the exotic force of empire seems to combine with this anxiety about power to create some of Conan Doyle's most remarkable and unforgettable effects, as respectable humans exhibit new forms of degeneracy. The effect can be as direct as physical trauma—Watson's own wound, Jonathan Small's

Figure 18. Conan Doyle's "The Crooked Man" meets Nancy again. Illustration by Sidney Paget to "The Crooked Man," Arthur Conan Doyle, *Sherlock Holmes, The Short Stories* (London, Murray, 1928), p. 353.

lost leg in *The Sign of the Four*, the effect of apparent leprosy on Godfrey Emsworth in "The Blanched Soldier," and the physical debilitation of Henry Wood in "The Crooked Man." The damage may be psychic as with Dr. Roylott in "The Speckled Band," Colonel Sebastian Moran in "The Empty House," or Stapleton in *The Hound of the Baskervilles*, returned from South America with evil in his heart for his wealthy English family, and especially the admirable returnee from North America, Sir Henry Basker-ville—that related pair is another sign of the negative and positive doubling that Siddiqi finds in the imperial domain, and she discusses this as another form of "insurgency."[41]

A critical awareness of the negative possibilities of empire may be a result of Conan Doyle's own distance as being Scottish (and in part Irish), so giving him a sense not of Englishness but of British semi-colonial mar-ginality, as Barsham suggested in the context of *The Mystery of Cloomber*, or it may be a lesson learnt in his time as a ship's doctor on the Africa run as he saw empire in raw close-up. His vision, through the processes of crime fiction, of the dialectically negative impact of the skills and practices of imperial authority, when brought home, is quite searching, as was noticed by Edward Said in *Culture and Imperialism* when, speaking of Conan Doyle's Holmes and Colonel Creighton in Kipling's *Kim*, he said, "Colonial rule and crime detection almost gain the respectability and order of the classics or chemistry."[42]

Conan Doyle's imperially-conditioned criminals are officers retaining their rank, not outcasts, and their status and their legitimized authoritarian practices are part of the problem. The general in *The Mystery of Cloomber* is the most dramatic version, but the theme recurs, from the jewel-stealing officers of *The Sign of the Four* on. The colonel in "The Crooked Man" had the military power over his rival in love and used it as he would on a legit-imate enemy. Dr. Roylott mobilized his sexual obsessions with medico-scientific energy. After Conan Doyle, others will envisage the same potent figures, up to Conrad's partly benign Lord Jim and his wholly negative Mr. Kurtz. This reversed imperial activist, authority becoming malign, does not seem to be substantially realized before Conan Doyle: Collins' Herncastle is at most a partial, unexplored, off-stage indication of the possibility of this figure.

Conan Doyle Accepts Empire

But Conan Doyle did not keep up this critique. Towards the end of the second series the anxious self-representations of criminality, both domestic and imperial, were displaced and euphemized by the simplicity of an external master criminal in Moriarty. After Holmes was killed off by that anxiety-resolving force in 1893, Conan Doyle himself turned to other empires, the medieval English, the Napoleonic, and that of emergent science fiction. When he returned to a contemporary imperial topic, it was in a fully approbatory tone. He defended English practices in the Boer War against dissent in England, where the criticism included charges of cruel degeneracy inculcated by the exigencies of imperial rule—just what Conan Doyle had himself previously outlined. He first wrote an account of his own activities in Africa entitled *The Great Boer War* (1900), and in another, *The War in South Africa* (1901), he defended the empire against his own earlier kind of charges. For this he received a knighthood, though his own charitable medical activities in Africa themselves, as well as his literary fame, might well have contributed to the award.

Another major event was that in 1901 Conan Doyle agreed, for the then massive sum of £100 a thousand words (today at least a hundred times as much), to write a new Holmes story. Protecting his position, he set it back before Holmes died, but *The Hound of the Baskervilles* (1902) effectively initiated the second phase of Holmes stories. Having a primarily Gothic set-up with the alleged ghostly hound roaming the darkly romantic wastes of the south-western Dartmoor, the novella also exposed two quite differing views of criminality. Real London brutish crime was represented in the escaped convict, Selden, a savage murderer, a representative of simple native English bestiality. Yet he is hardly demonized: hiding among the stone-age huts, seen only at night, sympathized with by his respectable sister, herself working for the gentry, he seems a sadly lost part of the human family, and the plot makes him in fact another victim of the real criminal, Mr. Stapleton, the former school-master with his distant but obsessive claim to the Baskerville estate.

This rogue bourgeois is familiar in Conan Doyle's own stories from the past and is the sort of figure who is central to the clue-puzzle of the so-called "Golden Age" that is in full swing by the 1920s, when Holmes was still appearing. Stapleton's envy of family status and money are basically forms of domestic degeneracy, and no less threatening for that, and his alarming propinquity. But Conan Doyle over-determines such a local threat with a striking set of overseas features, positive and negative. The Baskerville wealth is of recent South African origin (just like Conan Doyle's own new dignities); Sir Henry, who inherits it, has spent most of his life in America, mostly north. As a result of this bracing location, it seems, he is an "alert, dark-eyed man," "very sturdily built, with thick, black eyebrows and a strong, pugnacious face" and is morally strong as well with "a steady eye and the quiet assurance of his bearing which indicated the gentleman."[43] Conan Doyle has Sir Henry bring new Yankee energy to the enervated English aristocracy: he belongs to it, strengthens it, and is in no way foreign.

It is that "deep-lying race-feeling" again: imperial wealth can have its own version of native authenticity.

But other characters are essentially foreign, in both origin and behavior. Stapleton, it turns out, is an overlooked Baskerville cousin brought up in Costa Rica, part of non–English speaking and so especially threatening Central America, and he has married a Costa Rican, "darker than any brunette whom I have seen in England," as Watson notes, with some racist undertone (307). Like any un–English husband, in theory at least, Stapleton treats her badly, and he elaborates the whole fiendish plot with its Gothic overtones and degenerate brutalities. Symbolized elsewhere by Dr. Roylott's swamp adder, here these are focused in the fearful marsh that both protects Stapleton's hound and finally swallows the aberrant regressive criminal in an English version of the naturalized vengeance found in imperial fiction with its fires, floods, and ferocious animals.

This finely-paced novella, the height of Conan Doyle's fictional craft, is also the last complex statement of his anxiety about invasive degeneracy, now located outside the empire. When he agreed to bring Holmes back to life in the third series of stories, *The Return of Sherlock Holmes* (serialized 1902–03, as collection, 1905), there are some flickers of the earlier "white savage" excitements but they tend to be contained or redirected. The first villain, assistant to the apparently dead Moriarty, is the brutal Colonel Moran, tiger hunter and human beast, who cheated at cards and "made India too hot to hold him" (581), but there is nothing more than his past to upbraid in imperial terms. It is true that he contributes to the "dark jungle of criminal London" (570), but his acts are London-located, not in any way imported from empire: he stalks Holmes with a western weapon, a high-powered airgun. The beasts, obsessions and degenerate narratives of the east are left behind: indeed the idea of using dum-dum bullets in an airgun has such a strained improbability that it seems imperial features are now used as inauthentic cranking-up of brief horror, not a structural source of degeneracy.

Similarly reduced and strained is the effect of the action and reference of "The Solitary Cyclist" in the third series. The usual pleasant maiden is harassed in the familiar false-lover way. The motive is, harking back to Boscombe Valley, colonial hostilities, but in South Africa this time—after the Boer War this country becomes Conan Doyle's favored and, if challenging, usually positive location. But here the crime is fully local in effect and impact. Woodley, the master-mind of the appropriation plot, may be like "a savage wild animal" (651) but nothing in the action has the melodrama or the excited perversity of the earlier imperial degeneracy stories.

In a later story in this third series, "Black Peter," the hero himself is an improbably extreme figure of violence. He was a South American whaler, and while certainly savage he is doubly displaced—he has not practiced his evil in England and in any case he is now dead, and Holmes both solves and forgives his murder. This is far indeed from a pygmy blowing deadly darts on the Thames or a maddened doctor assaulting young ladies with a deadly snake in the home counties.

Empire gains value in positive ways as well as by being displaced as the impetus of degeneracy. At the end of "The Three Students" the athletic young hero goes off to join the Rhodesian police, while in "The Abbey Grange" the South Australian beauty is the truest of all the characters and survives English malpractice. Villainy may now derive from American criminals ("The Dancing Men") and European threats ("The Golden-Pince Nez" and "The Six Napoleons"), or, mostly, from native British sources. Overall, empire is fading as a danger.

In the fourth series, *His Last Bow* (1917), some stories seem consciously to reverse the old imperial degeneracy theme. There is an Australian confidence man in "Lady Frances Carfax" but also a fine, if rough-looking, Englishman from South Africa; the displaced villain of "Wisteria Lodge," the "Tiger of San Pedro" (917) is evidently Hispanic, and Euro-villains are becoming visible—with Italians in part at least of "The Red Circle." The only real imperial drama is "The Devil's Foot" where an apparently fiendish South African poison is actually employed by a former explorer, but it is to avenge a crime, not to commit it. In the last collection, *The Case-Book of Sherlock Holmes* (1927) the tone of reversing earlier imperial critique is strong in "The Blanched Soldier," where it sounds as if, as actually occurred in "The Creeping Man," some terrible imperial crime is being covered up. In fact what Holmes eventually, and with some tact, reveals is that this family's son contacted leprosy through his soldierly courage in a native hospital, and he is now being lovingly and secretly tended at home. The Boers themselves are not as easily relieved of disgrace, appearing in this sequence, Siddiqi suggests, "as hapless victims, but degenerates nonetheless."[44] This reversal of the degeneracy theme is compounded when Holmes brings in an expert who shows it is not in fact true leprosy: the implication is that imperialism itself was never the disabling sickness that many adventures made us think, but just a challenging experience for brave young men and their families. The blanched soldier himself is a memory of the pale, decrepit isolated Watson with his wound, not an avatar of the maddened criminals with their imperially trained violence now let loose on their own fellow-citizens.

Goodbye to All That Imperial Crime

The later stories have some increasing emphasis on European villainy and even the South Americans are redeemed when, in "The Sussex Vampire," a melodramatically pitched and apparently heavily anti-foreigner story goes into reverse: the Peruvian wife is shown to the be the long-suffering protector of the child she shares with a true Briton—against her brutal but equally English stepson. In "Thor Bridge" there is a surviving South American fiend in the jealous Brazilian wife, but the worst she can do is commit suicide in an unsuccessful attempt to frame for her own murder the beautiful English governess of whom she is jealous. This strained improbability, a knee-jerk memory of foreign onslaught on English maidens, and failed at that, is a long way from the well-sustained pirates, killers and perverts of Conan Doyle's earlier vision of imperial degeneracy.

From 1902 on Conan Doyle revisits his old imperial theme basically to vary and dilute it, and to disavow the doubts about empire he communicated before. He has plenty of new enemies, mostly from the continent of Europe as the arms race grows—though never from France. Himself named Conan after a part–Breton relative and godfather, and awarding Holmes a French grandmother, Conan Doyle was *avant la lettre* an emblem of the *entente cordiale*. Italians and increasingly Germans are seen as potential degenerates, but without any of the tragic misdirection of the English imperial renegades of the early stories. American professional criminals continue to be a recurring theme, going back it would seem to Conan Doyle's earliest reading among the tough adventures of the American cheap press. Yet they too can be varied. The novella *The Valley of Fear* (1915) appears to return to the late 19th century in a story based on the "Molly Maguires," a violent labor gang operating in the 1880s, but Conan Doyle's account makes it clear that he is in fact responding with hostility to the new organization of the anarcho-syndicalist "Wobblies," the International Workers of the World, who were themselves infiltrated by the Pinkertons.

The American material was always for Conan Doyle in part a fantasy world of freedom—and also of fine sales and good commissions, going back to *The Sign of the Four*, but it was also a para-empire, a sadly lost land where white English culture could thrive and, alarmingly, sometimes go askew. In that way America was a benignly unforeign version of that wider world of empire and foreignness where Conan Doyle was one of the first to note that violence and cruelty were instruments of government, and that the negative impact on those who wielded those instruments could be substantial.

Conan Doyle and imperial crime travel a long journey from early anxieties, through mature concerns to senescent complacency. Watson's wound was loyal English painful suffering, part of the white man's imperial burden: the fact that it wandered from his shoulder in *A Study in Scarlet* to his leg in *The Sign of the Four* (and in "The Noble Bachelor" Watson only recalls it as being "in one of my limbs" [224]) suggests its systematic rather than symptomatic character. But the swamp adder that delivered to another English doctor returned from the tropics a wound both fatal and symbolic was of a much higher order of fictional imagination. It showed that Conan Doyle could offer a strikingly powerful critique of some aspects of his society, in advance of writers usually thought more politically and imperially searching, notably Stevenson and Conrad.

It does also suggest the question what he had in mind by giving his hero the domestic surname Holmes—just what was he suggesting were the disturbing forces at work in the homes of English bourgeois, in their uneasy comfort in their post-imperial society, a world and a world-view at times so well-revealed in the equally contemporary, equally complex, equally complicit, empire of crime fiction.

Chapter Notes

Chapter 1

1. *The Oxford Companion to Crime and Mystery*, ed. Rosemary Herbert (New York: Oxford University Press, 1999).

2. Larry N. Landrum, *American Mystery and Detective Novels: A Reference Guide* (Westport, CT: Greenwood, 1999).

3. Régis Messac, *Le "Detective Novel" et l'influence de la penseé scientifique* (Paris: Champion, 1929), 207.

4. Worldcat records a Philadelphia version of Camden Pelham's *Calendar*, which it dates as "1800?," but this came out in London in 1841; it cites another Philadelphia-published Calendar dated "18–?" but as its publisher F.C. Wemyss was born in 1797, this too is likely to come from the 1830s or 1840s.

5. Daniel A. Cohen, *Pillars of Salt, Monuments of Grace: New England Crime Literature and the Origins of American Popular Culture, 1674–1860* (New York: Oxford University Press, 1993); Karen Halttunen, *Murder Most Foul: The Killer and the American Gothic Imagination* (Cambridge: Harvard University Press, 1998).

6. For a description of the Calendar pattern, see Stephen Knight, "The Newgate Calendar" in *Form and Ideology in Crime Fiction* (Bloomington: Indiana University Press, 1980), 8–20.

7. Halttunen, 107; "The Continuation of Murder as Mystery" is the title of her Chapter 4, 91–134.

8. Cohen, Chap. 9, "The Prostitute and the Somnambulist: Rufus Choate and the Triumph of Romantic Advocacy," 195–246.

9. On Lippard see Stephen Knight, "The Philadelphia Version: George Lippard's *The Quaker City*," Chap. 4 of *The Mysteries of the Cities, Urban Crime Fiction in the Nineteenth Century* (Jefferson, NC: McFarland, 2012), 131–55.

10. Michael Denning, *Mechanic Accents* (London: Verso, 1987): for his discussion of Lippard see Chap. 6, "Mysteries and Mechanics of the City," 85–117; Gary Hoppenstand, "Introduction" to *The Dime Novel Detective*, ed. Gary Hoppenstand (Bowling Green, OH: Bowling Green University Press, 1982), 1–8; for his discussion of the "Avenger Detective" see 3.

11. On Judson, see Stephen Knight "'A Perfect Daguerreotype of This Great City': Edward Zane Carroll Judson's *The Mysteries and Miseries of New York*," Chap. 5 of *The Mysteries of the Cities*, 156–81.

12. For the six Americans who imitated Judson in using "Miseries" as well as "Mysteries" in their titles, see Knight, *Mysteries of the Cities*, 215–16, note 12.

13. Cohen, 212.

14. "Introduction" to George Lippard, *The Quaker City or, the Monks of Monks Hall* (Amherst: University of Massachusetts Press, 1995), vii–xliv, see vii.

15. Heather Worthington, *The Rise of the Detective in Early Nineteenth-Century Popular Fiction* (London: Palgrave Macmillan, 2005).

16. "Pages from The Diary of a Philadelphia Lawyer," *The Gentleman's Magazine* (Philadelphia), vol. 2 (1838): "The Murderess," 107–12; "The Counterfeiter," 193–6; "A Chapter on Aristocracy," 248–50; "The Un-

natural Prosecution," 334–7; vol. 3 (1839), "The Will," 54–7; "The Reprieve," 195–8; "The Fatal Shot," 208–11.

17. Lippard, "The Origin and Object of This Book," *The Quaker City*, 3–4, see 3.

18. William L. Keese notes, "Articles of his own appeared in it from time to time," *William E. Burton, Actor, Author and Manager: A Sketch of His Career* (New York: Putnam, 1885), 16.

19. These stories were collected as Samuel Warren, *Passages from the Diary of a Late Physician*, three vols. (Edinburgh: Blackwood's, vols. 1 and 2, 1832, vol. 3, 1837); for a discussion see Worthington, 49–74.

20. The U.S. National Union catalogue records an 1831 Harper edition in New York entitled *Passages*, but also a pirate edition in the same year re-titled as *Affecting Scenes: being passages from the diary of a physician*. *Blackwood's* two-volume edition of 1832 and third volume of 1837 were available in New York at once.

21. See Dorothy L. Sayers, "Introduction," *The Omnibus of Crime* (London: Gollancz, 1928), 9–47.

22. Messac, 237–44.

23. Messac, 237.

24. Alexandre Dumas, *The Mohicans of Paris*, translated and adapted John Laty Jun (New York: Routledge, 1875), 21.

25. Messac, 429.

26. Messac, 437.

27. Régis Messac, *Influences Françaises dans l'oeuvre d'Edgar Poe* (Paris: Picart, 1929).

28. Sxxx Xxxxxx Xxxxxx D.C.L., *Experiences of a Barrister* (London: Brown, 1856).

29. Eric Osborne, "Introduction" to the reprint of the 1875 double series edition of *The Recollections of a Detective Police-Officer* (London: Covent Garden Press, 1975), unpaginated.

30. James Brampton, ed. John B. Williams, M.D., *Leaves from the Note-book of a New York Detective: The Private Records of James Brampton* (New York: Dick and Fitzgerald, 1865).

31. Allan J. Pinkerton, "Preface" to *The Expressman and the Detective* (Chicago: Keen and Crook, 1874), unpaginated.

32. "Old Sleuth," *A Mystery of One Night*, *Old Sleuth's Own*, no. 111 (New York: Parlor Car Publishing, 1898), 7.

33. For the "Young Sleuth" detail, see J.

Randolph Cox, *The Dime Novel Companion: A Source Book* (Westport, CT: Greenwood, 2000), 295.

34. Denning, Chap. 4 "The Uses of Literacy: Class, Culture, and Dime Novel Controversies," 47–61; Pamela Bedore, *Dime Novels and the Roots of American Detective Fiction* (London: Palgrave Macmillan, 2013), 13–17.

35. Messac, Livre 6, Chapitre 4, "Les morts de Nick Carter," 555–79.

36. "In the Cellar" and the second Furbush story "In the Maguerriwock" are both included in *The Amber Gods and Other Stories*, ed. Alfred Bendixen (Rutgers: Rutgers University Press, 1989): though this uses the title of Spofford's 1863 collection it is in fact a wider selection. The other detective story, "Mr Furbush," appeared under her maiden name Harriet Prescott in *Harper's Magazine* 30 (1865), 623–26.

37. For a description of Victor's fiction see Kate Watson, *Women Writing Crime Fiction, 1860–1880: Fourteen American, British and Australian Authors* (Jefferson, NC: McFarland, 2012), 99–101.

38. See Catherine Ross Nickerson, "Introduction" to Metta Fuller Victor, *The Dead Letter and The Figure Eight* (Durham: Duke University Press, 2003), 1–10, see 5; also see Watson, 114–15.

39. Lucy Sussex, *Women Writers and Detectives in Nineteenth-Century Crime Fiction: the Mothers of the Mystery Genre* (London: Palgrave Macmillan, 2010), 161.

40. On Davitt, see Sussex, *Women Writers*, 124–5.

41. The melodramatic sub-title was *The Stains and Splendors of New York Life. A Story of Our Day and Night.* Williams was the son of the identically named publisher of *Julia Bicknell* in 1844, and was himself an energetic hack-writer and translator from French, especially the crime writers. His version of Sue's *Les Mystères de Paris* would appear in New York in 1892.

42. R.F. Stewart, *And Always a Detective* (Newton Abbot: David and Charles, 1980); see his bibliography for details of reviews in *The Saturday Review* of *L'Affaire Lerouge* (1866) and *Les Esclaves de Paris* (1869); there was also an essay by A. Innes Shand on French detective fiction in *Blackwood's* in 1879.

43. For a discussion of Green's life and work see Patricia D. Maida, *Mother of Detective Fiction: The Life and Works of Anna Katharine Green* (Bowling Green, OH: Bowling Green State University Popular Press, 1989).

44. It is conceivable that the name was influenced by Collins' Matthew Grice, from *Hide and Seek*.

45. Messac, 577.

46. For Alcott's thrillers see Madeleine B. Stern, "Dime Novels by 'The Children's Friend,'" in *Pioneers, Passionate Ladies and Private Eyes: Dime Novels, Series Books, and Paperbacks*, Larry E. Sullivan and Lydia Cushman Schurman, eds. (New York: Haworth, 1996), 197–213.

47. Douglas G. Greene, "Introduction" to Mary Roberts Rinehart, *The Circular Staircase* (New York: Dover, 1997), v–vii, see vi.

48. See J. Randolph Cox, "Paperback Detective: The Evolution of the Nick Carter Series from Dime Novel to Paperback, 1886–1990," in *Pioneers, Passionate Ladies and Private Eyes*, Sullivan and Schurman, eds., 119–32.

49. Denning, 148.

Chapter 2

1. Arthur Conan Doyle, "The Greek Interpreter," in *The Complete Sherlock Holmes Short Stories* (London: Murray, 1928), 478.

2. Arthur Conan Doyle, *A Study in Scarlet*, in *The Complete Sherlock Holmes Long Stories* (London: Murray, 1929), p. 23.

3. François Eugène Vidocq, *Memoirs of Vidocq: Master of Crime*, translated Edwin Gile Rich (Edinburgh: AK Press/Nabat, 2003), 138.

4. See James Morton, *The First Detective: The Life and Revolutionary Times of Vidocq: Criminal, Spy and Private Eye* (London: Ebury, 2011), Chap. 16, "Vidocq and his Agency," 217–38.

5. Paul Féval, as "Sir Francis Trolopp," *Les Mystères de Londres* (Paris: Imprimeurs Unis, 1844), serialized in *Courrier français*, 1843–4, translated Henry Champion Deming as *The Mysteries of London* (New York: Judd and Taylor, 1845).

6. Paul Féval, père et fils, *Le Bossu: le roman de Lagardère* (Paris: Presses de la Cité, 1997).

7. Brian Stableford, "Introduction" to Paul Féval, *John Devil*, translated Brian Stableford (Encino, CA: Black Coat Press, 2005), 7–14, see 12.

8. Paul Féval, *Les Habit Noirs: le Forêt Parisien* (Paris: Dentu, 1863), serialized in *Le Constitutionnel*, 1863, translated Brian Stableford as *The Blackcoats: The Parisian Jungle* (Encino, CA: Black Coat Press, 2008).

9. Yves Olivier-Martin, *Histoire du roman populaire en France de 1840 à 1980* (Paris: Michel, 1980), 50.

10. E.F. Bleiler, "Introduction" to Émile Gaboriau, *Monsieur Lecoq* (New York: Dover, 1975), v–xii, see vii.

11. Roger Bonniot, *Émile Gaboriau, ou le naissance du roman policier* (Paris: Vrin, 1985); for a discussion of the timing of the writing of the Lecoq novels, see 192.

12. Émile Gaboriau, *The Slaves of Paris* (London: Routledge, 1887), II.135.

13. Bonniot, 184.

14. Bonniot, 148–50.

15. Émile Gaboriau, *Monsieur Lecoq*, translated Bayard Jones (New York: Scribner, 1900), 25.

16. Bonniot, 161.

17. Régis Messac, *Le "Detective Novel" et l'influence de la penseé scientifique* (Paris: Champion, 1929), 516.

18. Tzvetan Todorov's well-known account of the "whodunit" being based on one apparent but baffling narrative and one other, concealed by the criminal and slowly elucidated by the detective is set out in "The Typology of the Detective Story," in his essay-collection *The Poetics of Prose*, translated Richard Howard (Oxford: Blackwell, 1977), 70–8.

19. Arthur Conan Doyle, *A Study in Scarlet*, *Sherlock Holmes: The Complete Long Stories* (London: Murray, 1929), 23.

20. Marius Topin, *Romanciers contemporains* (Paris: Charpentier, 1876), 324.

21. Fortuné du Boisgobey, *The Omnibus Crime*, translated Nina Cooper (Waitesfield, VT: Distinction Press, 2010), 14.

22. Messac, Livre 4, Chapitre 5, "Les Exploits de Rocambole," 466–94.

Chapter 3

1. R.S. Neale, *Class and Ideology in the*

Nineteenth Century (London: Routledge, 1972), see 30.

2. Julian Symons, *Bloody Murder: From the Detective Story to the Crime Novel: A History*, rev. ed. (London: Pan, 1994), 33.

3. Michael Foucault's argument is advanced in *Discipline and Punish*, translated Alan Sheridan (London: Lane, 1972), see especially "Docile Bodies," 135–69; this topic is discussed by Simon During in *Foucault and Literature: Towards a Genealogy of Writing* (London: Routledge, 1992), see chapter 6, "Discipline." In relation to crime fiction the topic has been discussed and developed by D.A. Miller, *The Novel and the Police* (Berkeley: University of California Press, 1988), see pp. 16–23.

4. Robert Morrison and Chris Baldick, eds, *Tales of Terror from Blackwood's Magazine*, World's Classics Series (Oxford: Oxford University Press, 1995); for a discussion see Heather Worthington, *The Rise of the Detective in Early Nineteenth-Century Popular Fiction* (London: Palgrave Macmillan, 2005), 30–45.

5. *Richmond: Scenes in the Life of a Bow Street Runner*, ed. E.F. Bleiler (New York: Dover, 1976), 205.

6. E.F. Bleiler, "Introduction" to *Richmond*, v–xiv, see xi.

7. Bleiler, "Introduction" to *Richmond*, vii.

8. Jerome McGann, "Introduction" to Edward George Bulwer-Lytton, *Pelham or the Adventures of a Gentleman* (Lincoln: University of Nebraska Press, 1972), xi–xxv, see xviii.

9. On Warren see Worthington, 55–68.

10. Samuel Warren, *Passages from the Diary of a Late Physician*, vols. 1–2 (Edinburgh: Blackwood, 1832), vol. 3 (Edinburgh: Blackwood, 1839), vol. 1. xii.

11. See Worthington, 71–72.

12. They are the first six of *The Confessions*, in slightly varied order and with the first titled "A Life Assurance," not "A Life Policy." However, they are introduced by the statement "The following papers, though included under the heading of 'Leaves form the Diary of a Law Clerk' purport, it will be seen, to have been written by one of the partners of the law firm of Flint and Sharp; they, like the 'Leaves,' are the records of a real experience," see *Leaves from the Diary of a Law-Clerk* (London: Brown, 1857), 159.

13. Anon., *The Experiences of a Barrister* (London: Brown, 1856), 46.

14. See the discussion in Eric Osborne, "The Publication History of *Recollections of a Detective Police-Officer*," in the reprint of the 1875 edition of *Recollections of a Detective Police-Officer* (London: Covent Garden Press, 1972), unpaginated.

15. Anon., *The Confessions of an Attorney* (London: Brown, 1857), 207.

16. "The Confessions of an Attorney" series of seven stories is printed after the eight stories in the "Law-Clerk" series attributed to "Russell" in *Leaves from the Diary of a Law-Clerk* (London: Brown, 1857): the book is on the title-page and in the short Preface said to be "By the author of 'Recollections of a Detective Police Officer' etc."

17. Anon., "The Incendiary" in "The Confessions of an Attorney," in *Leaves from the Diary of a Law Clerk*, 280.

18. Anthea Trodd, "The Policeman and the Lady," Chapter 2 in *Domestic Crime in the Victorian Novel* (London: Macmillan, 1989), 12–44.

19. *Diary of an Ex-Detective*, ed. "Charles Martel" (= Thomas Delf) (London: Ward and Lock, 1860), see 1.

20. See Stephen Knight, *Crime Fiction Since 1800: Detection, Death, Diversity*, second edition (London: Palgrave Macmillan, 2010), 36.

21. Kate Summerscale, *The Suspicions of Mr Whicher, or the Murder at Road Hill House* (London: Bloomsbury, 2008), see note to page 242, 331.

22. Judith Flanders, "The Hanky-Panky Way: Creators of the First Female Detectives: A Mystery Solved," *The Times Literary Supplement*, June 18, 2010, 14–15; *The Invention of Murder: How the Victorians Revelled in Death and Detection and Created Modern Crime* (New York: St. Martin's, 2011), 374.

23. Mike Ashley, "Introduction" to "Andrew Forrester," *The Female Detective* (London: British Library, 2012), vii–xi, see x–xi.

24. Anonyma" (= William Stephens Hayward?), *The Revelations of a Lady Detective* (London: Vickers, 1864), 200.

25. "Andrew Forrester," *The Female Detective* (London: Ward Lock, 1864), 175.

26. See his "Introduction" to *Three Nineteenth-Century Detective Novels* (New York: Dover, 1978), vii–xvi, see x.

27. "Andrew Forrester," *The Revelations of a Private Detective* (London: Ward Lock, 1863), 295.

28. "Andrew Forrester," *Secret Service, or Recollections of a City Detective* (London: Ward Lock, 1864), 35.

29. E.F. Bleiler, "Introduction" to Arthur Morrison, *Best Martin Hewitt Detective Stories* (New York: Dover, 1976), vii–xiv, see vii.

30. Arthur Morrison, "The Case of the Dixon Torpedo," in *Best Martin Hewitt Detective Stories*, pp. 17–30, see 17.

31. Catherine Louisa Pirkis, *The Experiences of Loveday Brooke, Lady Detective* (London; Hutchinson, 1894), 7.

Chapter 4

1. On this topic see Stephen Knight, *Crime Fiction Since 1800: Detection, Death, Diversity*, rev. ed. (London: Palgrave Macmillan, 2010), 170.

2. Brenda Ayres, "*Apis Trollopiana*: An Introduction to the Nearly Extinct Trollope," in *Francis Trollope and the Novel of Social Change*, ed. Brenda Ayres (Westport, CT: Greenwood, 2002), 1–10, see 3.

3. Lucy Sussex, "'A Most Preposterous Organ of Wonder': Catherine Crowe," Chapter 3 of *Women Writers and Detectives in Nineteenth-Century Crime Fiction: The Mothers of the Mystery Genre* (London: Palgrave, 2010), 45–63, see 46 and 49.

4. "Andrew Forrester" "Tenant for Life," in *The Female Detective*, sec. ed. (London: British Library, 2012) , 6–96, see 41–2.

5. E.F. Bleiler, "Introduction" to *Three Victorian Detective Novels* (New York: Dover, 1978), vii–xvi, see x.

6. Bleiler, x.

7. Bleiler, x; Kathleen Gregory Klein, *The Woman Detective: Gender and Genre*, sec. ed. (Urbana: University of Illinois Press, 1995), 18.

8. Klein, 18 and 23.

9. "Anonyma," *Revelations of a Lady Detective*, sec. ed. (London: British Library, 2013), 19 and 17.

10. Mike Ashley, "Introduction" to *Revelations of a Lady Detective*, 7–14, see 13–14.

11. Joseph A. Kestner, *Sherlock's Sisters: The British Female Detective, 1864–1913* (Aldershot: Ashgate, 2003), 7.

12. Klein, 26.

13. Klein, 29.

14. Nicola Imogen Bowes, "Damned Whores and God's Detectives," Chap. 4 of *Criminal Nation: The Crime Fiction of Mary Helena Fortune* (PhD, University of Queensland, 2008), 223–67.

15. Sussex, "The (Feminine) Eye of the Law," Chap. 7, *Women Writers*, 120–41.

16. Mike Ashley, "Introduction" to Leonard Merrick, *Mr Bazalgette's Agent*, sec. ed. (London: British Library, 2013), 6–12, see 8.

17. William Baker and Jeanette Roberts Shumaker, *Leonard Merrick: A Forgotten Novelist's Novelist* (Madison, NJ: Fairleigh Dickinson University Press, 2009).

18. Merrick, *Mr Bazalgette's Agent*, 18.

19. Kestner, 33 and 34.

20. Kestner, 40.

21. Catherine Louisa Pirkis, *The Experiences of Loveday Brooke, Lady Detective*, sec. ed. (Rockville, MD: Wildside Press, 2012), 4.

22. Klein, 68.

23. Kestner, see 73 and 83.

24. Klein, 71.

25. Klein, 71.

26. Elizabeth Carolyn Miller, "Trouble with She-Dicks: Private eyes and Public Women in *The Adventures of Loveday Brooke, Lady Detective*," *Victorian Literature and Culture* 33 (2005), 47–65, see 48.

27. Christopher Pittard, *Purity and Contamination in Late Victorian Detective Fiction* (Farnham: Ashgate, 2011), 150.

28. Douglas G. Greene, "Introduction" in L.T. Meade and Robert Eustace, *The Detections of Miss Cusack* (Shelbourne, Ontario: Battered Silicon Despatch Box, 1998), vii–xiii, see x.

29. Jack Adrian, "Afterword" to *The Detections of Miss Cusack*, 107–10, see 107.

30. Kestner, 157.

31. Baroness Orczy, *Lady Molly of Scotland Yard*, sec. ed. (New York: Akadine, 1999), see 244.

32. Kestner, 193 and 197.

33. Klein, 63.

34. Klein, 64; Kestner, 103.

35. Mary Craig and Patricia Cadogan, *The Lady Investigate: Women Detectives and Spies in Fiction* (London: Gollancz, 1981), 23.

36. See Vanessa Warne and Colette Colligan, "The Man Who Wrote a New Woman

Novel: Grant Allen's 'The Woman Who Did' and the Gendering of New Woman Authors," *Victorian Literature and Culture* 33 (2005), 21–46.

37. Clarissa J. Suranyi, "Introduction" to Grant Allen, as "Olive Pratt Rayner," *The Type-Writer Girl*, sec. ed. (Peterborough, Ontario: Broadview, 2004), 9–16, see 11.

38. Grant Allen, *Hilda Wade: A Woman with Tenacity of Purpose*; Project Gutenberg Ebooks, 2006, unpaginated.

39. Kestner, 170.

40. Mathias McDonnell Bodkin, *Dora Myrl, the Lady Detective* (London: Chatto and Windus, 1900).

41. Mathias McDonnell Bodkin, *The Capture of Paul Beck* (London: Fisher Unwin, 1909), see 75 and 115–16.

42. Klein, 61.

43. Fergus Hume, *Hagar of the Pawn Shop*, Project Gutenberg Ebooks, 2006, unpaginated.

44. Carolyn Wells, *The Technique of the Mystery Story*, sec. ed. (London: Pearl Necklace Books, 2014), 225. The four Americans in addition to Rinehart are Mary E. Wilkins (Freeman), Natalie Lincoln, Stella M. Düring and A.M. Barbour; the English are Baroness Orczy and Florence Warden; the Austrian is Augusta Gröner.

Chapter 5

1. Anthea Trodd, *Domestic Crime in the Victorian Novel* (London: Macmillan, 1989), 42.

2. Charles Dickens, *The Life and Adventures of Martin Chuzzlewit* (London: Oxford University Press, 1951), 447.

3. Edward Bulwer Lytton, "Preface" to *Night and Morning* (London: Routledge, 1845), vii–xii, see x.

4. Jean Fernandez, *Victorian Servants, Class, and the Politics of Literacy* (London: Routledge, 2010), 42.

5. Lucy Sussex, *Women Writers and Detectives in Nineteenth-Century Crime Fiction: The Mothers of the Mystery Genre* (London: Palgrave Macmillan, 2010), 47.

6. John Forster, review of *Susan Hopley*, *Examiner*, February 28, 1841, 132; see Sussex, *Women Writers*, 46–47.

7. Elizabeth Gaskell, *Mary Barton* (London: Penguin, 1994), 11.

8. Kate Watson, *Women Writing Crime Fiction, 1860–1880: Fourteen American, British and Australian Authors* (Jefferson, NC: McFarland, 2012), 39.

9. G.W.M. Reynolds, *The Mysteries of London*, four vols. (London: Vickers, 1845–48), vol. 1, 126.

10. Like the other *Household Words* police essays this is reprinted in Charles Dickens, *Hunted Down: The Detective Stories of Charles Dickens*, ed. Peter Haining (London: Peter Owen, 1996), 61–70, see 61.

11. Haia Shpayer-Makov, *The Ascent of the Detective: Police Sleuths in Victorian and Edwardian England* (Oxford: Oxford University Press, 2011), 200.

12. Dickens' letters appeared on November 14 and 19, 1849; they are summarized in Philip Collins, *Dickens and Crime*, London, Macmillan, 1965, 236–7.

13. For example, the London *Daily News* for October 27, 1849, praised "the intelligence, energy, and organization of the police their prompt and skilful use of the railroad, steamboat, and electric telegraph; the sagacity with which they elicited and combined the conclusive train of circumstantial evidence."

14. Sussex, *Women Writers*, 82.

15. Haining, 18.

16. Charles Dickens, *Bleak House* (Ware: Wordsworth, 1993), 604.

17. Julian Symons, *Bloody Murder: From the Detective Story to the Crime Novel: A History*, sec. rev. ed. (London: Pan, 1994), 57; Ronald R. Thomas, "Detection in the Victorian Novel," in *The Cambridge Companion to the Victorian Novel*, Deirdre David, ed. (Cambridge: Cambridge University Press, 2000), 169–92, see 172.

18. Dagni Bredesen, "Investigating the Female Detective in Victorian Fiction," (Review of Joseph A. Kestner, *Sherlock's Sisters: The British Female Detective, 1864–1913* [Aldershot; Ashgate, 2003]), *Nineteenth-Century Gender Studies* 3.1 (2007), electronic unpaginated.

19. Trodd, 32.

20. Trodd, 1.

21. Deborah Wynne, *The Sensation Novel and the Victorian Family Magazine* (London: Palgrave, 2001), 54–57.

22. *Armadale: Wilkie Collins and the Dark Threads of Life*, ed. Mariaconcetta Costantini, *Studia di Anglistica* 17 (Rome: Aracne, 2009).

23. Eliot opened his "Introduction" to the novel by saying it "is the first, the longest and the best of modern English detective novels," Wilkie Collins, *The Moonstone*, Worlds Classics ed. (Oxford: Oxford University Press, 1928), v–xii, see v. The introduction repeats many points made in an essay in *The Times Literary Supplement*, August 4, 1927, 525–26, reprinted in T.S. Eliot, *Selected Essays* (London: Faber and Faber, 1932), 460–70, though the essay more simply says the novel is "the first and greatest of English detective novels," 465, and curiously is well aware of Sergeant Cuff's limitations, where the introduction finds him "the perfect detective," xii. Symons called *The Moonstone* "the first detective novel written in English," *Bloody Murder*, 61.

24. See his letter to W.H. Wills, July 26, 1868, in *The Letters of Charles Dickens*, G. Storey, ed. (Oxford: Oxford University Press, 2002), vol. 12, 159.

25. Charles Dickens, *The Mystery of Edwin Drood* (London: Penguin Classics, 2002), 18.

26. Datchery, in his hat and with full and fair hair, appears to be the figure in the main bottom illustration who appears, presumably in the crypt, to have been waiting for Jasper to appear, carrying a lantern: this may well be the scene where Edwin's body is discovered, after which Jasper is presumably arrested. Datchery also appears to be one of the figures mounting the stairs on the right, and some have thought he, as Tartar, is the man seated with Rosa on the left, who looks quite different from Edwin, who appears with her at the top of the page on the left in their projected wedding.

27. For a survey of the possibilities for Datchery's identity and the possible outcomes of the story, see the exhibition summary *Dickens at 2000–1812–2012*, curated by Jaime Margalotti at the University of Delaware Library, www.lib.udel.edu/ud/spec/exhib/dickens/drood.html.

28. John Forster, *The Life of Charles Dickens*, four vols. (London: Chapman and Hall, 1872–76), vol. 1, 451–52.

29. On this genre see Jennifer Carnell and Graham Law, "Our Author: Braddon in the Provincial Weeklies," in *Beyond Sensation: Mary Elizabeth Braddon in Context*, Marlene Trump, Pamela K. Gilbert and Aeron Haynie, eds. (New York: State University of New York Press, 2000), 127–63, see 151.

30. Trodd, 105.

31. Jenny Bourne Taylor, "Introduction" to Mary Elizabeth Braddon, *Lady Audley's Secret* (London: Penguin, 1998), vii–xli, see xix.

32. Trodd, 6.

33. Janice M. Allan, "To See is to Suspect: Investigating the Private in Sensation Fiction," in *Private Investigators*, Alastair Rolls and Rachel Franks, eds. (Chicago: Intellect, University of Chicago Press, 2016), 172–82, see 175.

34. Anne-Marie Beller, *Mary Elizabeth Braddon: A Companion to the Mystery Fiction* (Jefferson, NC; McFarland, 2012), 84.

35. Ellen Wood, *Wyllard's Weird: A Romance* (London: Maxwell, 1885), 241.

36. Sussex, *Women's Writing*, 113.

37. See Watson, note 162, 201.

38. Quoted in Sussex, *Women's Writing*, 111.

39. Ellen Wood, *Roland Yorke* (London: Bentley, 1869), 418.

40. Ellen Wood, "Lost in the Post," *Johnny Ludlow*, Second Series (London: Bentley, 1880), 1–18.

41. Quoted in Elton E. Smith, *Charles Reade* (Boston: Twayne, 1976), 73.

42. John Carter, "Introduction" to *Victorian Detective Fiction: A Catalogue of the Collection Made by Dorothy Glover and Graham Greene, Bibliographically Arranged by Eric Osborne* (London: Bodley Head, 1966), ix–xv, see xiii–xiv.

Chapter 6

1. Lucy Sussex, *Blockbuster! Fergus Hume and The Mystery of a Hansom Cab* (Melbourne: Text, 2015), see 55–6.

2. Susan Martin and Kylie Mirmohamadi, *Sensational Melbourne: Reading Sensational Fiction and Lady Audley's Secret in the Victorian Metropolis* (Melbourne: Australian Scholarly Publishing, 2011), 9.

3. Hume's "Preface" is found in the revised edition, The *Mystery of a Hansom Cab* (London: Jarrolds, 1895), 5–9, see 7.

4. John Holroyd, *George Robertson of Melbourne, 1825–1898, Pioneer Bookseller & Publisher* (Melbourne; Robertson and Mullens, 1968), 56.

5. Hume, "Preface," 7.

6. Sussex, *Blockbuster*, 114.

7. Sussex, *Blockbuster*, 134–35.

8. October 6, 1888, 410; see Sussex, *Blockbuster*, 278, note 267.

9. Eric Sinclair Hill, "The Publishing History of Fergus Hume's *The Mystery of a Hansom Cab*," "Appendix" to *Victorian Detective Fiction: A Catalogue of the Collection Made by Dorothy Glover and Graham Greene, Bibliographically Arranged by Eric Osborne* (London: Bodley Head, 1966), 123–6; see 123–4.

10. Fergus Hume, *The Mystery of a Hansom Cab* (Melbourne: Text, 1999), 49.

11. Hume, "Preface," 8.

12. Hume and his sister arrived on May 8 and the serial ran in Melbourne until the end of May; it had not been serialized in the Dunedin papers before Hume left New Zealand. I am most grateful to Lucy Sussex for these two details.

13. On these topics see Stephen Knight, *Continent of Mystery: a Thematic History of Australian Crime Fiction* (Melbourne: Melbourne University Press, 1997).

14. For biographical data about Fortune see Lucy Sussex, *The Fortunes of Mary Fortune* (Melbourne: Penguin, 1989). The two 1880 *Australian Journal* urban stories are "The Window on the 'Willows,'" 15, 350–59 and "Checkmate and Revenge," 15, 455–61; the 1886 story where Sinclair leaves Melbourne for a bush case is "My Dream at Walworth's," 22, 45–52.

15. Martin and Mirmohamadi, "Watching Lady Audley," Chap. 4, 81–98; Sussex, "Three Readers: Maudie, Edith and Minnie," *Blockbuster*, Chap. 16, 136–40.

16. For a discussion of the novel see Stephen Knight, "Mysteries Across the World: Donald Cameron's *The Mystery of Melbourne Life*," Chap. 6 in *The Mysteries of the Cities: Urban Crime Fiction in the Nineteenth Century* (Jefferson, NC: McFarland, 2012), 182–204.

17. Though most people think Ian Rankin comes from Edinburgh, at a talk he gave in Cardiff in 2005 he expressed shock at the suggestion, made by myself, that he was a rarity among crime writers in having grown up in the city he has made famous: he insisted he was born and brought up "in the Kingdom of Fife"—Fife is 34 miles away across the Firth of Forth Road Bridge.

18. Hume, "Preface," 8; the 1902 *Bulletin* quotation is reprinted by Sussex, *Blockbuster*, 89.

19. See Robert Dixon, *Writing the Colonial Adventure: Race, Gender and Nation in Anglo-Australian Popular Fiction, 1875–1914* (Cambridge: Cambridge University Press, 1995), 158–61, and Christopher Pittard, "'A Strange Inverted World': Sensation and Social Purity in *The Mystery of a Hansom Cab*," Chap. 1 of *Purity and Contamination in Late Victorian Detective Fiction* (Aldershot: Ashgate, 2011), 27–62.

20. Hume, "Preface," 9.

21. Sussex, *Blockbuster*, 156.

22. Sussex, *Blockbuster*, 159.

23. Peter Drexler, "Mapping the Gaps: Detectives and Detective Themes in British Novels of the 1870s and 1880s," in *The Art of Murder: New Essays on Detective Fiction*, H. Gustav Klaus and Stephen Knight, eds. (Tübingen: Stauffenburg, 1998), 77–89, see 81.

24. Coral Lansbury, *Arcady in Australia: The Evocation of Australia in Nineteenth-Century English Literature* (Melbourne: Melbourne University Press, 1970).

25. The world spread of much of the genre is discussed by Knight in *Mysteries of the Cities*, 182–84; for the Vatican see Maurizio Ascari, "The Mysteries of the Vatican: From Nineteenth-century Anti-clerical Propaganda to Dan Brown's Religious Thrillers," in *Crime Fiction in the City: Capital Crimes*, Lucy Andrew and Catherine Phelps, eds. (Cardiff: University of Wales Press, 2013), 107–225.

26. Hume, "Preface," 10.

27. Scott's review was reprinted in *Table Talk* (Melbourne), January 6, 1888, 4–7; For an edited version see Sussex, *Blockbuster*, 157–59: page references in the text are from this version.

28. For a reference to this being mentioned in Adams' letters, see A.H. Kellow, *Queensland Poets* (London: Harrap, 1939), 145.

29. See Knight, *Continent of Mystery*, 73.

Chapter 7

1. Dates given are of publication in book format; the stories had appeared in *The Strand* up to two years before being anthologized.

2. This version of the title was the American one and responds better to in-text references; *The Sign of Four* may be an English publisher's error.

3. Arthur Conan Doyle, *The Sign of the Four* (Philadelphia: Lippincott, 1890): references from this and other Holmes novellas are to *The Complete Sherlock Holmes Long Stories* (London: Murray, 1929), 140, 142, 170.

4. Joseph McLaughlin, *Writing the Urban Jungle: Reading Empire in London from Doyle to Eliot* (Charlottesville: University of Virginia Press, 2000), 51.

5. "Waters" (i.e., "William Russell"), "The Two Widows," in *Recollections of a Detective Police Officer*, Second Series (London: Kent, 1859), 72–99, 89.

6. Grace Moore, *Dickens and Empire: Discourses of Class, Race and Colonialism in the Works of Charles Dickens* (Aldershot: Ashgate, 2004), 13.

7. Coral Lansbury, *Arcady in Australia: The Evocation of Australia in Nineteenth-Century English Literature* (Melbourne: Melbourne University Press, 1970).

8. Coral Lansbury, "Samuel Sidney Discovers Arcady," Chap. 5 of *Arcady in Australia*, 60–78, see 73.

9. Patrick Brantlinger, *Rule of Darkness: British Literature and Imperialism, 1830–1914* (Ithaca: Cornell University Press, 1988), 121.

10. Lansbury, 119 and 121.

11. Lansbury, 122.

12. David Matthews, *Medievalism: A Critical History* (Cambridge: Brewer, 2015), 25 and 56.

13. U.P. Mukherjee, *Crime and Empire: The Colony in Nineteenth Century Fiction of Crime* (Oxford: Oxford University Press, 2003), see Chap. 5, "New Policing, India, and Thuggee," 96–122.

14. Mukherjee, 60.

15. Brantlinger, 86–90.

16. Brantlinger, 89.

17. Brantlinger, 202.

18. Mukherjee, 134.

19. Brantlinger, 215.

20. Moore, 108.

21. Moore, 121.

22. Yumna Siddiqi, *Anxieties of Empire and the Fiction of Intrigue* (New York: Columbia University Press, 2008), 92.

23. Garrett Ziegler, "The Perils of Empire: Dickens, Collins and the Indian Mutiny," Chap. 9 of *Pirates and Mutineers of the Nineteenth Century: Swashbucklers and Swindlers*, ed. Grace Moore (Farnham: Ashgate, 2011), 149–64, see 151.

24. Ashish Roy, "The Fabulous Imperialist Semiotic of Wilkie Collins's *The Moonstone*," *New Literary History*, 24 (1993), 657–81; Roy's views are discussed by Mukherjee, 177–80.

25. Alfred Tennyson, "The Passing of Arthur," *Idylls of the King* (1869), J.M. Gray, ed., sec. ed. (London: Penguin, 1996), 288–300, see 288, line 26.

26. Deborah Wynne, *The Sensation Novel and the Victorian Family Magazine* (London: Palgrave, 2001), 59.

27. Mukherjee, 190 and 22.

28. Arthur Conan Doyle, "The Gully of Bluemansdyke," reprinted in *Dead Witness: Best Australian Mystery Stories*, Stephen Knight, ed. (Melbourne: Penguin, 1989), 37–60, see 54.

29. Siddiqi, 38 and 61.

30. Siddiqi, 35–37.

31. Arthur Conan Doyle, *The Mystery of Cloomber* (London: Hodder and Stoughton, 1912), 217.

32. Diana Barsham, *Arthur Conan Doyle and the Meaning of Masculinity* (Aldershot: Ashgate, 2003), 71.

33. Barsham, 74–75.

34. See Charles Higham, *The Adventures of Conan Doyle* (London: Cape, 1976), 79.

35. Arthur Conan Doyle, *The Complete Sherlock Holmes Short Stories* (London: Murray, 1928), 612.

36. McLaughlin, 39.

37. For a discussion of this illusion, see Stephen Knight, *Form and Ideology in Crime Fiction* (London: Macmillan, 1980), 86–7.

38. Brantlinger, 37 and 230.

39. The collected *Adventures* and *Memoirs* in fact only contain 23 stories: "The Cardboard Box" was originally one of the second series. The box which arrives in the post contains a human ear, and was sent in connection with an adulterous affair: Doyle asked Newnes to leave the story out of the second collection as he now found it

"sensational," and it did not appear in collected form until *His Last Bow* in 1917. On this, see Andrew Lycett, *Conan Doyle—The Man Who Created Sherlock Holmes* (London: Weidenfeld and Nicholson, 2007), 193.

40. Siddiqi, 74.

41. Siddiqi, 88–104.

42. Edward Said, *Culture and Imperialism* (London: Chatto and Windus, 1993), 184.

43. Arthur Conan Doyle, *The Hound of the Baskervilles*, in *The Complete Sherlock Holmes Long Stories* (London: Murray, 1929), 242–405, see 267.

44. Siddiqi, 68.

Bibliography

Items listed are those receiving some analysis in the text, rather than passing mentions; where books have received extensive discussions, modern available reprints and editions are mentioned when available. Pseudonyms have been used for main entries, with cross-references from real names.

Primary Works

Adams, Charles Warren, see "Felix, Charles."

Allen, Grant. *Hilda Wade: A Woman with Tenacity of Purpose.* London: Grant Richards, 1899; Project Gutenberg, 2006.

_____, see "Rayner, Olive Pratt."

Anon. *The Confessions of an Attorney.* New York: Cornish, Lamport, 1852. In *Leaves from the Diary of a Law-Clerk*, see "Russell, William."

Anon. *The Experiences of a Barrister.* London: Brown, 1856.

Anon. "Pages from The Diary of a Philadelphia Lawyer." *The Gentleman's Magazine* (Philadelphia), vol. 2 (1838): "The Murderess," 107–12; "The Counterfeiter," 193–96; "A Chapter on Aristocracy," 248–50; "The Unnatural Prosecution," 334–37; vol. 3 (1839), "The Will," 54–57; "The Reprieve," 195–98; "The Fatal Shot," 208–11.

Anon. (= Thomas Gaspey?). *Richmond: Scenes in the Life of a Bow Street Runner, Drawn up from his Private Memoranda.* London: Colburn, 1827; E.F. Bleiler, ed. New York: Dover, 1976.

"Anonyma" (= William Stephens Hayward?). *Revelations of a Lady Detective.* London: Vickers, 1864; London, British Library, 2013.

Baldick, Chris, see Morrison, Robert.

Balzac, Honoré de. *Père Goriot.* Paris: Werdet, 1835; *Old Goriot*, trans. David Bellos, Cambridge: Cambridge University Press, 1987.

Bodkin, Mathias McDonnell. *The Capture of Paul Beck.* London: Fisher Unwin, 1909.

Braddon, Mary Elizabeth. *Aurora Floyd.* London: Tinsley, 1863.

_____. *Dora Myrl, the Lady Detective.* London: Chatto and Windus, 1900.

_____. *Eleanor's Victory.* London: Tinsley 1863.

_____. *Henry Dunbar.* London: Maxwell, 1864.

_____. *Lady Audley's Secret.* London: Tinsley, 1862; London: Penguin Classics, 1998.

_____. *The Trail of the Serpent.* London: Maxwell, 1861.

_____. *Wyllard's Weird.* London: Maxwell, 1885.

Brown, Charles Brockden. *Arthur Mervyn Part 1.* Philadelphia: Maxwell, 1799; *Part 2.* New York: Hopkins 1800; Parts 1 and 2, Kent, OH: Kent State University Press, 2002.

_____. *Edgar Huntly, or the Memoirs of a Sleepwalker.* Philadelphia: Dobson and Dickins, 1799; Norman S. Grabo, ed. New York: Viking, 1981.

_____. *Wieland.* New York: Caritat, 1798; Indianapolis: Hackett, 1009.

Bulwer Lytton, Edward. *Pelham, or the Adventures of a Gentleman.* London: Colburn, 1828.

_____. "Preface" to *Night and Morning.* London: Routledge, 1845.

Collins, Wilkie. *Armadale.* London: Smith, Elder, 1866; London: Penguin Classics, 1995.

_____. *Hide and Seek.* London: Bentley, 1854; New York: Dover, 1981.

_____. *The Law and the Lady.* London: Chatto and Windus, 1875.

_____. *The Moonstone.* London: Tinsley, 1868; World's Classics edition, Oxford; Oxford University Press.

_____. *No Name.* London: Sampson and Low, 1862; New York: Oxford University Press, 1998.

_____. *The Woman in White.* London: Sampson and Low, 1860; London: Penguin Classics, 2003.

Conan Doyle, Arthur. *The Complete Sherlock Holmes Long Stories.* London: Murray, 1929.

_____. *The Complete Sherlock Holmes Short Stories.* London: Murray, 1928; *Sherlock Holmes: The Complete Stories, with Illustrations from the "Strand Magazine,"* Ware: Wordsworth, 1989.

_____. "The Gully of Bluemansdyke," *London Society,* 1881, in *The Gully of Bluemansdyke and Other Stories.* London: Scott, 1892, pp. 7–49; Kindle, 2012.

_____. "J. Habbakuk Jephson's Statement." *Cornhill Magazine* 2 (1884), 1–32, in Arthur Conan Doyle, *The Captain of the Pole-Star and Other Stories.* London: Longmans, 1890; ebooks.adelaide.edu.au, 2014.

_____. *Memories and Adventures.* London: Murray, 1926.

_____. *The Mystery of Cloomber.* London: Hodder and Stoughton, 1912.

_____. "The Mystery of Uncle Jeremy's Household." *Boys' Own Paper,* January 8, 1887–February 19, 1887; reprinted in Arthur Conan Doyle, *The Final Adventures of Sherlock Holmes,* Peter Haining, ed. New York: Barnes and Noble, 1993, pp. 41–79.

Crowe, Catherine. *Men and Women: or Manorial Rights.* London: Saunders and Otley, 1843.

_____. *Susan Hopley, or Circumstantial Evidence.* London: Nicholson, 1841.

Delf, Thomas, see "Martel, Charles."

Dickens, Charles. *Bleak House.* London: Bradbury and Evans, 1853; New York: Vintage Classics, 2008.

_____. "A Detective Police Party," *Household Words,* 27 July and 10 August, 1850; in *Hunted Down,* ed. Haining, 71–90.

_____. *Hunted Down: The Detective Stories of Charles Dickens.* Peter Haining, ed. London, 1996.

_____. *The Letters of Charles Dickens.* G. Storey, ed. Oxford: Oxford University Press, 2002.

_____. *The Life and Adventures of Martin Chuzzlewit.* London: Chapman and Hall, 1844; World's Classics edition, London: Oxford University Press, 1951.

_____. "The Modern Science of Thief-Taking." *Household Words* 16 (July 1850); in *Hunted Down,* ed. Peter Haining, 61–70.

_____. *The Mystery of Edwin Drood.* London: Chapman and Hall, 1870; London: Penguin Classics, 2002.

_____. *Oliver Twist.* London: Bentley, 1838.

_____, with Wilkie Collins. *The Perils of Certain English Prisoners. Household Words.* December 1857; Kindle, 2012.

du Boisgobey, Fortuné. *Le Crime d'un Omnibus.* Paris: Plon, 1881; as *The Omnibus Crime,* translated Nina Cooper. Waitesfield. VT: Distinction Press, 2010.

Dumas, Alexandre. *Les Mohicans de Paris.* Paris: Cadot, 1856–57; as *The Mohicans of Paris,* translated and adapted John Laty Jun. New York: Routledge, 1875.

Eustace, Robert, see Meade, L.T.

"Felix, Charles" (= Charles Warren Adams). *The Notting Hill Mystery.* London: Saunders and Otley, 1865.

Féval, Paul, as "Sir Francis Trolopp." *Jean Diable.* Paris: Dentu, 1863; as *John Devil,* translated Brian Stableford. Encino, CA: Black Coat Press, 2005.

_____. *Les Habits Noirs: le Forêt Parisien.* Paris: Dentu, 1863; as *The Blackcoats: The Parisian Jungle,* translated Brian Stableford. Encino, CA: Black Coat Press, 2008.

_____. *Les Mystères de Londres.* Paris: Imprimeurs Unis, 1844; as *The Mysteries of London,* translated Henry Champion Deming. New York: Judd and Taylor, 1845.

"Forrester, Andrew." *The Female Detective.* London: Ward and Lock, 1864.

_____. *The Revelations of a Private Detective.* London: Ward and Lock, 1863.

_____. *Secret Service: Recollections of a City Detective.* London: Ward and Lock, 1864.

Gaboriau, Émile. *L'Affaire Lerouge*. Paris: Dentu, 1866.

_____. *Le Crime d'Orcival*. Paris: Dentu, 1867.

_____. *Le Dossier no. 113*. Paris: Dentu, 1867; as *File no. 113*, translator not stated. New York: Munro, 1875.

_____. *Les Ésclaves de Paris*. Paris: Dentu, 1868; as *The Slaves of Paris*, translator not stated. New York: Munro, 1879.

_____. *Monsieur Lecoq*. Paris: Dentu, 1869; translated Bayard Jones. New York: Scribner, 1900; E.F. Bleiler, ed. New York: Dover, 1975.

_____. *Le Petit Vieux des Batignolles*. Paris: Dentu, 1876; as *The Little Old Man from the Batignolles*, translator not stated. New York: Munro, 1880.

Gaskell, Elizabeth. *Mary Barton*. London: Chapman and Hall, 1848; London: Penguin, 1994.

_____. *North and South*. London: Chapman and Hall, 1854.

Gaspey, Thomas, see Anon., *Richmond*.

Godwin, William. *Things as They Are, or Caleb Williams*, 3 vols. London: Crosby, 1794.

Green, Anna Katharine. *The Leavenworth Case*. New York: Putnam, 1878.

Halsey, Harlan Page, see "Old Sleuth."

Hayward, William Stephens, see "Anonyma."

Hume, Fergus. *Hagar of the Pawn Shop*. London: Skeffington, 1898; Project Gutenberg Ebooks, 2006.

_____. *The Mystery of a Hansom Cab*. Melbourne: Kemp and Boyce, 1886; London: Hansom Cab Publishing, 1887; revised edition, London: Jarrolds, 1895; Melbourne, Text, 1999.

_____. "Preface." The *Mystery of a Hansom Cab*. London: Jarrolds, 1895, 5–9.

Lippard, George. *The Quaker City, or The Monks of Monks' Hall*. Philadelphia: Peterson, 1844; David S. Reynolds, ed. Amherst: University of Massachusetts Press, 1995.

Lytton, Edward Bulwer, see Bulwer Lytton, Edward.

"Martel, Charles" (= Thomas Delf). *A Detective's Notebook*. London: Ward Lock, 1860.

_____. *The Diary of an Ex-Detective*. London: Ward Lock, 1860.

Meade, L.T., and Robert Eustace. *The Detections of Miss Cusack*. *Harmsworth's Magazine*, April 1899–June 1901; Shelbourne, Ontario: Battered Silicon Despatch Box, 1998.

Merrick, Leonard. *Mr Bazalgette's Agent*. London: Routledge, 1888; London: British Library, 2013.

Morrison, Arthur. *Adventures of Martin Hewitt*. London: Ward Lock, 1896.

_____. *Best Martin Hewitt Detective Stories*. New York: Dover, 1976.

_____. *Chronicles of Martin Hewitt*. London, Ward Lock, 1895.

_____. *Martin Hewitt: Investigator*. London, Ward Lock, 1894.

Morrison, Robert, and Chris Baldick, eds. *Tales of Terror from Blackwood's Magazine*. World's Classics Series. Oxford: Oxford University Press, 1995.

"Old Sleuth" (= Harlan Page Halsey). *A Mystery of One Night*, Old Sleuth's Own, no. 111. New York: Parlor Car Publishing, 1898.

Orczy, Baroness Emma. *Lady Molly of Scotland Yard*. London: Cassell, 1910; New York: Akadine, 1999.

Pinkerton, Allan J. *Claude Melnotte as a Detective and Other Stories*. Chicago: Keen and Cooke, 1875.

_____. *The Expressman and the Detective*. Chicago: Keen and Cooke, 1874.

Pirkis, Catherine Louisa Pirkis. *The Experiences of Loveday Brooke, Lady Detective*. London: Hutchinson, 1894; Rockville. MD: Wildside Press, 2012.

Poe, Edgar Allan. "The Murders in the Rue Morgue." *Graham's Magazine*, April 1841; *Tales of Mystery and Imagination*. London: Everyman, 1908, 378–410.

_____. "The Mystery of Marie Rogêt." *Snowden's Ladies' Companion*, November 1842, December 1842 and February 1843; *Tales of Mystery and Imagination*. London: Everyman, 1908, 410–54.

_____. "The Purloined Letter." *The Gift*, January 1845; *Tales of Mystery and Imagination*. London: Everyman, 1908, 545–71.

"Rayner, Olive Pratt" (= Grant Allen). *The Type-Writer Girl*. London: Pearson, 1897; Peterborough, Ontario: Broadview, 2004.

Reade, Charles. *Griffith Gaunt, or Jealousy*. London: Chapman and Hall, 1866.

"Regester, Seeley." *The Dead Letter: An American Romance*. New York: Beadle, 1867; Catherine Ross Nickerson, ed. Durham: Duke University Press, 2003.

Reynolds, G.W.M. *Ellen Percy: The Memoir of an Actress.* London: Dicks, 1857.

_____. *Joseph Wilmot, or The Memoirs of a Man Servant.* London: Dicks, 1855.

_____. *Mary Price, or The Memoirs of a Servant-Maid.* London: Dicks, 1852.

_____. *The Mysteries of London,* 4 vols. London: Vickers, 1845–48.

_____. *The Mysteries of the Court of London,* 8 vols. London: Dicks, 1849–56.

_____. *Rosa Lambert.* London: Dicks, 1854.

Rinehart, Mary Roberts. *The Circular Staircase.* Indianapolis: Bobbs Merrill, 1908.

"Russell, William" as "T. Waters." *Leaves from the Diary of a Law Clerk.* London: Brown, 1857.

_____. *The Recollections of a Detective Police-Officer.* London: Kent, 1856; London: Covent Garden Press, 1975.

_____. *The Recollections of a Detective Police-Officer,* Second Series. London: Kent, 1859.

_____. *The Recollections of a Police-Officer.* New York: Cornish, Lamport, 1853.

Sims, George. *Dorcas Dene, Detective.* London: White, 1897.

Spofford, Harriet Prescott. "In a Cellar." *Atlantic Monthly,* February 1859, 151–72; in Spofford, *The Amber Gods,* 1–36.

_____. "In the Maguerriwock." *Harper's New Monthly Magazine,* August 1868, 348–55; in Spofford, *The Amber Gods,* 1989, 97–114.

_____. "Mr Furbush." *Harper's New Monthly Magazine,* February, 1865, 623–32.

_____. *The Amber Gods and Other Stories,* ed. Alfred Bendixen. Rutgers, NJ: Rutgers University Press, 1989.

Taylor, Philip Meadows. *Tippoo Sultaun: A Tale of the Mysore War.* London: Bentley, 1840.

Venables, Terry, see "Yuill, P.B."

Victor, Metta Fuller, see "Regester, Seeley."

Vidocq, Eugène François. *Les Mémoires,* 4 vols. Paris: Tenon, 1827–8; as *Memoirs of Vidocq: Master of Crime,* translated Edwin Gile Rich. Edinburgh: AK Press/Nabat, 2003.

Warren, Samuel. *Passages from the Diary of a Late Physician,* vols. 1–2, Edinburgh: Blackwood, 1832. vol. 3, Edinburgh: Blackwood, 1839.

_____. *Ten Thousand a Year.* Edinburgh: Blackwood, 1841.

Wells, Carolyn. *The Clue.* Philadelphia: Lippincott, 1909.

Williams, Gordon, see "Yuill, P.B."

Williams, John Babbington. *Leaves from the Note Book of A New York Detective.* New York: Dick and Fitzgerald, 1865; Westholme, PA: Yardley, 2008.

Wood, Ellen. *East Lynne.* London: Bentley, 1861.

_____. "Lost in the Post," in *Johnny Ludlow,* Second Series. London: Bentley, 1880, 1–18.

_____. *Roland Yorke.* London: Bentley, 1869.

"Yuill, P.B."(= Gordon Williams and Terry Venables). *Hazel Plays Solomon.* London: Penguin, 1977.

Secondary Works

Adrian, Jack. "Afterword" to C.L. Pirkis, *The Detections of Miss Cusack,* 107–10.

Allan, Janice M. "To See Is to Suspect: Investigating the Private in Sensation Fiction," in *Private Investigator.* Alastair Rolls and Rachel Franks, eds. Chicago: Intellect, University of Chicago Press, 2016, 172–82.

Ascari, Maurizio. *A Counter-History of Crime Fiction: Supernatural, Gothic, Sensational.* London: Palgrave Macmillan, 2007.

_____. "The Mysteries of the Vatican: from Nineteenth-century Anti-clerical Propaganda to Dan Brown's Religious Thrillers," in *Crime Fiction in the City: Capital Crimes.* Lucy Andrew and Catherine Phelps, eds. Cardiff: University of Wales Press, 2013, 107–25.

Ashley, Mike. "Introduction" to "Andrew Forrester," *The Female Detective,* vii–xi.

_____. "Introduction" to "Anonyma," *Revelations of a Lady Detective,* 7–14.

_____. "Introduction" to Leonard Merrick, *Mr Bazalgette's Agent,* British Library edition, 6–12.

Ayres, Brenda. "*Apis Trollopiana*: An Introduction to the Nearly Extinct Trollope," in *Francis Trollope and the Novel of Social Change,* ed. Brenda Ayres. Westport, CT: Greenwood, 2002, 1–10.

Baker, William, and Jeanette Roberts Shumaker. *Leonard Merrick: A Forgotten Novelist's Novelist.* Madison, NJ: Fairleigh Dickinson University Press, 2009.

Barsham, Diana. *Arthur Conan Doyle and the Meaning of Masculinity.* Aldershot: Ashgate, 2003.

Bedore, Pamela. *Dime Novels and the Roots of American Detective Fiction.* London: Palgrave Macmillan, 2013.

Beller, Anne-Marie. *Mary Elizabeth Braddon: A Companion to the Mystery Fiction.* Jefferson, NC: McFarland, 2012.

Bleiler, E.F. "Introduction" to Anon., *Richmond*, v–xiv.

_____. "Introduction" to Arthur Morrison, *Best Martin Hewitt Detective Stories*, vii–xiv.

_____. "Introduction" to Émile Gaboriau, *Monsieur Lecoq*, v–xxiv.

_____. "Introduction" to *Three Victorian Detective Novels*, ed. E.F. Bleiler, New York: Dover, 1978, vii–xvi.

Bonniot, Roger. *Émile Gaboriau, ou le naissance du roman policier.* Paris: Vrin, 1985.

Bowes, Nicola Imogen. "Damned Whores and God's Detectives," Chap. 4 of *Criminal Nation: The Crime Fiction of Mary Helena Fortune.* PhD, University of Queensland, 2008, 223–67.

Brantlinger, Patrick. *Rule of Darkness: British Literature and Imperialism, 1830–1914.* Ithaca: Cornell University Press, 1988.

Bredesen, Dagni. "Investigating the Female Detective in Victorian Fiction." *Nineteenth-Century Gender Studies* 3.1 (2007), electronic, unpaginated.

Cadogan, Patricia, see Craig, Mary.

Carnell, Jennifer, and Graham Law. "Our Author: Braddon in the Provincial Weeklies," in *Beyond Sensation: Mary Elizabeth Braddon in Context*, Marlene Trump, Pamela K. Gilbert and Aeron Haynie, eds. New York: State University of New York Press, 2000, 127–63.

Cohen, Daniel A. *Pillars of Salt, Monuments of Grace: New England Crime Literature and the Origins of American Popular Culture, 1674–1860.* New York: Oxford University Press, 1993.

Colligan, Colette, see Warne, Vanessa.

Collins, Philip. *Dickens and Crime.* London: Macmillan, 1965.

Costantini, Mariaconcetta, ed. *Armadale: Wilkie Collins and the Dark Threads of Life.* Studia di Anglistica 17. Rome: Aracne, 2009.

Cox, J. Randolph. *The Dime Novel Companion: A Source Book.* Westport, CT: Greenwood, 2000.

_____. "Paperback Detective: The Evolution of the Nick Carter Series from Dime Novel to Paperback, 1886–1990," in *Pioneers, Passionate Ladies and Private Eyes*, Sullivan and Schurman, eds., 119–32.

Craig, Mary, and Patricia Cadogan. *The Lady Investigates: Women Detectives and Spies in Fiction.* London: Gollancz, 1981.

Denning, Michael. *Mechanic Accents.* London: Verso, 1987.

Dixon, Robert. *Writing the Colonial Adventure: Race, Gender and Nation in Anglo-Australian Popular Fiction, 1875–1914.* Cambridge: Cambridge University Press, 1995.

Drexler, Peter. "Mapping the Gaps: Detectives and Detective Themes in British Novels of the 1870s and 1880s," in *The Art of Murder: New Essays on Detective Fiction*, H. Gustav Klaus and Stephen Knight, eds. Tübingen: Stauffenburg, 1998, 77–89.

During, Simon. *Foucault and Literature: Towards a Genealogy of Writing.* London: Routledge, 1992.

Eliot, T.S. "Introduction" to Wilkie Collins, *The Moonstone*, World's Classics edition. Oxford: Oxford University Press, 1928, v–xii.

_____. *Selected Essays.* London: Faber and Faber, 1932.

Fernandez, Jean. *Victorian Servants, Class, and the Politics of Literacy.* London: Routledge, 2010.

Flanders, Judith, J. "The Hanky-Panky Way: Creators of the First Female Detectives: A Mystery Solved." *Times Literary Supplement*, 18 June 2010, 14–15.

_____. *The Invention of Murder: How the Victorians Revelled in Death and Detection and Created Modern Crime.* New York: St Martin's, 2011.

Forster, John. *The Life of Charles Dickens*, four vols. London: Chapman and Hall, 1872–76.

_____. Review of *Susan Hopley. Examiner*, 28 February 1841, 132.

Greene, Douglas G. "Introduction" in Mary Roberts Rinehart, *The Circular Staircase.* New York: Dover, 1997, v–vii.

_____. "Introduction" in L.T. Meade and Robert Eustace, *The Detections of Miss Cusack*, vii–xiii.

Halttunen, Karen. *Murder Most Foul: The Killer and the American Gothic Imagination.* Cambridge: Harvard University Press, 1998.

Herbert, Rosemary, ed. The *Oxford Companion to Crime and Mystery*. New York: Oxford University Press, 1999.

Higham, Charles. *The Adventures of Conan Doyle*. London: Cape, 1976.

Holroyd, John. *George Robertson of Melbourne, 1825–1898, Pioneer Bookseller & Publisher*. Melbourne: Robertson and Mullens, 1968.

Hoppenstand, Gary, ed. *The Dime Novel Detective*. Bowling Green, OH: Bowling Green University Press, 1982.

Hoveyda, Fereydoun. *Histoire du roman policier*. Paris: Le Pavilion, 1965.

Kellow, A.H. *Queensland Poets*. London: Harrap, 1939.

Kestner, Joseph A. *Sherlock's Sisters: The British Female Detective 1864–1913*. Aldershot: Ashgate, 2003.

Klein, Kathleen Gregory. *The Woman Detective: Gender and Genre*, sec. ed. Urbana: University of Illinois Press, 1995.

Knight, Stephen. *Crime Fiction Since 1800: Detection, Death. Diversity*, sec ed. London: Palgrave Macmillan, 2010.

_____. *Continent of Mystery: A Thematic History of Australian Crime Fiction*. Melbourne: Melbourne University Press, 1997.

_____ . *Form and Ideology in Crime Fiction*. London: Macmillan, 1980.

_____. *The Mysteries of the Cities: Urban Crime fiction in the Nineteenth Century*. Jefferson, NC: McFarland, 2012.

Landrum, Larry N. *American Mystery and Detective Novels: A Reference Guide*. Westport, CT: Greenwood, 1999.

Lansbury, Coral. *Arcady in Australia: The Evocation of Australia in Nineteenth-Century English Literature*. Melbourne: Melbourne University Press, 1970.

Law, Graham, see Carnell, Jennifer.

Lycett, Andrew. *Conan Doyle—The Man Who Created Sherlock Holmes*. London: Weidenfeld and Nicholson, 2007.

Maida, Patricia D. *Mother of Detective Fiction: The Life and Works of Anna Katharine Green*. Bowling Green, OH: Bowling Green State University Press, 1989.

Martin, Susan, and Kylie Mirmohamadi. *Sensational Melbourne: Reading Sensational Fiction and Lady Audley's Secret in the Victorian Metropolis*. Melbourne: Australian Scholarly Publishing, 2011.

Matthews, David. *Medievalism: A Critical History*. Cambridge: Brewer, 2015.

McCann, Sean. *Gumshoe America: Hard-Boiled Crime Fiction and the Rise and Fall of New Deal Liberalism*. Durham: Duke University Press, 2000.

McGann, Jerome. "Introduction" to Edward George Bulwer Lytton, *Pelham or the Adventures of a Gentleman*. Lincoln: University of Nebraska Press, 1972, xi–xxv.

McLaughlin, Joseph. *Writing the Urban Jungle: Reading Empire in London from Doyle to Eliot*. Charlottesville: University of Virginia Press, 2000.

Messac, Régis. *Le "Detective Novel" et l'influence de la penseé scientifique*. Paris: Champion, 1929.

_____ *Influences Françaises dans l'oeuvre d'Edgar Poe*. Paris: Picart, 1929.

Miller, D.A. *The Novel and the Police*. Berkeley: University of California Press, 1988.

Miller, Elizabeth Carolyn. "Trouble with She-Dicks: Private Eyes and Public Women in *The Adventures of Loveday Brooke, Lady Detective*." *Victorian Literature and Culture* 33 (2005), 47–65.

Mirmohamadi, Kylie, see Martin, Susan.

Moore, Grace. *Dickens and Empire: Discourses of Class, Race and Colonialism in the Works of Charles Dickens*. Aldershot: Ashgate, 2004.

Morton, James. *The First Detective: The Life and Revolutionary Times of Vidocq: Criminal, Spy and Private Eye*. London: Ebury, 2011.

Mukherjee, U.P. *Crime and Empire: The Colony in Nineteenth Century Fiction of Crime*. Oxford: Oxford University Press, 2003.

Neale, R.S. *Class and Ideology in the Nineteenth Century*. London: Routledge, 1972.

Nickerson, Catherine Ross. "Introduction" to "Seeley Regester," *The Dead Letter and The Figure Eight*, ed. Catherine Ross Nickerson. Durham: Duke University Press, 2003, 1–10.

Olivier-Martin, Yves. *Histoire du roman populaire en France de 1840 à 1980*. Paris: Michel, 1980.

Osborne, Eric. "The Publication History of *Recollections of a Detective Police-Officer*," in 1875 edition of *Recollections of a Detective Police-Officer*, London, Covent Garden Press, 1972, unpaginated.

_____, ed. *Victorian Detective Fiction: A Catalogue of the Collection Made by Dorothy Glover and Graham Greene, Bibliographi-*

cally Arranged by Eric Osborne. London: Bodley Head, 1966.

Pittard, Christopher. *Purity and Contamination in Late Victorian Detective Fiction*. Farnham: Ashgate, 2011.

Reddy, Maureen. *Sisters in Crime: Feminism and the Crime Novel*. New York: Continuum, 1988.

Reynolds, David S. "Introduction" to George Lippard, *The Quaker City or, the Monks of Monks Hall*. Amherst: University of Massachusetts Press, 1995, vii–xliv.

Roy, Ashish. "The Fabulous Imperialist Semiotic of Wilkie Collins's *The Moonstone*." *New Literary History* 24 (1993), 657–81.

Said, Edward. *Culture and Imperialism*. London: Chatto and Windus, 1993.

Sayers, Dorothy L. "Introduction" to *The Omnibus of Crime*. Dorothy L. Sayers, ed. London: Gollancz, 1928, 9–47.

Scott, Clement. Review of Fergus Hume, *The Mystery of a Hansom Cab. Echoes of the Week*, 3 December 1887; reprinted in *Table Talk* (Melbourne), 6 January 1888, 4–7.

Shpayer-Makov, Haia. *The Ascent of the Detective: Police Sleuths in Victorian and Edwardian England*. Oxford: Oxford University Press, 2011.

Shumaker, Jeanette Roberts, see Baker, William.

Siddiqi, Yumna. *Anxieties of Empire and the Fiction of Intrigue*. New York: Columbia University Press, 2008.

Smith, Elton E. *Charles Reade*. Boston: Twayne, 1976.

Stableford, Brian. "Introduction" in Féval, *John Devil*, translated Brian Stableford. Encino, CA: Black Coat Press, 2005, 7–14.

Stern, Madeleine B. "Dime Novels by 'The Children's Friend,'" in *Pioneers, Passionate Ladies and Private Eyes: Dime Novels, Series Books, and Paperbacks*, Larry E. Sullivan and Lydia Cushman Schurman, eds. New York: Haworth, 1996, 197–213.

Stewart, R.F. *And Always a Detective*. Newton Abbot: David and Charles, 1980.

Summerscale, Kate. *The Suspicions of Mr Whicher, or The Murder at Road Hill House*. London: Bloomsbury, 2008.

Suranyi, Clarissa J. "Introduction" to "Rayner." *The Type-Writer Girl*. Peterborough, Ontario: Broadview, 2004, 9–16.

Sussex, Lucy. *Blockbuster! Fergus Hume and The Mystery of a Hansom Cab*. Melbourne: Text, 2015.

_____. *The Fortunes of Mary Fortune*. Melbourne: Penguin, 1989.

_____. *Women Writers and Detectives in Nineteenth-Century Crime Fiction: The Mothers of the Mystery Genre*. London: Palgrave Macmillan, 2010.

Symons, Julian. *Bloody Murder: From the Detective Story to the Crime Novel: A History*, sec rev. ed. London: Pan, 1994.

Taylor, Jenny Bourne. "Introduction" to Braddon, *Lady Audley's Secret*. London: Penguin Classics, 1998, vii–xli.

Thomas, Ronald R. "Detection in the Victorian Novel," in *The Cambridge Companion to the Victorian Novel*, Deirdre David, ed. Cambridge: Cambridge University Press, 2000, 169–92.

Topin, Marius. *Romanciers contemporains*. Paris: Charpentier, 1876.

Trodd, Anthea. *Domestic Crime in the Victorian Novel*. London: Macmillan, 1989.

Warne, Vanessa, and Colette Colligan. "The Man Who Wrote a New Woman Novel: Grant Allen's 'The Woman Who Did' and the Gendering of New Woman Authors." *Victorian Literature and Culture* 33 (2005), 21–46.

Watson, Kate. *Women Writing Crime Fiction, 1860–1880: Fourteen American, British and Australian Authors*. Jefferson, NC: McFarland, 2012.

Wells, Carolyn. *The Technique of the Mystery Story*. Springfield, IL: Home Correspondence School, 1913; London: Pearl Necklace Books, 2014.

Wynne, Deborah. *The Sensation Novel and the Victorian Family Magazine*. London: Palgrave, 2001.

Worthington, Heather. *The Rise of the Detective in Early Nineteenth-Century Popular Fiction*. London: Palgrave Macmillan, 2005.

Ziegler, Garrett. "The Perils of Empire: Dickens, Collins and the Indian Mutiny," Chap. 9 of *Pirates and Mutineers of the Nineteenth Century: Swashbucklers and Swindlers*, Grace Moore, ed. Farnham: Ashgate, 2011, 149–64.

Index

Numbers in **_bold italics_** refer to pages with photographs.